Star-Hopping

for Backyard Astronomers

Star-Hopping

for Backyard Astronomers

Alan M. MacRobert

Foreword by Fred Schaaf

Sky Publishing Corp.

Cambridge, Massachusetts

Published by:

Sky Publishing Corp.
49 Bay State Rd.
Cambridge, MA 02138

First published September 1993.

Library of Congress Cataloging-in-Publication data:

MacRobert, Alan M., 1951–
      Star-hopping for backyard astronomers / by Alan M. MacRobert ;
   foreword by Fred Schaaf.
      p.   cm.
      Includes bibliographical references and index.
      ISBN 0-933346-68-9 :
      1. Stars–Amateurs' manuals. 2. Astronomy–Observers' manuals.
   QB63.M33 1993
   523.8'022'3–dc20   93-25106

Printed and bound by Horowitz/Rae, Fairfield, New Jersey

Printed on acid-free paper

10 9 8 7 6 5 4 3 2

ISBN 0-933346-68-9

For Lucy and Andrew

Contents

Foreword

Some of the best ideas get overlooked for a long time. One such idea is a book built around the easy, enjoyable, and informative telescopic tours of the starry sky called "star-hops." We've had to wait a long time for a book of this kind, but through the one you are now holding in your hands you'll begin to see that it has been well worth the wait.

What's so great about star-hops? In a nutshell, they are the practical action-oriented way to learn (or master) much of observational astronomy, become familiar (or more familiar) with your telescope, see the greatest variety of sights in the starry sky, and know the heavens in the most detailed form. This approach to astronomy makes it fun and accessible to observers at all knowledge levels.

A star-hop is a telescopic journey through a small, selected part of the heavens using a detailed map. By carefully comparing the map to what you see, you make your way from one recognizable star, or little pattern of dim stars, to another and another until you reach your destination. This can be especially easy if you make your whole journey with each object's field of view at least slightly overlapping the next.

Of course, if you have a good equatorial mount, precise polar alignment, and large, accurately adjusted setting circles – or a computer-assisted telescope – *and* the proper celestial coordinates for objects you want to look at, you can find the sights you want without a map. But not everyone has all this equipment. Furthermore, and most importantly, star-hopping gives you a chance to see everything along the way for yourself. Instead of dialing the positions from someone else's list of suggested sky objects and looking at only them, you, the star-hopper, view all the fascinating sights along your path. Along that path there may be among the "sidelights" (objects you weren't targeting) double stars, star clusters, and galaxies that are granted nothing more than a line of statistics in a few observer's guides but which you personally find captivating. And you also won't find in any catalog the countless simple starscapes of great beauty that you will cross on the way. What better means could there be to learn your way around the heavens?

Star-hopping allows you to take the scenic route, see the backcountry of the heavens, get a real feeling for those "lands" you are visiting. But whenever you want adventures off the beaten track, want to become an explorer in your own right, you initially need a knowledgeable guide who will keep you from getting lost and teach you the pathfinding techniques that will eventually make you self-sufficient.

That is where this book and its author, Alan MacRobert, enter in.

Mapping out a good star-hop requires careful planning, and a great one requires no less than a deep familiarity and experience with the heavens. This book offers you many great star-hops, a variety for every time of the year. Alan MacRobert, a *Sky & Telescope* associate editor, makes the selection of routes and notable objects seem easy, as if the choices were already written up there in the heavens. And after you've sampled the star-hop tours in this book, you will be able to plan interesting tours of your own.

Another measure of MacRobert's success is how suitable and productive his star-hops are for everyone from the novice to the veteran amateur astronomer. If you're a beginner with a small telescope, there is plenty for you to see on his tours, and the more challenging objects can be goals for your future runs of the star-hop routes, perhaps someday with a larger telescope. I also highly recommend this book for advanced amateur astronomers. Only the most experienced of deep-sky observers will have encountered all the objects MacRobert examines, yet even these observers will learn some new things and get some fresh insights from viewing the featured objects in a new context.

The star-hops in this book originally appeared as popular articles in the pages of *Sky & Telescope*. Here they are enhanced and accompanied by sections that clearly explain the basics of observational astronomy that the beginner needs to know to try the star-hops. If you are just starting out, this book can serve as a good working introduction to the practice of observational astronomy beyond the solar system.

The ultimate goal for many astronomy books is to get the reader actually outside, actually observing the universe's wonders. No book will succeed in overcoming all personal apathy and inertia. But this program of star-hops is so inviting when read, so stimulating when tried, that I expect it to be a major success. I believe it will help great numbers of people to discover, and some to rediscover, the thrill and other rewards of exploring the starry heavens.

Fred Schaaf
Millville, New Jersey
August 1993

About This Book

The hobby of astronomy – the biggest and most mind-boggling branch of amateur nature study – is attracting more people than ever before. You can see this in the vigor of the telescope market, in magazine subscription figures, and in the number of astronomy books being published, but most tellingly in the social climate that astronomy enthusiasts face.

Back in the mid-1960s when I first took up the hobby, amateur astronomers were considered geeks, if they were considered at all. A starwatching enthusiast was assumed to be the stereotypical science nerd who couldn't make it anywhere else in life. If you were a male (and you almost certainly were), females thought you were drippy. It was rough.

All that has changed. Five times as many Americans now read an astronomy magazine every month as did in 1968 at the height of the space program. When I mention at a party that I'm into the stars and have a telescope, people perk up and ask about comet impacts, quasars, and the Big Bang. Hints are dropped (by members of both sexes) about maybe getting invited some evening when I have the telescope out.

Starting Right

It is wonderfully captivating to learn, understand, and *see with your own eyes* tremendous cosmic immensities that float overhead every clear night – things unsuspected by most people as they go about their tiny routines on this tiny planet. But many who get fired up by the idea don't make it very far and soon quit.

What goes wrong? Almost always, they didn't get hold of practical information about what to observe and how. "I just can't find much of anything with this telescope," is the sort of thing I hear. "Do you think it needs a new eyepiece?" What it needs are the right books and sky charts to go with it. Astronomy is very much a learning hobby. Paper and ink are more important than glass and metal, especially for anyone starting out.

A lot of mass-market astronomy books contain little or no useful information for new observers. Others try but botch the job. New telescope users may never even learn *how* to find out what they *need* to find out. So they conclude that astronomy is hard and mysterious or that their brain power must be short a few watts.

This is deplorable and unnecessary. Compare the disorganization of entry-level astronomy with, say, amateur radio, which perfected its newcomer-welcoming machinery decades ago – or birdwatching, where widely available and straightforward field guides start everyone out just right.

The book you're holding is one attempt to help. It is intended to jump-start novice telescope users into hunting and finding some astronomical big game. It provides 14 selected doses of major-league sky hunting that anyone can do outdoors with a telescope, even with little or no experience and only modest astronomy book learning. We've culled through major references of the sort used by "serious amateurs," the hobby's self-defined elite, to produce guided tours along well-marked celestial nature trails that anyone can walk.

Most chapters in this book first appeared as articles in the Backyard Astronomy department of *Sky & Telescope* magazine, where I've worked since 1982. Much material in Star-Hops 1 and 7 was scouted by *Sky & Telescope* writer Philip Harrington, author of *Touring the Universe through Binoculars*. I field-tested all the telescopic tours using a 6-inch reflector telescope that I built when I was 15 years old. A 6-inch reflector is one of the best "real" (as opposed to toy) telescopes for starting out. I'm still happy with mine 25 years later, though nowadays I spend more time with a second scope twice its size permanently mounted in an observatory shed. A 6-inch reflector is big enough to show quite a lot, yet small enough to carry, set up, manage, and store without too much trouble. And it's relatively low priced for what it does.

The term "6-inch" refers to a telescope's *aperture*, the diameter of the main lens or mirror that collects and focuses the light. The bigger the aperture, the fainter you can see and the sharper the image. If your telescope is smaller than a 6-inch, some of the sights described in this book will be out of reach, but plenty of others will still be visible. If your scope is larger than a 6-inch, you'll probably have an easier time seeing the sights than I did.

In addition to aperture, the other major factor governing what you can see is *light pollution*. This is the murky veil of artificial skyglow that washes out the stars over heavily populated areas. I live in the outer suburbs of Boston where light pollution is a problem but not overwhelmingly so, a more or less average situation for amateur astronomers. Light pollution, incidentally, is by no means a necessary evil of civilization. About three-fourths of it is *waste light* from badly designed, energy-inefficient outdoor fixtures. "Waste light" is light that goes directly from the fixture sideways or up into the sky, not down toward the ground where it was intended to go.

Greater Boston's light pollution usually limits my naked-eye view to stars brighter than about magnitude 5.2. If your sky is darker than this, consider yourself blessed.

The Maps

Using star maps is the most essential skill for an amateur astronomer to develop. The first step is simply to learn the bright stars and constellations (star patterns) that you can see with the naked eye. The constellations are the basic geography of the heavens – what you need to know to find your way around and get where you want to go. After all, if you were a newcomer to the planet Earth, you'd need a map of the continents before you could find your way to a street address in Paducah or Sendai. The naked-eye constellations are the "continents" of the sky.

The constellations appear to rotate around the Earth through the night and throughout the year. Consequently, you need maps showing where they are at different months and at different hours of night. The next chapter gives you enough maps and instructions to get started.

Each of the 14 star-hop chapters is built around a much more detailed close-up map of a small area. The all-sky charts on pages 16 to 27 show where these close-up areas are located (they're the small, numbered rectangles). Most of the close-up maps are adapted from *Sky Atlas 2000.0,* a grand work by the Dutch sky cartographer Wil Tirion that has become the world standard amateur atlas. It shows 43,000 stars – all stars to as faint as 8th magnitude, fainter than the naked-eye limit – along with 2,500 galaxies, star clusters, and nebulae.

Some chapters use even more detailed, larger-scale charts adapted from the *Uranometria 2000.0* atlas by Tirion, Barry Rappaport, and George Lovi. This two-volume work comprises 473 charts with 332,000 stars to magnitude 9.5, plus over 10,000 other objects.

Every summer nearly 2,000 amateur astronomers gather on a hill near Springfield, Vermont, for the annual Stellafane convention – a weekend of observing the sky at night and comparing home-built telescopes by day. Stellafane began in 1926 after local amateur telescope makers built the clubhouse on the hilltop. The convention now spawns traffic jams and has inspired at least a half dozen similar big gatherings across North America, most of them in better facilities. Spiritually, however, Stellafane remains the "high holy ground" of amateur astronomy.

We've put numbered circles on the maps highlighting the points of interest on our tours. The circles are either 1°, 2°, or 3° in diameter; the caption tells which.

The chapter entitled "Star-Hopping: Using a Map at the Telescope" (page 49) tells how to use these or other detailed maps outdoors to pinpoint faint objects with your telescope. This is the most important chapter in the book.

Keep Reading...

A big part of this hobby is getting familiar with the astronomy shelves at your local public library. Most libraries have a very mixed collection – a couple of British observing manuals from the 1950s, gorgeous art books of astronomical photographs, naked-eye constellation guides of good, bad, or indifferent quality, how-to-use-a-telescope manuals, Halley's Comet books from the comet's last return in 1985-86, a freshman-year college textbook, a Victorian treatise on the lore of star names.... Browse through all of it, picking what appeals to you for detailed study or bedtime reading. Look especially, however, for beginner-oriented books that focus on do-it-yourself backyard observing.

The more you learn, the easier it is to learn more. This book will go more smoothly if you have at least a little background in the basics. A recommended reading list begins on page 149.

Finding Your Way in the Sky

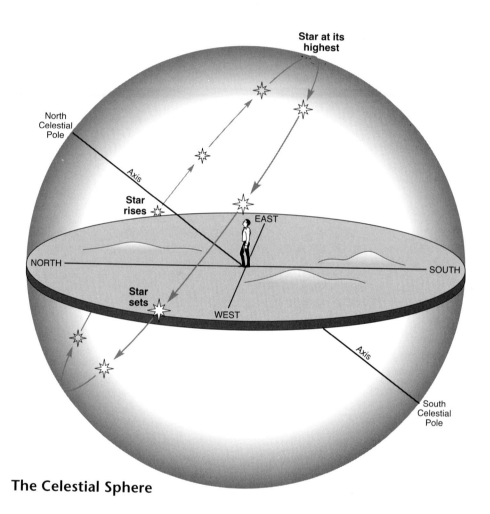

The Celestial Sphere

Standing on the ground and looking up at the sky, you appear to be on a flat Earth enclosed in a "celestial sphere" studded with the Sun, Moon, and stars. The celestial sphere appears to rotate as the hours pass, with its western side moving down and setting while its eastern side rises.

Stargazing is easy, and astronomy is something anyone can do and enjoy. *If,* that is, you get started on the right foot. Leave your equipment behind. The first step, regardless of whether you have a telescope, is to learn the stars as they appear to the naked eye.

Imagine yourself standing in an open field on a clear night. The starry firmament appears to be a great dome over the flat landscape of the Earth, with the bottom rim of the dome resting on the distant horizon all around you. This is how the universe actually *looks* from our humble viewpoint within it. For most of human history, people assumed that what you saw was what you got – that the Earth was indeed flat, and that the stars were attached like nailheads to a big dome enclosing us.

As the hours of the night pass at your open field, you'll see stars in the west move downward and set, those overhead shift westward, and new stars rise in the east. It's as if the entire starry dome is slowly rotating. Of course it's the Earth that's turning, but we're only paying attention now to how things *look*. You would quickly conclude that the sky dome extends down below the western horizon and that there's more of it below the eastern horizon waiting to rise.

If you watched all night, as shepherds and hunters did at their campfires millennia ago, you'd soon realize that the starry dome continues all the way around beneath the Earth to form a complete *celestial sphere,* with you at the center. Half of the celestial sphere shows above the horizon at any given time. The picture on the previous page shows the celestial sphere enclosing your flat landscape.

The round maps on the next few pages show the sky dome – the half of the celestial sphere that's above you – on any date at whatever time of night you care to look.

How To Use the All-Sky Maps

Each of the maps on pages 16 to 27 flattens out the sky dome above you and shrinks it to fit onto a page. Leaf through the 12 maps. Check the dates and times in the lower corners to find the one most appropriate for your date and hour of night.

Each map's *edge* is the horizon all around you, as you would see if you stood gazing horizontally and turned around in a complete circle. The map's *center* is the point straight overhead, called the *zenith*. Thus, a star halfway from the edge of the map to the center can be spotted in the sky about halfway from the horizon to straight up. Compass points are labeled around the map's horizon – North, Northeast, East, and so on. When you go outdoors to find stars you'll need to start with a rough idea of direction. Check a map of your neighborhood or use a compass.

Outdoors, hold the map vertically in front of you and turn it around so the horizon edge *labeled with the direction you're facing* is down. The stars above this edge are now oriented the way that they appear in front of you in the sky. For example, suppose it's 9 p.m. in mid-November. Looking at the legends, we choose the next to the last of the maps, the one labeled "Midevening in November." Suppose you have a view to the northeast. Turn the page around so the chart's "NE" horizon is down. About halfway from this edge to the center is the bright star Capella. Go outside, face northeast, look halfway up the sky – and there's Capella sparkling away! The two numbered rectangles on the map at Capella refer to star-hop chapters later in this book. The rectangles show the sky areas covered by the close-up charts in those chapters, intended for use with a telescope.

Turn to face north, and rotate the page so the north horizon is down. Very high up, almost at the zenith overhead, is a W-shaped pattern of five stars labeled "Cassiopeia." Crane your neck high up as you face north – and there it is. You've just found a constellation. Cassiopeia is supposed to be a queen of Ethiopia sitting in a chair, but don't expect to see her. Forget people and chairs. Just remember the W, which is what you actually see.

Turn east-southeast (between due east and southeast) and rotate the map accordingly. There, low down near the horizon, is the constellation Orion. Simple, isn't it?

Here are some tips to help you over possible rough spots.

Look for the bright stars. When you start out, look only for the brightest stars on the map, those with the biggest dots. Mentally blank out the fainter ones if

Midevening in January

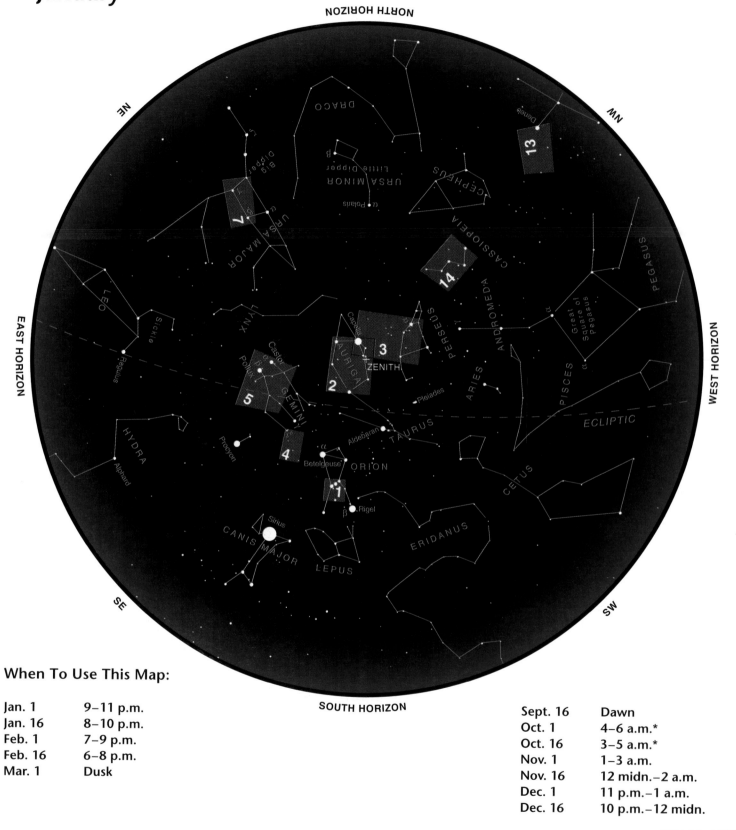

NORTH HORIZON

DRACO

URSA MINOR
Little Dipper
α Polaris
β

Big Dipper

13
Deneb

NW

CEPHEUS

CASSIOPEIA

14

PEGASUS

7

URSA MAJOR

Great Square of Pegasus
α
α

LYNX

PERSEUS

ANDROMEDA

LEO

Sickle

γ

AURIGA

Capella

3

ZENITH

Pleiades

ARIES

PISCES

ECLIPTIC

Regulus

Castor
Pollux

2

WEST HORIZON

EAST HORIZON

5

GEMINI

Aldebaran

TAURUS

Procyon

4

α
Betelgeuse

ORION

CETUS

HYDRA

Alphard

1

β
Rigel

ERIDANUS

Sirius

CANIS MAJOR

LEPUS

NE

SE

SW

SOUTH HORIZON

When To Use This Map:

Jan. 1	9–11 p.m.
Jan. 16	8–10 p.m.
Feb. 1	7–9 p.m.
Feb. 16	6–8 p.m.
Mar. 1	Dusk

Sept. 16	Dawn
Oct. 1	4–6 a.m.*
Oct. 16	3–5 a.m.*
Nov. 1	1–3 a.m.
Nov. 16	12 midn.–2 a.m.
Dec. 1	11 p.m.–1 a.m.
Dec. 16	10 p.m.–12 midn.

*Daylight Saving Time

Midevening
in February

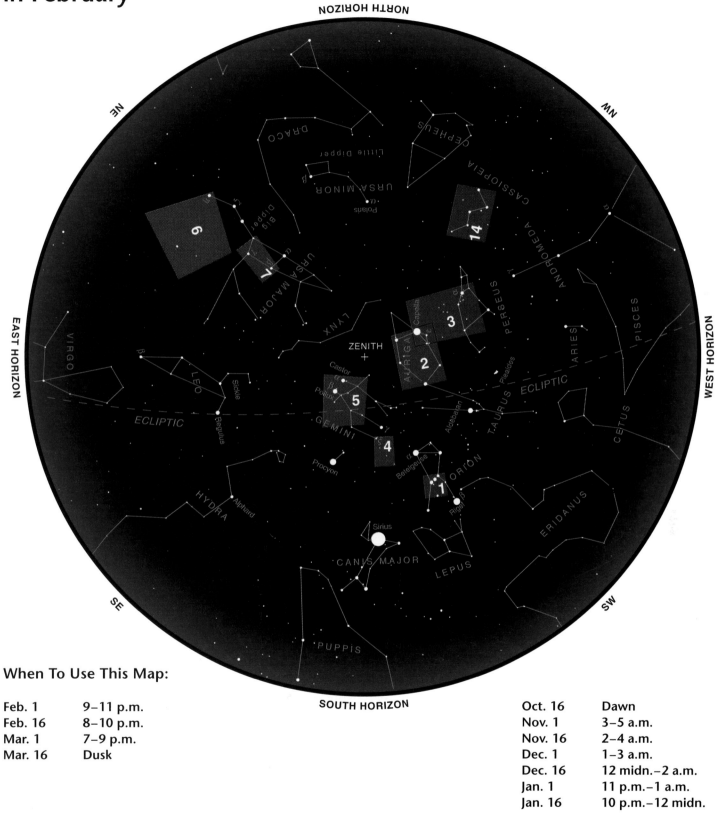

NORTH HORIZON

NE

NW

DRACO

Little Dipper

CEPHEUS

URSA MINOR

CASSIOPEIA

Polaris

β

Big Dipper

6

7

ANDROMEDA

URSA MAJOR

14

LYNX

PERSEUS

α

VIRGO

EAST HORIZON

β

Capella

3

PISCES

WEST HORIZON

LEO

Sickle

ZENITH
+

AURIGA

2

ε

Castor
α
β
Pollux

5

Pleiades

ARIES

Aldebaran

ECLIPTIC

Regulus

ECLIPTIC

γ

TAURUS

CETUS

GEMINI

4

Procyon

α

Betelgeuse

ORION

HYDRA

Alphard

1

β

Rigel

ERIDANUS

Sirius

CANIS MAJOR

LEPUS

SE

SW

PUPPIS

SOUTH HORIZON

When To Use This Map:

Feb. 1	9–11 p.m.
Feb. 16	8–10 p.m.
Mar. 1	7–9 p.m.
Mar. 16	Dusk

Oct. 16	Dawn
Nov. 1	3–5 a.m.
Nov. 16	2–4 a.m.
Dec. 1	1–3 a.m.
Dec. 16	12 midn.–2 a.m.
Jan. 1	11 p.m.–1 a.m.
Jan. 16	10 p.m.–12 midn.

Midevening
in March

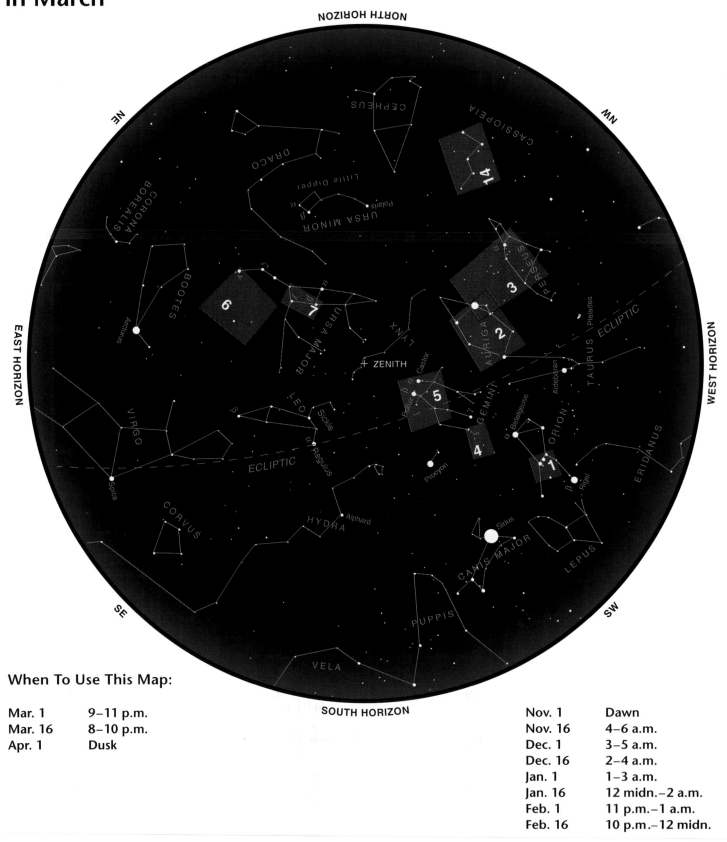

NORTH HORIZON

NE

NW

CEPHEUS

CASSIOPEIA

DRACO

14

CORONA BOREALIS

Little Dipper

URSA MINOR

α Polaris

β

PERSEUS

Pleades

BOOTES

6

7

3

ECLIPTIC

Arcturus

URSA MAJOR

LYNX

AURIGA

2

TAURUS

Aldebaran

EAST HORIZON

+ ZENITH

β

Castor

Pollux

5

GEMINI

γ

α Betelgeuse

ORION

WEST HORIZON

LEO

Sickle

4

α Regulus

VIRGO

ECLIPTIC

Procyon

β Rigel

ERIDANUS

Spica

Sirius

CORVUS

HYDRA

Alphard

CANIS MAJOR

LEPUS

PUPPIS

SE

SW

VELA

SOUTH HORIZON

When To Use This Map:

Mar. 1	9–11 p.m.
Mar. 16	8–10 p.m.
Apr. 1	Dusk

Nov. 1	Dawn
Nov. 16	4–6 a.m.
Dec. 1	3–5 a.m.
Dec. 16	2–4 a.m.
Jan. 1	1–3 a.m.
Jan. 16	12 midn.–2 a.m.
Feb. 1	11 p.m.–1 a.m.
Feb. 16	10 p.m.–12 midn.

Midevening in April

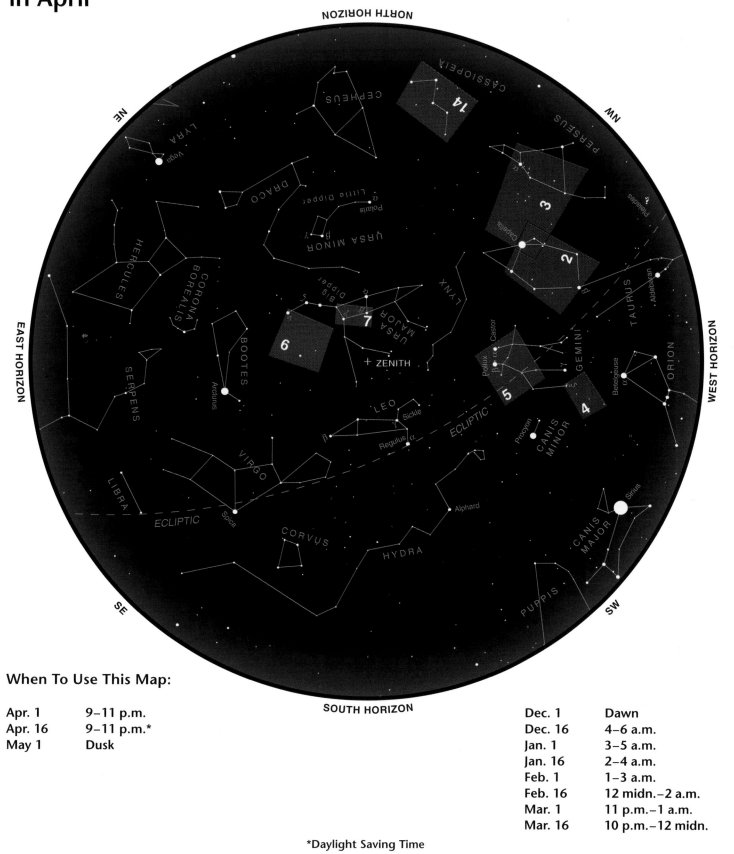

NORTH HORIZON

NE

NW

CASSIOPEIA

14

CEPHEUS

PERSEUS

Capella

LYRA

Vega

DRACO

3

Pleiades

α

Little Dipper

2

β

Polaris

β

γ

TAURUS

Aldebaran

HERCULES

URSA MINOR

LYNX

CORONA BOREALIS

Big Dipper

Castor

Pollux

GEMINI

δ

Orion

BOOTES

7

Castor

ORION

EAST HORIZON

6

URSA MAJOR

c

WEST HORIZON

+ ZENITH

5

4

Betelgeuse

α

SERPENS

Arcturus

LEO

Sickle

Procyon

CANIS MINOR

β

Regulus

α

ECLIPTIC

VIRGO

Spica

HYDRA

Alphard

LIBRA

ECLIPTIC

CORVUS

Sirius

CANIS MAJOR

SE

HYDRA

PUPPIS

SW

SOUTH HORIZON

When To Use This Map:

Apr. 1	9–11 p.m.
Apr. 16	9–11 p.m.*
May 1	Dusk

Dec. 1	Dawn
Dec. 16	4–6 a.m.
Jan. 1	3–5 a.m.
Jan. 16	2–4 a.m.
Feb. 1	1–3 a.m.
Feb. 16	12 midn.–2 a.m.
Mar. 1	11 p.m.–1 a.m.
Mar. 16	10 p.m.–12 midn.

*Daylight Saving Time

Midevening in May

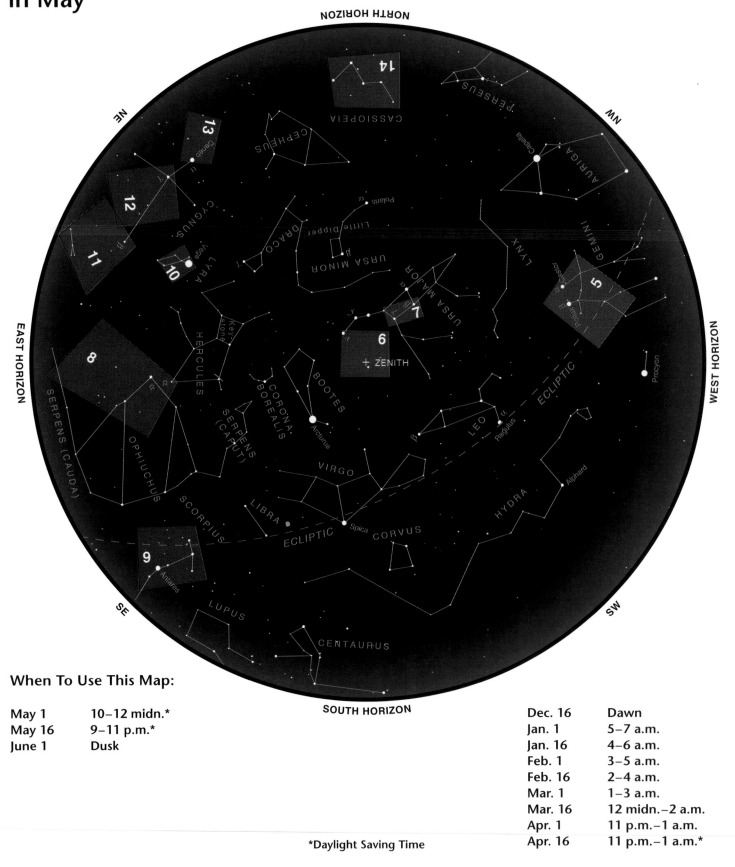

When To Use This Map:

May 1	10–12 midn.*
May 16	9–11 p.m.*
June 1	Dusk

Dec. 16	Dawn
Jan. 1	5–7 a.m.
Jan. 16	4–6 a.m.
Feb. 1	3–5 a.m.
Feb. 16	2–4 a.m.
Mar. 1	1–3 a.m.
Mar. 16	12 midn.–2 a.m.
Apr. 1	11 p.m.–1 a.m.
Apr. 16	11 p.m.–1 a.m.*

*Daylight Saving Time

Midevening in June

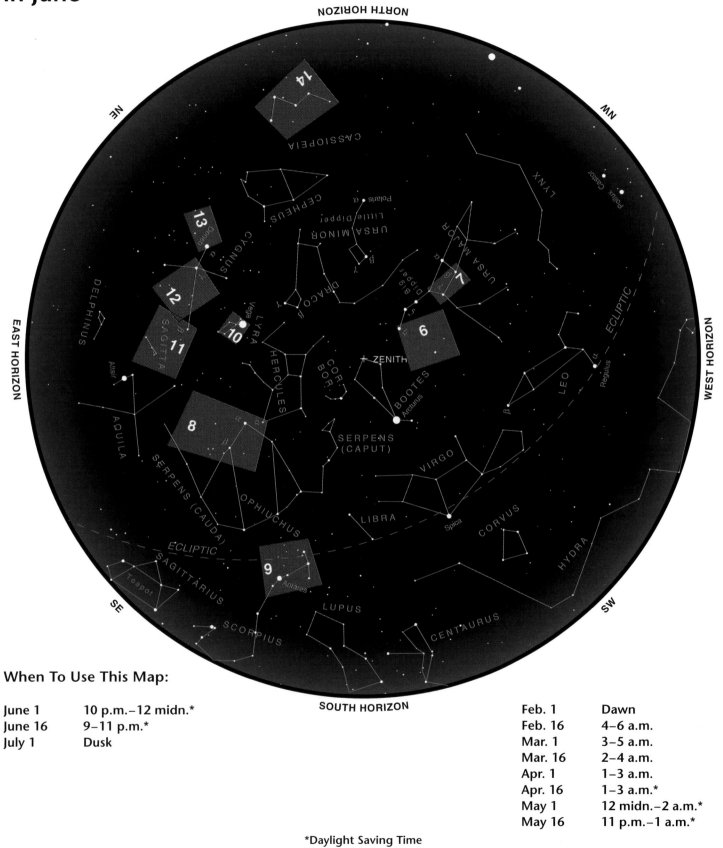

When To Use This Map:

June 1	10 p.m.–12 midn.*
June 16	9–11 p.m.*
July 1	Dusk

Feb. 1	Dawn
Feb. 16	4–6 a.m.
Mar. 1	3–5 a.m.
Mar. 16	2–4 a.m.
Apr. 1	1–3 a.m.
Apr. 16	1–3 a.m.*
May 1	12 midn.–2 a.m.*
May 16	11 p.m.–1 a.m.*

*Daylight Saving Time

Midevening
in July

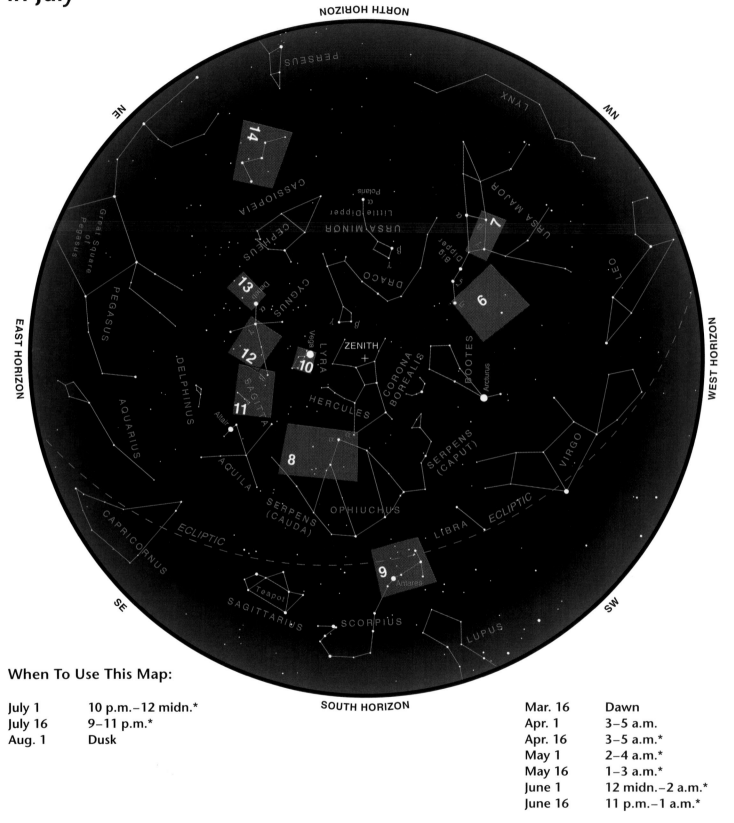

NORTH HORIZON

PERSEUS

NE

LYNX

NW

Polaris

CASSIOPEIA

Little Dipper

α

URSA MINOR

URSA MAJOR

14

β

Big Dipper

7

Great Square of Pegasus

CEPHEUS

γ

DRACO

α

6

PEGASUS

13

CYGNUS

Deneb

α

EAST HORIZON

WEST HORIZON

β

γ

LEO

Vega

LYRA

ZENITH

BOOTES

DELPHINUS

12

10

+

CORONA BOREALIS

Arcturus

SAGITTA

AQUARIUS

11

HERCULES

Altair

SERPENS (CAPUT)

8

VIRGO

AQUILA

SERPENS (CAUDA)

OPHIUCHUS

ECLIPTIC

CAPRICORNUS

LIBRA

ECLIPTIC

SE

9

Antares

Teapot

SAGITTARIUS

SCORPIUS

SW

LUPUS

SOUTH HORIZON

When To Use This Map:

July 1	10 p.m.–12 midn.*
July 16	9–11 p.m.*
Aug. 1	Dusk

Mar. 16	Dawn
Apr. 1	3–5 a.m.
Apr. 16	3–5 a.m.*
May 1	2–4 a.m.*
May 16	1–3 a.m.*
June 1	12 midn.–2 a.m.*
June 16	11 p.m.–1 a.m.*

*Daylight Saving Time

Midevening
in August

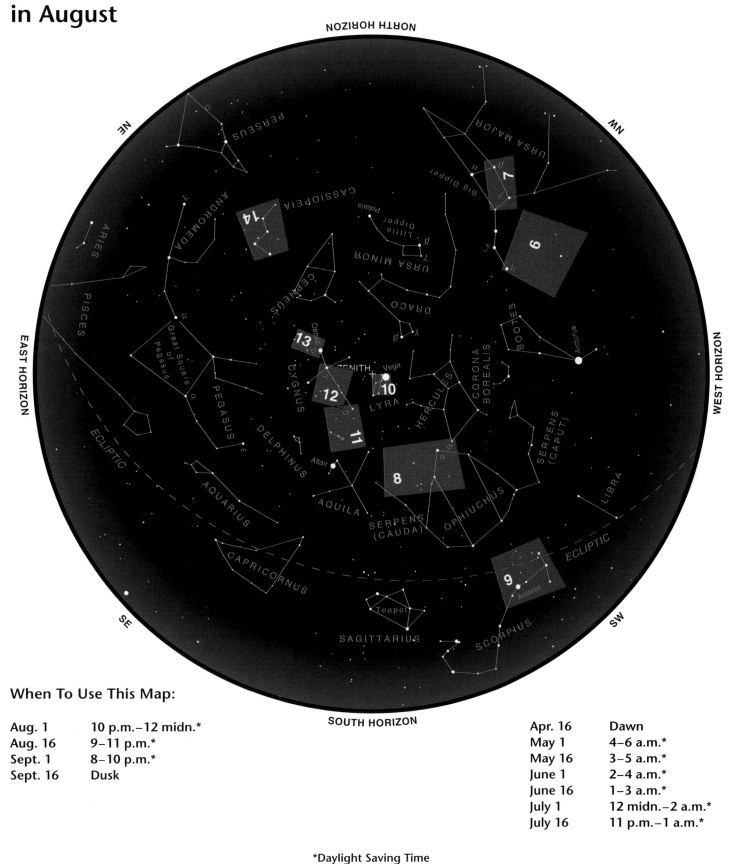

NORTH HORIZON

NE

NW

PERSEUS

ANDROMEDA

CASSIOPEIA

URSA MAJOR

14

Big Dipper

α
β
γ

7

ARIES

γ

Little Dipper
β
γ

Polaris

DRACO

URSA MINOR

6

PISCES

CEPHEUS

β

γ

BOOTES

Arcturus

EAST HORIZON

α

Great Square
of Pegasus

Deneb

13

ZENITH

Vega

HERCULES

CORONA
BOREALIS

WEST HORIZON

CYGNUS

12

10

LYRA

α

PEGASUS

β

11

SERPENS
(CAPUT)

ECLIPTIC

DELPHINUS

Altair

8

OPHIUCHUS

LIBRA

ε

AQUILA

AQUARIUS

SERPENS
(CAUDA)

ECLIPTIC

CAPRICORNUS

9

Antares

SE

Teapot

SCORPIUS

SW

SAGITTARIUS

SOUTH HORIZON

When To Use This Map:

Aug. 1	10 p.m.–12 midn.*
Aug. 16	9–11 p.m.*
Sept. 1	8–10 p.m.*
Sept. 16	Dusk

Apr. 16	Dawn
May 1	4–6 a.m.*
May 16	3–5 a.m.*
June 1	2–4 a.m.*
June 16	1–3 a.m.*
July 1	12 midn.–2 a.m.*
July 16	11 p.m.–1 a.m.*

*Daylight Saving Time

Midevening
in September

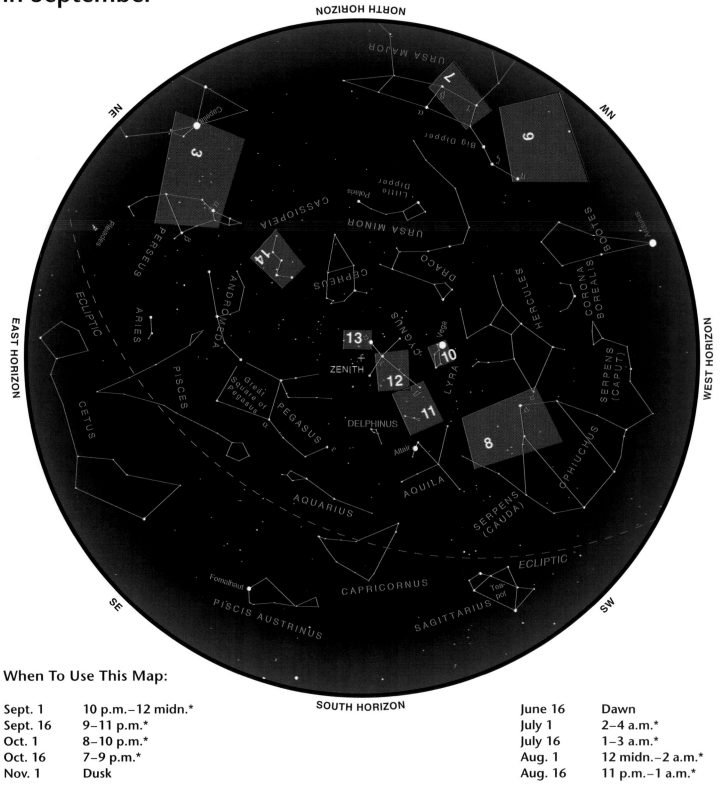

NORTH HORIZON

NE

NW

URSA MAJOR

7

3

Capella

Big Dipper

6

Pleiades

PERSEUS

Little Dipper

Polaris

URSA MINOR

CASSIOPEIA

14

ANDROMEDA

CEPHEUS

DRACO

BOOTES

Arcturus

ARIES

ECLIPTIC

EAST HORIZON

PISCES

Great Square of Pegasus

13

ZENITH

CYGNUS

HERCULES

CORONA BOREALIS

SERPENS (CAPUT)

WEST HORIZON

Vega

10

12

LYRA

11

CETUS

PEGASUS

DELPHINUS

8

α

OPHIUCHUS

Altair

AQUARIUS

AQUILA

SERPENS (CAUDA)

Fomalhaut

ECLIPTIC

CAPRICORNUS

Tea-pot

SE

PISCIS AUSTRINUS

SAGITTARIUS

SW

SOUTH HORIZON

When To Use This Map:

Sept. 1	10 p.m.–12 midn.*
Sept. 16	9–11 p.m.*
Oct. 1	8–10 p.m.*
Oct. 16	7–9 p.m.*
Nov. 1	Dusk

June 16	Dawn
July 1	2–4 a.m.*
July 16	1–3 a.m.*
Aug. 1	12 midn.–2 a.m.*
Aug. 16	11 p.m.–1 a.m.*

*Daylight Saving Time

Midevening
in October

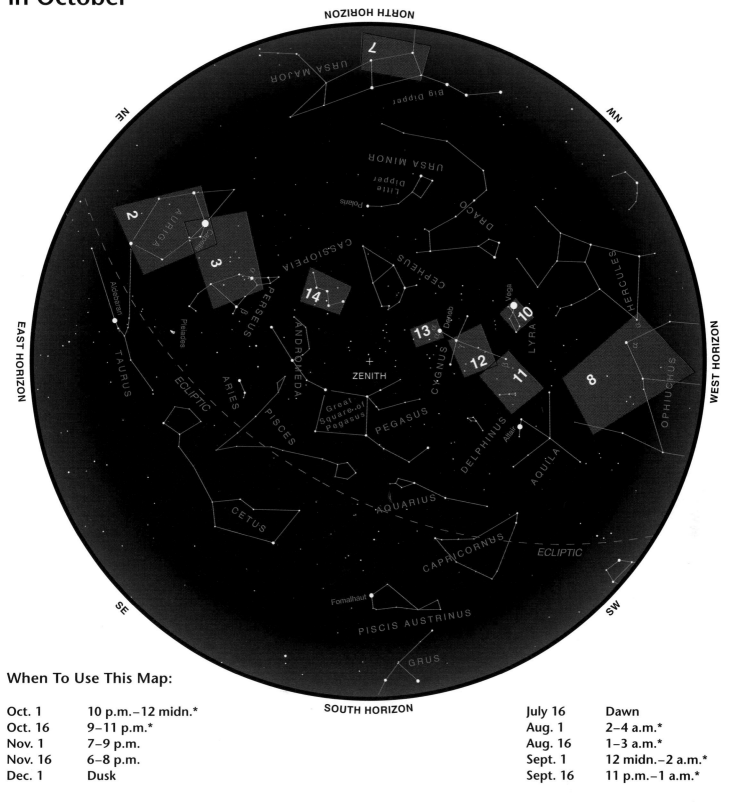

NORTH HORIZON

NE · NW

URSA MAJOR

Big Dipper

URSA MINOR
Little Dipper
Polaris

DRACO

CASSIOPEIA

CEPHEUS

HERCULES

7

2 AURIGA
Capella

3 PERSEUS

14

Vega

10 LYRA

Deneb

13 CYGNUS

12

11

8 α OPHIUCHUS

α

Aldebaran

Pleiades

TAURUS

ANDROMEDA

ARIES

ECLIPTIC

PISCES

ZENITH
+

Great Square of Pegasus

PEGASUS

DELPHINUS

Altair

AQUILA

EAST HORIZON

WEST HORIZON

CETUS

AQUARIUS

CAPRICORNUS

ECLIPTIC

SE · SW

Fomalhaut

PISCIS AUSTRINUS

GRUS

SOUTH HORIZON

When To Use This Map:

Oct. 1	10 p.m.–12 midn.*
Oct. 16	9–11 p.m.*
Nov. 1	7–9 p.m.
Nov. 16	6–8 p.m.
Dec. 1	Dusk

July 16	Dawn
Aug. 1	2–4 a.m.*
Aug. 16	1–3 a.m.*
Sept. 1	12 midn.–2 a.m.*
Sept. 16	11 p.m.–1 a.m.*

*Daylight Saving Time

Midevening in November

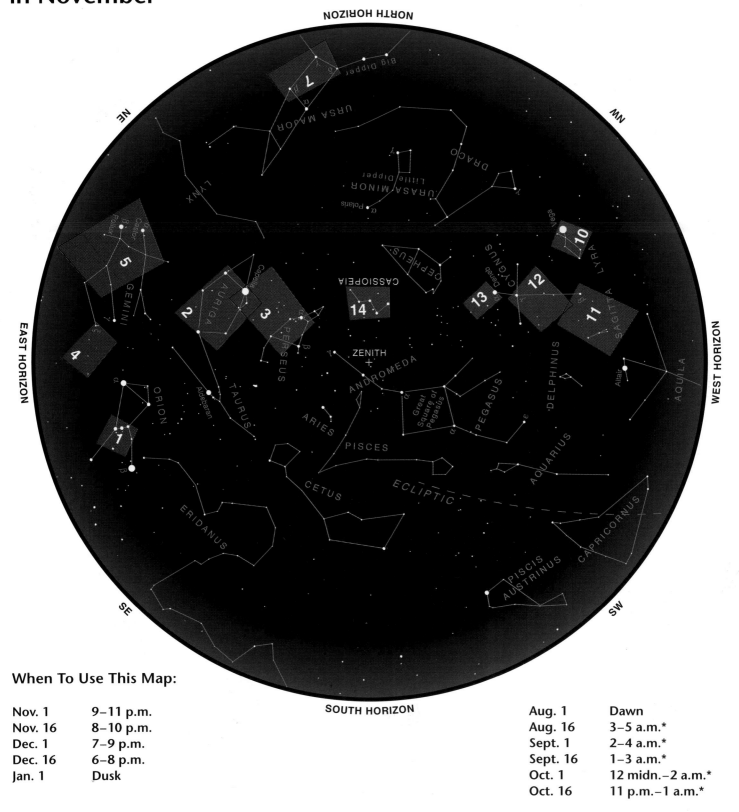

When To Use This Map:

Nov. 1	9–11 p.m.
Nov. 16	8–10 p.m.
Dec. 1	7–9 p.m.
Dec. 16	6–8 p.m.
Jan. 1	Dusk

Aug. 1	Dawn
Aug. 16	3–5 a.m.*
Sept. 1	2–4 a.m.*
Sept. 16	1–3 a.m.*
Oct. 1	12 midn.–2 a.m.*
Oct. 16	11 p.m.–1 a.m.*

*Daylight Saving Time

Midevening
in December

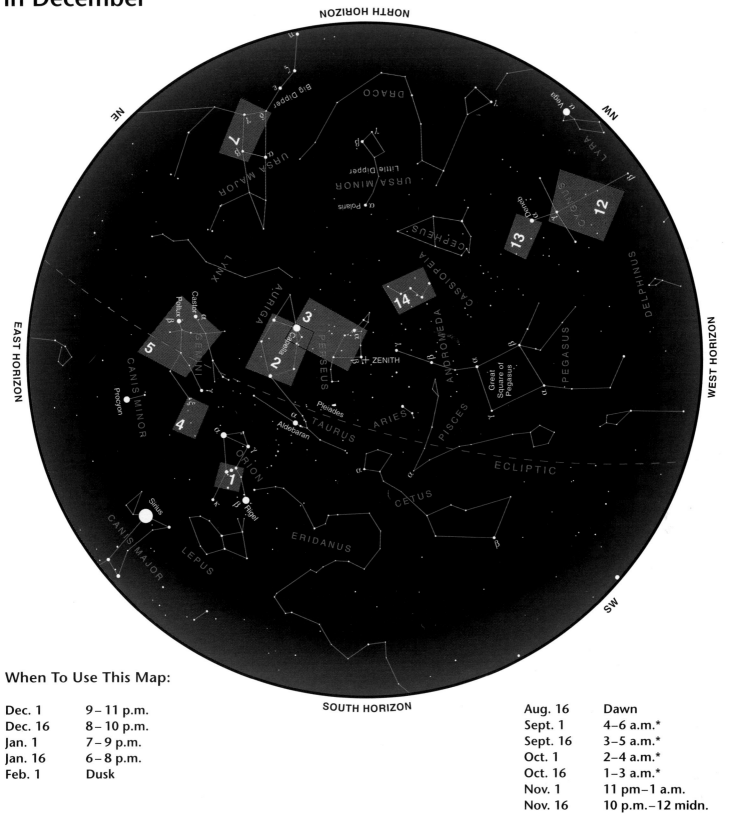

NORTH HORIZON

NE

NW

DRACO

Big Dipper

LYRA

α Vega

URSA MAJOR

7

LYNX

Little Dipper

URSA MINOR

α Polaris

CYGNUS

12

α Deneb

13

CEPHEUS

DELPHINUS

Castor α

Pollux β

GEMINI

AURIGA

3

Capella α

PERSEUS

14

β

CASSIOPEIA

ANDROMEDA

γ

α

β

PEGASUS

5

2

+ ZENITH

γ

β

Great Square of Pegasus

Procyon

CANIS MINOR

Pleiades

α

α

ARIES

PISCES

α

γ

4

Aldebaran

TAURUS

ORION

α

ECLIPTIC

γ

α

κ

β Rigel

CETUS

1

β

Sirius

CANIS MAJOR

ERIDANUS

LEPUS

β

EAST HORIZON

WEST HORIZON

SOUTH HORIZON

SW

When To Use This Map:

Dec. 1	9 – 11 p.m.
Dec. 16	8 – 10 p.m.
Jan. 1	7 – 9 p.m.
Jan. 16	6 – 8 p.m.
Feb. 1	Dusk

Aug. 16	Dawn
Sept. 1	4–6 a.m.*
Sept. 16	3–5 a.m.*
Oct. 1	2–4 a.m.*
Oct. 16	1–3 a.m.*
Nov. 1	11 pm–1 a.m.
Nov. 16	10 p.m.–12 midn.

*Daylight Saving Time

you are in suburbs or a city (or in bright moonlight), because faint stars will be invisible or nearly so through the light pollution. But even if your sky is very dark, there's still a lot more difference between bright and faint stars than the maps suggest.

Expect patterns to be big. Remember that the chart is a *very* reduced representation of the whole sky dome. To see just how reduced, hold your fist out at arm's length and sight past it with one eye. Your fist at arm's length is somewhat smaller than Cassiopeia. Compare this with how little Cassiopeia looks on the map. A fist width in the sky is only about ½ *inch* on the maps. Pretty tiny!

Planets look like bright stars. Planets are not plotted on the maps because they're always changing position. Find the dashed line arcing across each map. This is the *ecliptic,* the line near which the Sun, Moon, and planets always travel. If you find a bright "star" near the ecliptic that's missing from the map, you've discovered a planet.

Your latitude. The maps are drawn for an observer at latitude 40° north. This is near the latitude of New York, Indianapolis, Denver, and Northern California. If you're far south of there, stars in the southern part of your sky will appear somewhat higher than the maps indicate and stars in the north will be lower. Seen from locations far north of 40°, the reverse is true. (The maps won't work at all near the equator or in the Southern Hemisphere.)

If you live anywhere in the world's north temperate latitudes, these maps are all you need for spotting the major constellations of every season and locating the areas of the telescopic charts later in the book.

The Next Step: Sky Distances and Directions

Navigating on the celestial sphere is a bit different from finding your way on land with a map. The differences are in the two kinds of measures you use on any map: *distance* and *direction.*

Newcomers to astronomy often have trouble expressing distances on the sky: "Do you see that star? About eight inches below the bright one?"

"I see one about six feet below it. Is that the one you mean?"

Distances on the sky can't be given in feet or inches, because to one person the sky may look like it's 100 yards away while another sees it as being a half mile away. Actually, the celestial sphere can be considered infinitely distant. So instead of familiar linear measures like feet or inches, we need a different scheme: *angular* measure. The faint star may be *one degree* below the bright one. This means that if lines were drawn from your eye to the stars, the lines would form a 1° angle.

Hold your fist at arm's length and sight past it with one eye, as you did for measuring Cassiopeia. Your fist covers about 10° from thumb to little finger, as shown on the next page. Your hand at arm's length with fingers outstretched as wide as possible covers about 20° from thumb-tip to little fingertip. A fingertip at arm's length is roughly 1° wide, if you have narrow fingers. Cassiopeia is 13° long. The Big Dipper measures 25° from end to end – a little longer than one fully outstretched hand span. Now you know just what size dipper to look for. The Sun and Moon have almost exactly the same angular size, ½°. People usually don't believe they're both so small, but an outstretched fingertip easily covers each. From the horizon to the zenith overhead is 90°. Try measuring this with fists. Maybe you'll find your fist is not exactly 10° wide, but it's close enough for finding your way around.

Everyday objects can also serve as angular gauges. To find the angular size of anything in degrees, divide its linear width, such as inches or feet, by its distance from you measured in the same units, then multiply by 57. For instance, a 1-foot ball 57 feet away from you appears 1° wide – twice the width of the Sun or Moon.

A pair of binoculars typically shows a field about 7° wide. A finderscope (the small sighting aid mounted on the side of an astronomical telescope) typically shows a field about 5° wide. A 50-power telescope magnifies a piece of sky that's just 1° wide.

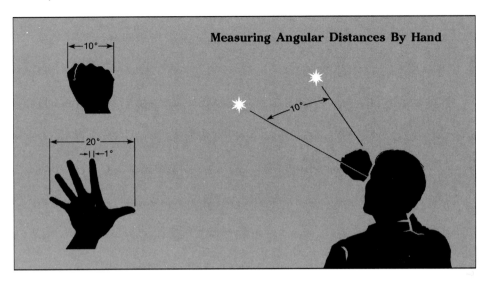

Measuring Angular Distances By Hand

Distances on the sky are given in angular measurement, which loses its mystery when explained in terms of hand widths at arm's length. Finding angular distances this way is the first step in learning to use a sky map.

Try your binoculars or finderscope on the Big Dipper, if it's on your all-sky map for tonight, and see which of the Dipper's stars just fit into the edges of the field. Compare this with the chart of the Big Dipper at left, which gives angular distances between its stars.

Degrees, minutes, and seconds. Sometimes you'll encounter angular sizes smaller than a degree. An *arc minute* is ¹⁄₆₀ of a degree. It's written '. An *arc second* is ¹⁄₆₀ of an arc minute. It's written ". The smallest things the naked eye can resolve, whether in the far distance or in front of you on a piece of paper, are 1' or 2' in angular size, and that's in bright light with good vision. The smallest things a telescope can resolve in the sky are roughly 1" across, 60 times finer, though this depends on the telescope and especially on the atmospheric *seeing* – the steadiness of the air.

Sky directions. When using the all-sky maps on the previous pages, you can make your way from constellation to constellation just by thinking in terms of up, down, left, and right. But that's only possible because these maps show your horizon. That limits each one to particular times and dates. More general star charts, like the ones later in this book, are meant for use at any time. But this versatility comes at a price. Up, down, left, and right lose their meaning. Instead, most star charts are based on *celestial coordinates* – celestial north, south, east, and west. These directions stay fixed with respect to the stars – no matter how the stars happen to be oriented with respect to your horizon.

Don't confuse celestial directions with north, south, east, and west on the ground. On the sky, celestial north is always the direction toward the *north celestial pole*. This is a point about halfway up the northern side of the sky dome that's closely marked by Polaris, the North Star. Polaris is at the end of the handle of the Little Dipper, about halfway between Cassiopeia and the Big Dipper.

You can find Polaris by an age-old trick. The two stars at the front of the Big Dipper's bowl point to it, from about 30° away (three fist widths). Check the maps on the previous pages to see that this is so. Polaris is rather dim, but there's not much else in this dull part of the sky to confuse it with.

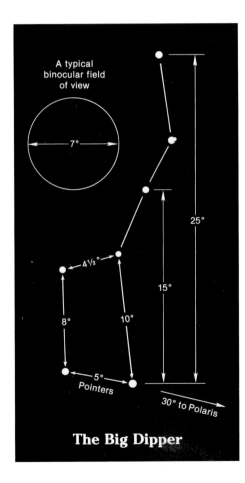

A typical binocular field of view

7°

25°

4½°

15°

8° 10°

5°
Pointers

30° to Polaris

The Big Dipper

The stars of the Big Dipper provide a variety of convenient angular measurements.

Once you find Polaris from a given site, finding it again is easy. Polaris will remain right there all night and all year for centuries to come. This is the point around which the whole celestial sphere seems to rotate.

Celestial north is always the direction toward Polaris, no matter what strange angle this happens to be. Celestial east is the direction at right angles to north that stars move *from* as the sky turns; this more or less corresponds to east on the ground, depending on the part of the sky you're looking at. Celestial west is the direction stars move *toward* as the sky turns. A tricky point: east is *left* on a sky map when north is up, the opposite of east on a land map. This is a consequence of the sky being above us while the land is below.

The rest of this chapter covers some other useful things to know. They're not essential for now, so you can skip over them if you wish.

Right Ascension and Declination

To identify a star's position on the celestial sphere, astronomers use a system much like latitude and longitude on the sphere of the Earth. Sky "latitude" is called *declination;* sky "longitude" is called *right ascension.*

Like latitude on Earth, declination runs from 90° at the north celestial pole to 0° on the *celestial equator.* The celestial equator is the imaginary line on the dome of the sky directly above the Earth's equator. As seen from our latitudes, the celestial equator runs from the east point on the horizon high across the southern part of the sky and down to the west. Declinations in the part of the sky south of this line are negative.

Right ascension, the longitude equivalent, is usually written not in degrees but in hours, minutes, and seconds of time, from 0 hours to 24 hours. This corresponds to the once-daily turning of the celestial sphere. For example, the celestial coordinates of the star Vega are declination 38° 47′ 01″, right ascension 18h, 36m, 56s. This is like specifying where Boston, Massachusetts, is by saying it's at latitude 42° 22′ 10″ north, longitude 71° 07′ 10″ west.

Right ascension and declination are printed around the edges of many star maps, including some of those later in this book. Remember, north is the direction toward greater declination values, and right ascension *increases* to the *east.*

When using a telescope, you can always tell north in the field of view by nudging the telescope slightly toward Polaris. New stars will come into view from the north edge of the field. With the telescope's drive switched off, the turning of the celestial sphere makes stars *enter* from the *east.* These rules work regardless of whether the telescope's view is upside down, mirror-imaged, or both.

Star Names

The names of stars can seem pretty confusing. "Vega," "Alpha Lyrae," "3 Lyrae," and "SAO 67174" all refer to the same object! Here's a quick summary that will explain most star names you'll encounter.

1. A few dozen stars have well-known proper names, such as Vega and Polaris.

2. The brighter stars in each constellation are named with lower-case Greek letters. Vega, for instance, is the Alpha star of Lyra. The letter is used with the Latin genitive of the constellation name: "Alpha Lyrae." This just means "the Alpha of Lyra." The Greek alphabet, and the Latin genitives of all 88 constellations, are listed in Appendixes A and B, respectively. Sooner or later, every astronomer needs to sit down and memorize them.

3. The Greek alphabet doesn't go very far. So star mappers started using numbers instead, giving us star names like 3 Lyrae (Vega again) and 61 Cygni.

4. Still fainter stars are usually listed by their numbers in massive catalogs, such as the *Smithsonian Astrophysical Observatory Star Catalog* (SAO) and the *Henry Draper Catalogue* (HD). Vega, as we've seen, is SAO 67174.

5. Variable stars, those that change brightness, have their own designations in a special system that has grown over time. Within each constellation, if a variable star lacked a Greek letter it was given a capital Roman letter in a sequence from R through Z. The letter is used with the genitive of the constellation name; for example, R Leonis. After Z was used up in a given constellation, astronomers named variables RR, RS, and so on to RZ, then SS to SZ, on up to ZZ.

But new variable stars kept getting discovered. After ZZ, astronomers decided to go to AA, AB, and on to AZ (omitting J since in some languages it could be confused with I), then BB to BZ, on up to QZ. Even these 334 designations finally proved inadequate in some crowded constellations, so all further variables are simply designated V335, V336, and so on.

6. In addition, there are many special lists of particular kinds of stars named for the astronomer who compiled the list. For example, Struve 1138 is the 1,138th double star listed in the catalogue of doubles that was compiled over 150 years ago by the German astronomer Wilhelm Struve.

Magnitudes

The brightnesses of stars and other celestial objects are given in "magnitudes," an odd system that dates from ancient times. The magnitude system was born when the Greek astronomer Hipparchus divided stars into brightness classes. He called the brightest ones "1st magnitude," by which he simply meant "the biggest." Those a little fainter he called 2nd magnitude, or second biggest, and so on down to the faintest he could see: 6th magnitude. When the telescope was invented around 1610, it revealed stars fainter still. Thus 7th, 8th, and 9th magnitudes were added. Today a pair of binoculars will show stars about as faint as 9th magnitude, and an amateur's 6-inch telescope can see to about 13th magnitude. The largest telescopes in the world can reach 25th magnitude or fainter with sensitive electronic detectors.

Some "1st magnitude" stars, it was realized, are a lot brighter than others. To accommodate them, the scale had to be extended the other way into negative numbers. Vega and Capella are 0 magnitude, and Sirius, the brightest in the sky, is magnitude –1.5. Venus is usually magnitude –4, the full Moon is –12, and the Sun shines in our sky at magnitude –27.

More than a century ago this system was mathematically formalized. A brightness difference of one magnitude was defined to be a difference of 2.512 times in the amount of light. This number is the 5th root of 100; it was chosen so that 5 magnitudes are exactly a 100-fold difference in light.

Spectral Types of Stars

A star's light can be divided up into its constituent colors or *wavelengths*, just the way a prism can divide the Sun's light into its rainbow colors. By analyzing this *spectrum* of light, astronomers can tell a great deal about a star: its temperature, chemical composition, surface gravity, rotation, magnetic-field strength, and the star's motion toward or away from us.

The strongest influence is temperature. This determines a star's basic *spectral type*. Some stars are only red hot. Others are orange, yellow, or yellow-white hot (such as the Sun). Those with the highest temperatures are white or even blue-white hot. This temperature sequence corresponds to the *spectral sequence* of star types. From hottest on down, stars are called type *O, B, A, F, G, K*, and *M*. The time-honored way to remember this sequence is by the phrase "Oh Be A Fine Guy/Gal, Kiss Me." To divide the sequence more finely, astronomers use numbers from 0 to 9 after the letter. *F*5, for instance, is halfway between *F*0 and *G*0. The Sun is a type *G*2 star. Hot, white Rigel is type *B*8; orange-red Betelgeuse is *M*2. All but a few unusual stars fit somewhere into this sequence.

Binoculars: Halfway To a Telescope

One December evening when I was 14 years old, I was playing with a large magnifying glass and happened to hold it up in line with a Christmas light at the other end of the house. Suddenly the lens was filled with a blinding glare. How could such a dim light, I wondered, produce such a dazzle? Would it work on an even fainter light – a distant streetlight, say, or a star? I ran out into the cold night to try. The results were disappointing. But my father, who came out to see me holding the magnifying glass up to the stars, suggested I try the family binoculars instead. I did, and the sight that night of the Pleiades and the Belt of Orion helped start me on an astronomical path that continues to this day.

It seemed so easy! I had never realized that ordinary binoculars could be an astronomical instrument. Like most kids I knew a little astronomy from books. But *seeing* celestial objects seemed to be something only scientists could do. As I found out in the following weeks, however, a pair of binoculars opens up endless opportunities for serious sky exploring.

Binoculars are the ideal starter instrument because they are so simple to use. You see the image right-side up and in front of you. The large field of view makes it easy to find what you point at. Yet binoculars reveal many sights that most people think require a telescope – including craters, mountains, and plains on the Moon, planets and their satellites, the brightest asteroids at favorable times, an occasional comet, countless double and variable stars, dozens of star clusters, and some nebulae and galaxies.

The observing and chart-reading skills you'll gain from searching out these things are the same skills needed to put a telescope to good use. But binoculars are far cheaper as a first investment – not to mention being much more convenient to carry in and out and easier to store in a closet. In fact, a good pair of binoculars gives as much improvement over the naked-eye view as a large amateur telescope gives over the binoculars. In other words binoculars get you halfway there – but for a lot less than half the price.

If you don't have a telescope, binoculars are powerful enough to show some of the brighter objects in the guided tours later in this book. In fact, the first tour – Orion's Belt and Sword – is specifically designed for binoculars only.

These instruments are so useful and handy, yet so often unappreciated by beginners fixated on the idea of a telescope, that we're going to sidetrack for a bit to see some of the other things they can do.

The Solar System

The brightest sights are the easiest to begin with. The Moon shows at least as much detail in binoculars as Galileo saw with his primitive telescopes. The mountains, craters, and plains he discovered in 1610 established for the first time that the Moon is a world, like the Earth, overturning the long-established belief that it was a perfect sphere made of some ideal heavenly substance.

Binoculars show more in the sky, and are more pleasant to use, when they are rigidly supported on a convenient mount. This flexible mounting allows binoculars to be aimed comfortably anywhere overhead from anyone's eye height.

The first glance through binoculars reveals the major dark areas, the so-called seas or *maria* (plural of the Latin word for sea, *mare,* pronounced MARray). The maria are flat lava plains. The major maria and other landmarks are named on the full-Moon photograph below. After you spend a few nights outdoors identifying the Moon's features, its geography will begin to grow as familiar as that of the Earth.

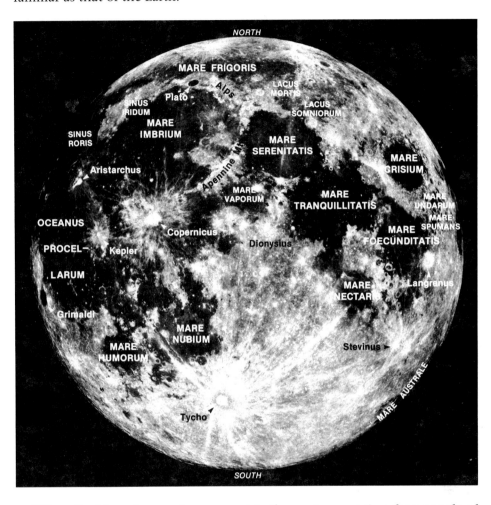

The Moon's major landmarks are easy for binocular users to learn. In addition to the features identified here, scores of smaller details can be seen in even a 5 × instrument. Features often change appearance at different lunar phases. For instance, the bright rays spreading from Tycho (the white crater near bottom) are prominent at full Moon but hardly seen at other times.

When the Moon is a waxing crescent in the western evening sky a couple of days after new, only Mare Crisium is visible. The *terminator,* the line dividing lunar day and night, moves across the disk to unveil ever more features as the Moon's phase grows to first quarter, gibbous, then full. Night by night more seas are revealed – Mare Tranquillitatis, Serenitatis, Imbrium, and finally Oceanus Procellarum. Near the terminator the slanting sunlight casts long shadows, making mountains and valleys stand out prominently. They become more easily visible if you brace the binoculars tightly against something to hold them very still.

The planet **Mercury** can sometimes be located during twilight with the naked eye, but binoculars make it much easier to pick up. Once found, however, this little planet only appears starlike. As with many astronomical objects, the accomplishment lies in finding it at all. Every month the Stars and Planets pages of *Sky & Telescope* tell where to locate this and other planets.

Venus will show its crescent phase in high-quality binoculars. In the summer and fall of 1610, Galileo watched Venus change phases in the evening sky. If the traditional Earth-centered idea of the solar system had been correct, with

Venus always staying between us and the Sun, Venus would *always* appear as a crescent. Instead Galileo saw it as gibbous – proving that it circles behind the Sun, thus providing crucial evidence for the Copernican system that would shake religion and philosophy for the next century. Can you repeat Galileo's observation?

Mars just looks like a bright orange star. **Jupiter**, on the other hand, is one of the binocular showpieces of the sky. Its four bright Galilean moons (so named for their discoverer) are lined up on either side of the planet in patterns that change every night. The outer two moons of Jupiter, Ganymede and Callisto, are the most easily seen in binoculars. Europa and Io remain hidden in Jupiter's bright glare until you catch them near their greatest elongation (distance) from the planet. The monthly Jupiter's Satellites diagram in *Sky & Telescope* can be used to identify the moons you spot. Each one is roughly the size of our own Moon or a little larger. Comparing these tiny pinpoints with the full Moon itself dramatizes how much farther away they are.

A much more difficult achievement is finding Titan, the lone binocular moon of **Saturn**. This 8th-magnitude speck only gets about as far from Saturn as 6th-magnitude Europa does from Jupiter. It needs large, high-power binoculars. Saturn's rings, unfortunately, cannot be seen very definitely with magnifications less than about 20× or 30×.

Uranus, **Neptune**, and the half dozen or so **asteroids** that reach 8th magnitude or brighter look like faint stars. Uranus and Neptune can be found in binoculars with the aid of charts in *Sky & Telescope*. Charts for bright asteroids are also printed in the magazine from time to time. To be sure which "star" is the object you're looking for, draw a map of the stars you see near the correct location and watch for the one that moves from night to night. This is the method by which all the major asteroids were discovered.

Deep-Sky Objects

A different kind of reward comes from seeking out the vanishingly faint glows of star clusters and galaxies thousands or millions of light-years away. Merely finding these eerie phosphorescences amid vast expanses of stars is most of the fun. To do this you will need to become handy with sky charts and adept at finding your way through star fields. This is much easier with binoculars than a telescope, so the binoculars are excellent training. If you have already learned some of the constellations with the naked eye, you'll discover that binoculars show countless new stars in what used to be blank spaces. Sweep from one star to another in familiar constellations to get used to finding your way around.

Pay attention to the size of your field of view; keep in mind how much sky it covers as shown on the map you're using. Locate two bright stars that just fit in the edges of your binoculars' field and see how many degrees apart they are on your map. As described in the chapter "Star-Hopping: Using a Map at the Telescope," you can make a wire ring with this diameter and place it on the chart. The ring will instantly show you the binoculars' field. By sliding it around on the chart you'll see how much territory you have to cross to get from one place to another.

If your sky is fairly dark and free of light pollution, a pair of 8×50 binoculars (see page 36 for an explanation of binocular numbers) should show all stars 9th magnitude and brighter and most deep-sky objects that are described as 7th magnitude or brighter.

As with a telescope, your charts and reference books are crucial to success. See Recommended Reading, page 149, for binocular observing guides.

Binocular Observing Tips

The biggest problem with binoculars, you'll quickly discover, is holding them steady. The constant dancing of the view prevents you from seeing the faintest objects and the finest detail. As a teenager I followed the moons of Jupiter by holding my binoculars against the side of a tree or wedging them between slats of a fence. Lying on your back and resting their weight on the bones below your eyes will reduce the dancing to a wiggle in time with your heartbeat.

Many binoculars can be attached to a photographic tripod with an L-shaped adapter. This holds them perfectly still for near-horizontal viewing, but you can't get underneath a tripod to look up. In recent years a number of special binocular mounts for astronomers have become available. These mounts tend to be a bit large and expensive, but the best of them work extremely well.

If you lack a binocular mount, a lawn chair makes for comfortable sky observing while allowing you to hold the binoculars fairly steady.

Short of buying a binocular mount, the usual way of coping with the shakes is to observe from a reclining lawn chair that has arms. By resting both elbows on the chair arms and the eyepieces against your face, the dancing is greatly reduced. You probably won't be able to set up a tripod over the lawn chair. But even if the binoculars are attached to a photographic tripod lying across your lap with its legs sticking sideways into the air, the images become wonderfully still. Merely attaching the binoculars to such a large, rigid object is enough to stop the troublesome rapid jittering. Many amateurs have constructed their own homemade supports that work well too. With the glasses held still, their performance will seem *at least doubled*. Compare the detail visible in solidly mounted 6×30 binoculars with hand-held 10×50s.

The comfort provided by the chair is also vital. Some of the most satisfying observations are made at the limit of visibility, where all your powers of concentration are called into play. The slightest discomfort or strain will interfere with this concentration and blind you to faint detail. This loss is critical. Half of the astronomical objects visible with *any* instrument – from opera glasses to the Hubble Space Telescope – are within ½ magnitude of the instrument's faint limit. (The reason is that by seeing ½ magnitude deeper, you double the volume of space examined.)

Rubber eyecups are also a boon, especially if artificial lights intrude on your observing site. Charts and notes should be handy, so you can glance back and forth from sky to chart without moving the binoculars. Your lap works fine in a lawn chair, whereas a telescope really requires a separate chart table. For a reading light, a flashlight covered with dark red paper or plastic works well, as red light interferes relatively little with night vision.

Lastly, start keeping an observing notebook or diary right away – even if you only write down the date, time, observing instrument, and such comments as "Sinus Iridum standing out prominently on Moon's terminator," or "M35 in Gemini a big, dim glow," or "NGC 457 not found." This turns an evening's sightseeing into a permanent collection of observations that will grow in value to you with the passage of time. A plain spiral-bound notebook is ideal for this purpose. The more structured records that some amateurs keep (such as a separate page or file card for each object) are best copied out later; they are a chore to organize in the dark and constrain your freedom to write down off-the-cuff remarks. It is often these asides – your first bright meteor; an especially clear, starry sky after a snowstorm; a night at a memorable site – that mean the most when you look back on them in years to come.

CHOOSING YOUR BINOCULARS

Any optical aid will bring deeper views of the sky than the naked eye, and any binoculars that happen to be available, no matter how poor or small, are enough to launch a rewarding observing program. But some kinds are much better for astronomy than others.

The variety of brands and models on the market can be bewildering. Prism binoculars of the basic type made today have been sold commercially for nearly 100 years – so manufacturers have long since discovered and incorporated every easy improvement that is possible. Therefore, when a particular model offers special advantages, you can expect these to be offset by corresponding disadvantages, either in performance, convenience, or price. Choosing the right instrument for your purpose is a matter of choosing where to compromise. The following guidelines will help.

Power. Every binocular has a two-number designation, such as 6×30 or 8×50. The first number is the magnifying power. The second is the diameter of the objective (front) lenses in millimeters.

Beginners usually assume that the higher the power the better. Higher powers do penetrate light pollution more effectively and are best for double stars, star clusters, and certain other objects such as the moons of Jupiter. But high power also narrows the field of view (making it harder to find your way among the stars), and, worst of all, magnifies the dancing of the stars when the instrument is held in the hands. For this last reason, 10 power is the maximum recommended for hand-held binoculars.

Aperture. The bigger the objective lenses the brighter the stars appear, and here the astronomer should compromise least. Most astronomical objects are hard to see not because they are small and need more magnification, but because they are faint and need more aperture. A pair of 8×50s collects twice as much light as all-purpose 8×35s and hence makes everything appear almost one magnitude brighter. The corresponding disadvantage (aside from higher price) is that the 8×50s are bigger and heavier, making them less appropriate for prolonged daytime hiking or birdwatching.

Focusing. Most binoculars are "center-focus," meaning you turn a knob in the center to focus both eyes at once. The right-hand eyepiece is also individually focusable so you can correct for differences between your eyes; in theory this only has to be done once. Center-focus binoculars are convenient for birdwatchers and others whose targets often shift from near to far.

But astronomers don't need this feature. Everything in the sky is at the same "infinity" distance as far as focusing is concerned. So you can save both money and mechanical complication (with its increased likelihood of problems) by choosing *individual focus* binoculars. With these you focus each eyepiece separately.

Quality vs. Price. Suppose you've decided on 8×50s or 10×50s – excellent all-around choices for astronomy. You may find three similar-looking instruments offered for $49, $180, and $1,000. Do these prices really reflect the range of value? This is a matter of opinion, though it's certainly true that a pair costing 20 times more than another won't show 20 times as much. Moving away from the price extremes toward, say, the $75 to $300 range, you basically get what you pay for.

Some manufacturers offer different lines of binoculars having poor, moderate, and good quality (in sales talk: "good," "better," and "best") to provide a selection of prices and values. A cheap instrument may be the best buy for a casual user. But quality is *very* important in the stringent applications of astronomy, so the amateur should consider the better grades. However, having decided on a make and model, you may get a bargain on it by checking with discount stores and dealers.

Used binoculars can be bought at great savings at yard sales, secondhand stores, and pawn shops, but you risk getting stuck with a lemon. The following tests, which can be done in less time than it takes to read them, will enable you to judge the value of any binoculars, new or used.

Three sizes of binoculars: pocket 7×25s, medium-large 10×50s, and giant 20×80s. All of them are useful for amateur astronomy, but the bigger the objective (front) lenses, the brighter the view and the fainter the things you'll be able to see. Many sizes, shapes, and special capabilities are offered on today's binocular market.

Testing Binoculars

1. Pick up the instrument and compare its overall workmanship with other brands; some will seem better made than others. Hold the two barrels and try to twist them slightly. If there is any play in the joints or anything rattles, reject the pair. Move the barrels together and apart; the hinges should work smoothly, with steady resistance. So should the focusing motions for both eyepieces. On center-focus binoculars, the eyepiece frame should not tilt back and forth when you turn the focus in and out.

2. Next, look into the large objective lenses with a light shining over your shoulder so the inside of the barrel is illuminated. Reject the pair if a film of dirt or mildew is visible on any glass surface. (Dust on the outside is not a problem.) Look at the two reflections of the light from the front and back of the objective lens, which will appear to float a little above and behind it. If the lens is antireflection coated – as it should be – both reflections will have a purple, amber, or greenish cast, instead of white. Move the binoculars around until you see a third reflection deep inside, from the first surface of the prisms. This too should be colored, not white. Then, still looking in the front, aim the eyepiece at a nearby light bulb and move the glasses around to view a row of internal reflections. The ratio of colored to white images suggests the percentage of coated to uncoated surfaces.

The coatings increase light transmission and contrast, and reduce "ghost" reflections, all of which is especially important in astronomy. "Multicoating" is the best kind. In top-notch models, all glass-to-air surfaces are multicoated. Don't take vague advertising terms such as "fully coated" too literally; this could mean one lens is "fully" coated and the rest are not.

3. Turn the binoculars around and repeat your examination of lenses and coatings from the eye end. Then, holding the glasses a foot or so in front of you, aim them at the sky or a bright wall. Look at the little disks of light seen floating just outside the eyepieces. These are the *exit pupils*. If they have four shadowy edges, rendering them squarish instead of round, the prisms are not the best and are cutting off some light. In good binoculars the exit pupils are uniformly bright to their round edges. Also, they should be surrounded by darkness, not by reflections from inside the barrels.

4. Finally, look through the binoculars. Adjust the separation of the barrels to match the separation of your eyes, then focus each side separately. A noticeably filmy or gray image indicates an unacceptable contrast problem. If you wear glasses to correct for astigmatism, make sure you can get your eyes close enough to view the full field with the glasses on. If your glasses do not correct for astigmatism, you can take them off.

Each barrel should point in the same direction! If you see a double image or feel eyestrain as your eyes compensate for the binoculars' misalignment, you have a reject. The eyestrain would soon become a real headache.

For a better alignment test, first make sure the barrels are adjusted exactly for the separation between your eyes, then look at something distant through the binoculars. Slowly move them a few inches out from your eyes while still viewing the object. It should not become double. This test is a bit tricky because your eyes will automatically try to fuse a double image. At the same time, even a correctly aligned pair of images will look double for a brief moment before your eyes get them into register. Gross misalignment due to flimsy prism supports is the worst problem of cheap binoculars; even a small knock can render a working pair worthless. More expensive instruments should survive minor accidents better.

Notice the size of the field of view: the wider the better. But the edges of a wide field usually have poor optical quality. Sweep the field at right angles across a straight line, such as a door frame or telephone wire. Watch whether the line bows in or out near the edges. This *distortion* should be slight.

Look at sharp lines dividing light and dark, such as dark tree limbs or the edge of a building against a bright sky. Do they have red or blue fringes? No instrument is perfectly free of this *chromatic aberration,* but some are better than others.

A star at night is the most stringent test of optical quality, so try the binoculars on real stars if you get a chance. If not, look for an "artificial star" such as sunlight glinting off the rounded edge of a distant car bumper. Center it in the field of view. Looking with one eye at a time, can you bring it to a perfect point focus? Or, as you turn the knob, do tiny rays start growing in one direction before they have shrunk all the way in the direction at right angles? This *astigmatism* is especially bothersome when viewing stars, and binoculars that are completely free of it can be forgiven some other faults.

Move the star from the center of the field to the edge. It will go out of focus unless you have a perfectly *flat field* and freedom from various other aberrations. As a rule of thumb, no degradation should be visible until the star is at least halfway to the edge of the field.

After running through these tests with several binoculars, you will have an excellent idea of their relative value.

One last word: Don't be discouraged if you can't find (or can't afford) perfection. Success in amateur astronomy depends more on the right attitude than the right instrument. This was driven home to me some years ago after I moved into downtown New Haven, Connecticut. The sky seemed hopelessly light polluted, my pair of 7×50s was mediocre, and there was no place to use them except through a plastic bubble skylight in the roof of my apartment. The plastic turned star images into shapes I felt no proper amateur would deign to look at. But they were there, all right, and I was so intrigued at being able to observe anything under such conditions that I kept at it. It turned out that stars could be detected down to 8th magnitude. I wound up spending a year following variable stars through the skylight, hunting clusters and doubles, comparing stellar colors, and becoming more familiar with the sky than ever before. So take what you've got and enjoy it.

About Telescopes

Binoculars are fine as far as they go. They're the only optical instrument I used for my first year as a skywatcher, and this turned out to be exactly the right approach to take. But during that time I was laboring toward a bigger goal: building a 6-inch reflector. Making the telescope was the only way I could afford it. I later realized that this constraint was a blessing in disguise. It kept me from getting the telescope too soon – before I knew what to do with it – and led me to value it like the crown jewels despite all the things a telescope of this fairly modest size cannot do.

Sooner or later, every beginning amateur faces up to the tricky question of what to do about getting a telescope. This is probably the most critical decision you will make in the hobby. Choose well, and the telescope will open up a lifetime of pleasurable evenings exploring the sky. Choose poorly, and it is liable to bring frustration and disillusionment and be sold off in the classified ads: "mint condition, rarely used."

If you've already cast the die and committed yourself to an instrument now proudly claiming space in your garage or closet, fine. Whatever it is, you can put it to good use. Once again: success in astronomy depends less on equipment than attitude – persistence, dedication, study. But if you haven't yet decided, this chapter will help sort out your options.

What makes for the right decision? This depends more on you than on the telescope itself. If you live in a fifth-floor city apartment with tiny storage closets and are fascinated by the Moon and planets, you should get an entirely different telescope than if you live on a farm in Vermont with a nice empty shed and your true love is galaxies. The money you can spend, the weight you can lift, and the amount of observing you've already done with the naked eye and binoculars are also crucial.

A telescope's most important characteristic is its *aperture*. This is the diameter of the main lens or mirror. The aperture determines the brightness and sharpness of everything you will see. A 3-inch-aperture telescope can never show stars as faint, or detail as fine, as a well-made 6-inch. The 6-inch in turn can never match a 10-inch of similar quality.

Power, or magnification, is *not* something to consider when purchasing. You can make any telescope magnify at essentially any power you want by using different eyepieces. An eyepiece is the little removable lens assembly you look into. Most telescopes come with several, and more can be bought separately. But it's pointless to use too high a power on a small-aperture telescope. You'll see nothing but highly magnified fuzz. Only a large-aperture scope (on a sturdy mounting!) can show a worthwhile image at 250× or more. In any case, the *lowest* powers are the easiest to use and provide the most pleasing views. You'll use them the most often.

The rule of thumb is that the maximum useful power is 50× per inch of aperture. This limits you to 300× on a 6-inch, and even that's usually pushing it a bit too far. Shun any telescope that is promoted for its high magnification. If you see a 2.4-inch (60-millimeter) department-store telescope advertised as

"475 power!!!", you know the manufacturer thinks you are ignorant and gullible. With that attitude he surely cut a lot of other corners too.

Since the aperture is so important, you might think choosing a telescope is easy – get the biggest aperture you can afford! But in practice it's not so simple. If a scope is too massive to lug outdoors easily and too time-consuming to set up, you'll rarely use it. Even among telescopes with the same aperture, some designs are more portable, others give somewhat sharper images, and others are more economical. The following advice will help you juggle all factors to make the best decision.

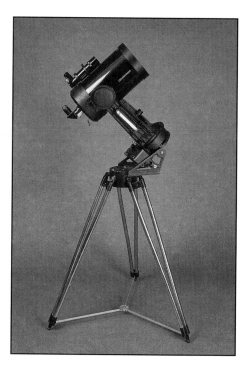

Left: A typical reflector. This is the author's old 6-inch Newtonian telescope, which was used for most of the observations in this book. It's on an equatorial mount. The eyepiece is on the side of the tube at the top.
Center: A refractor. This impressive 5-inch apochromat is shown on a state-of-the-art, computer-controlled, self-pointing equatorial mount. Sold by Meade Instruments Corp., it costs five or six times as much as a basic 6-inch reflector.
Right: A Schmidt-Cassegrain telescope. This 8-inch model is from Celestron International. It costs about twice as much as a 6-inch reflector.

Telescope Types

There are three basic kinds of telescope to choose from: the *reflector*, the *refractor*, and the *catadioptric*. Examples of each kind are illustrated above. Each has its strengths and weaknesses, which you should match to your lifestyle and observing desires.

Refractors have long, relatively thin tubes with an objective lens up front that collects and focuses the light. Refractors range from the very worst telescopes to the finest. "Department-store" refractors of the kind mass-marketed to the public are generally the worst. Their optical quality may be low, and their mountings are often so wobbly that the telescope can hardly be aimed at anything. If your astronomy budget limits you to this price range, stick with binoculars.

You say you *already have* a scope like this? Well, take heart; Galileo would have been overjoyed with it. Keep your expectations low, your patience intact, and don't blame yourself if it gives you trouble. Attitude is everything. Lots of amateurs started off successfully with a department-store refractor. For bright, easily found objects, it may work pretty well.

Very good refractors, on the other hand, are also on the market if you are willing to hunt them out and pay for them. New, complex lens designs offered by a few companies have created some of the most superb – and expensive – telescopes of all. These lens designs are called *apochromatic,* not to be confused with the ordinary *achromatic* refractor. With so much invested in the lens, the makers usually produce a smoothly working, high-quality mounting as well.

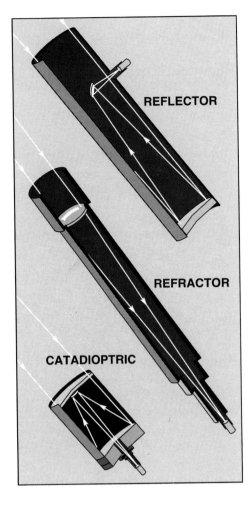

REFLECTOR

REFRACTOR

CATADIOPTRIC

Cutaway views of the three types of telescopes, showing the paths of light inside them.

Advantages. Refractors of all kinds are rugged, require little or no maintenance, and have sealed tubes that keep out dust and image-degrading air currents. If the lenses are good, a refractor provides very crisp, high-contrast images for the size of its aperture that are especially desirable for the Moon and planets.

Disadvantages. Refractors generally have small apertures, typically 3 to 5 inches. For many astronomical purposes this is too small. Faint objects such as galaxies and nebulae will appear very dim when you can detect them at all. A refractor usually requires a right-angle mirror (a "star diagonal") at the eyepiece for comfortable viewing. This mirror flips the image right-for-left, making it hard to compare with charts. And good-quality refractors cost more per inch of aperture than any other kind of scope.

Reflectors use a large, curved mirror instead of a lens to gather and focus light. You look through an eyepiece on the side of the tube up near the top. For decades the reflector was the undisputed king of amateur astronomy. Many would say it still is. From the beginner's standpoint, "reflector" means the Newtonian design illustrated at left.

Advantages. A reflector provides the most aperture per dollar. It is simple enough so the do-it-yourselfer can build it from scratch or tinker with a ready-made one. The optical quality can be very high. A reflector contains an even number of mirrors (two), so you see a "correct" image, not a mirror image. Dew is unlikely to condense on the optics in the night chill, a common annoyance with some other designs. The mounting can be stubby and low to the ground, providing stability while the eyepiece is still at a convenient height.

Disadvantages. Reflectors may require a little more care and maintenance. The tube is open to the air, which means dust on the optics no matter how well the tube is sealed during storage (though a little dust has zero effect on performance). The mirrors need occasional adjustment to keep them lined up exactly right, a simple but slightly tedious procedure of turning nuts on the mirror mounts. During observing, the open tube allows internal air currents that may fuzz up the image until the telescope comes to the same temperature as the surrounding air.

Different f/ratios. All telescopes, but reflectors especially, perform differently at different f/ratios (see box at left). In general, the higher the f/ratio the better. Lower than f/6 or f/5, a reflector's secondary mirror has to be relatively large and this reduces image sharpness. Distortions become more apparent near the edge of the field of view, and the entire optical system is more sensitive to tiny misalignments and other imperfections. Also, with a low f/ratio you have to use better, more expensive eyepieces to get sharp views. An f/4 reflector will almost never quite match an equally well-made f/8. On the other hand, the f/4 is much more handy and portable. A 10-inch reflector at f/4 is less than four feet long and will go in the back seat of a car for jaunts to dark sites. A 10-inch f/8 is about seven feet long and a major logistical problem to transport. Everything's a tradeoff.

Catadioptric or compound telescopes use both lenses and mirrors. The most popular design is the Schmidt-Cassegrain, which burst onto the market in the 1970s and quickly gained a place for itself alongside refractors and reflectors, which had been around for centuries. The following comments apply primarily to these commercial Schmidt-Cassegrains.

Advantages. The pluses of the "Schmidt-Cass" are in portability, convenience for photography, and special options, not visual performance. While most people can haul an 8-inch reflector in and out of doors, it is awkward and heavy. Most 8-inch Schmidt-Cassegrains come in a padded footlocker that can be hoisted with one hand. (The tripod is separate.) The footlocker can be stowed in a car or closet like a large piece of luggage, whereas a reflector tends to displace everything around it.

A Schmidt-Cassegrain's relatively short tube allows a motorized mounting to track the stars more reliably, making photography easier. These are excellent photographic telescopes. Elaborate electronic drive controls are available as options on Schmidt-Cass mountings, primarily for photographers.

Disadvantages. The image formed by a Schmidt-Cassegrain never seems to be quite as sharp as the image formed by a good reflector of the same aperture. This is most noticeable when observing planets. The cost is higher than for a reflector of the same aperture. A right-angle mirror (star diagonal) is generally used at the eyepiece to provide a comfortable viewing position, and this means your view is mirror-reversed. The focusing mechanism may be a bit sloppy and imprecise. You can't take the scope apart yourself; major adjustments mean shipping it back to the factory.

Special options. The newest options on Schmidt-Cassegrains, and on some high-performance refractors too, are robotic aiming motors controlled by an on-board computer with a database of celestial objects. Once you "initialize" the computer by aiming at a couple of known stars and doing some other setup, these telescopes will swing around to point automatically, by magic, at whatever you want. This is supposed to make astronomy easy; you don't have to know the sky.

Opinions about computerized scopes are heated and divergent. Some longtime observers rave about them, saying a computerized scope finally lets them spend more time looking *at* objects than looking *for* them. Others think a computerized scope for beginners is an expensive crutch that impedes learning and takes too much of the fun out. I lean to the latter opinion. After all, you wouldn't want to learn to fly an airplane by being told just to push a button labeled "autopilot."

Mountings

The best telescope is worthless if it is on a poor mounting. The tiniest wobble will be magnified into an earthquake by whatever power you are using. You can't see much in a view that's having earthquakes. Unfortunately, almost all telescope mountings are afflicted with undesirable wiggles. Often this is due to designers' oversights (or manufacturers' cost-cutting) at one or more key stress points. But to some degree it's the inevitable result of making any mount that's light enough to carry without a forklift.

There are two basic telescope mountings: the *equatorial* and the *altazimuth*. An equatorial mount is designed so you can easily track the motion of the sky as the Earth turns. Otherwise, the Earth's rotation carries things out of the field of view fairly quickly – in less than a minute at 100 power. Most equatorial mounts come with an electric "clock drive" to take care of this automatically. In addition, an equatorial mount is very useful in that its motions indicate celestial north-south and east-west in the eyepiece. This is a great help when you're trying to find your way among the stars with a chart.

An equatorial mounting must be aligned on the north celestial pole at the start of each observing session for these features to work. Fortunately, this doesn't need to be done accurately for visual observing. Just plunk the mount down so its polar axis is aimed more or less at Polaris by eyeball judgment.

Altazimuth mounts just swing up-down and side to side. You have to nudge the scope along every so often to follow the stars. An altazimuth mount is simpler, cheaper, and lighter for the same degree of stability, advantages that are exploited to the utmost in the *Dobsonian* mount design for giant, low-cost reflectors. Large altazimuth telescopes, however, require the user to be a skilled pathfinder among the stars. The big Dobsonians are best for experienced deep-sky observers hungry for aperture.

A homemade 20-inch reflector on an equatorial mount built from plywood. The 20-inch-diameter mirror is in the wooden box, and the eyepiece fits into the little projection at top left. You need a ladder to look into it. Ingenious, lightweight designs like this one – pioneered by ambitious do-it-yourselfers in basement workshops – have made observatory-size telescopes portable enough for carrying to star parties and campsites.

Whatever mount you get, don't compromise on its size and strength. Nothing kills your enthusiasm like a perpetually shaky view, but a solidly mounted telescope – one that wiggles only a trace as you focus it – is a joy to use.

Your Interests

Planets, the Moon, and close double stars require high power and sharp resolution, and if these objects are your main interest, a refractor or high-f/ratio reflector is probably the best bet. Very faint objects like galaxies and nebulae need aperture, aperture, aperture. A really big reflector is the logical choice if this will be your specialty. If you haven't specialized and don't intend to, an all-purpose midrange telescope should serve best – perhaps a 6- or 8-inch reflector with a focal ratio of f/8 or f/6, or an 8-inch Schmidt-Cassegrain.

One factor may force your choice of interests: light pollution. The Moon and major planets shine through light pollution unhindered. But faint objects such as galaxies and nebulae are devastated by it. The fifth-floor city dweller could clamp a small refractor to the rail of a fire escape and enjoy as fine a view of the Moon as the Vermont farmer. But most deep-sky objects would be invisible.

Your Living Situation

You don't just look through a telescope. You have to store it and carry it. You have to set it up *and* take it down at the end of a long day when most people are ready for bed. If this is a difficult chore, you won't observe very often no matter how burning your enthusiasm may be right now. Too many novices forget this and buy massive "white elephants" they hardly ever use. A lowly 3-inch telescope *will show more than a 16-inch* if you use it more.

The best scope for you is the scope you'll use the most. How much fun you have, and how good an astronomer you become, depend on how much time you spend observing – not the size of your aperture. Figure out where you'll use the telescope and where you'll store it. The farther apart these two places are, the smaller and lighter the instrument you should get. Does the route between them involve stairs? Then think carefully before getting a reflector bigger than a 6-inch.

An enclosed, unheated porch or a clean, well-ventilated, *dry* shed are excellent for storage. Not only will the telescope be close to where you'll use it, it will already be at the outdoor temperature when you set it up. This will save problems with the image-blurring "tube currents" of warm air that plague telescopes brought from a warm house into the cold night – and the massive dewing that can drench a cold scope brought back indoors.

Will you have to tote the telescope around to avoid trees and lights? If you have one permanent observing site, consider installing a pier rather than lugging the tripod in and out. A large, sand-filled pipe or a cut-off telephone pole planted deep in the ground will be steadier than any tripod. The ideal solution is a shelter or observatory around the entire telescope right where it will be used.

Buying Advice

Having narrowed your choices – perhaps to a 6- or 8-inch reflector or an 8-inch catadioptric – get all the manufacturers' catalogues and compare details, paying careful attention to size and weight. Call different dealers for the best price, but also ask the dealers' policies on returns and repairs (an unfortunate necessity for some brand-new scopes). Insist on an honest appraisal of the delivery date – which in certain cases could be a *year* from receipt of your order. In my opinion, good servicing and prompt delivery are worth more than getting the rock-bottom price.

Consider building the reflector yourself from parts. If you buy the mirror rather than grinding and polishing it yourself, the most complicated tool you'll need is an electric drill. You may save some money and you'll know your telescope literally inside out.

Optical Quality

If possible, star test a telescope before buying. This is especially important when considering a used one not covered by warranty. If you can't test before you buy, do so right after. Optical quality can vary quite a lot even among identical-looking instruments from the same assembly line. Large optical parts can't be mass-produced with reliable quality. Each one has to be hand-finished individually by a (hopefully) skilled worker. This means you never know for sure what you're getting till you test it.

Here is a simple but very stringent test. With the optics properly aligned or "collimated" (read the instructions that come with the scope), and after the telescope has come to the same temperature as the night air (an hour or two after it emerges from a warm house), focus on a 2nd- or 3rd-magnitude star using very high power (preferably without a Barlow lens, which in some cases might skew the test). Polaris is a good choice because it doesn't move. Turn the focus knob *slightly* to one side, then to the other side, of best focus. The star's fuzzy, shimmering, out-of-focus diffraction rings should *look the same* on both sides of best focus. That is, they should be the same shape and have the same distribution of light inside them. Poor atmospheric *seeing* – the quivering and blurring caused by the Earth's unsteady atmosphere – may make this test difficult. Keep trying on subsequent nights until you hit a spell of good seeing.

This test is so sensitive that few telescopes pass it perfectly. If the out-of-focus star image is *almost* the same on either side of focus, you still have a good scope. If it's obviously different, however, something is wrong. Before leaping to conclusions, try again on several other nights and remember to give the scope plenty of time to cool.

A telescope that fails the star test won't ever focus very sharply. At high power, the star will seem to gradually ooze or "shmush" through best focus as you turn the knob, compared to a fine scope where the star "snaps" through focus. The "snap test" is more of a judgment call than the either-side-of-focus star test, which is more exact. All stars are rendered "shmushy" to some degree by atmospheric seeing. But if you get a chance to test a good scope and a poor one side by side, the shmush-versus-snap effect is plain. Do this at high power, because imperfections in your own eye often make a star shmush through focus at low power no matter how good the telescope is.

If a scope is definitely bad, be bold about returning it for repair or refund. The better makers give lifetime guarantees and have excellent reputations for fixing problems fast. No matter who made the scope, you have a moral right to this treatment, so act accordingly.

The best advice when considering telescopes is to seek the opinions of other amateurs. Members of your local astronomy club will be glad to offer help and frank opinions. With luck you may even get to try out a variety of their telescopes, which will help you decide whether twice the aperture is really worth four times the cost and six times the weight. The addresses and phone numbers of over 400 clubs in the United States and Canada are listed in the Astronomical Directory available from Sky Publishing Corp.

Happy hunting!

There are other telescope designs than refractors, reflectors, and Schmidt-Cassegrains. Phil Rounsaville, an accomplished amateur telescope maker from Buckland, Massachusetts, resurrected the antique Gregorian optical design for this fine 6-inch f/31 scope.

Using Your Telescope

Once you've got a telescope, what can you expect of it? Both less and more than many new owners realize.

One of the most fun parts of being an amateur astronomer is showing off the heavens to others. The "oohs" and "aahs" at a public star party as people get their first good look at the Moon or Saturn are a pleasant reward for the telescope owner. Naturally, he or she will have aimed the scope at the most spectacular object above the horizon. Sometimes there's a temptation to show people more typical objects – ghostly, barely visible apparitions with obscure catalog numbers – "to give them an idea of *real* astronomy." The reactions then are not so encouraging, even when viewers are told they're looking at a recently recovered comet or a galaxy 40 million light-years away.

The truth is, most of the thousands of objects visible in amateur instruments are not the least bit spectacular. Anyone who gets a telescope for visual thrills is in the wrong hobby. The riches that astronomy offers are of a different sort. Visual observing outdoors in the dark usually means working to detect something extremely faint, tiny, hard to find, or all three. The more difficult the task, however, the greater the rewards of success. The excitement lies in finding and seeing first-hand remote marvels far beyond our planet – and in gaining skills and knowledge as an amateur scientist.

Too many people buy a telescope as if it were a TV, expecting it to show pictures all by itself. It's more like a piano, which gives back only as much value as the work you put into it. Learning to use a telescope well is a lot easier than learning a musical instrument, however. If you're reasonably persistent and careful and are willing to practice the techniques described here, you'll master the skies.

Know Your Equipment

Naturally, everyone first tries out a new telescope in the daytime. This is when to become familiar with its motions, pointing, focusing, different eyepieces, and magnifying powers, so you can then do everything in the dark.

The finder. Most telescopes have a finderscope attached to the side to help aim it. You need the finder because the main telescope has such a tiny field of view – that is, it shows such a tiny piece of sky – that you can't tell exactly where it's pointed just by looking.

The higher the power, the *smaller* the field of view. For example, at 50 power you're looking at a magnified piece of sky about as small as your little fingernail covers at arm's length. An 8× finderscope, on the other hand, displays about as much sky as a golf ball covers at arm's length. This is big enough to aim at something you see with the naked eye and get it in the finderscope's view. Once it's there, you center it in the finder's crosshairs. That should be a precise enough aim for the object to appear in the view of the main telescope.

First things first: you'll need to adjust the finder's mounting screws so it's aimed parallel to the main telescope. In daylight, point the main scope at

Observing the surface of the Sun through a special aluminized-Mylar solar filter. This one is fitted over the front of a small reflector on a Dobsonian altazimuth mount.

Amateur telescope making is a special branch of the astronomy hobby. Building your own telescope is not everyone's cup of tea, but it's not as hard as you might think; several good guidebooks are available. Everyone's product seems to come out different. This homemade wood-frame reflector was designed to collapse and stow easily in a small car.

something at least several hundred feet away using the lowest-power eyepiece. (But *not the Sun!* Never look in a telescope that might get aimed at the Sun or you could blind yourself.) A distant treetop is ideal. Never mind if it appears upside down. Now look in the finder. See the treetop? Is it centered in the crosshairs? Adjust the screws holding the finder until the crosshairs line up on the target. Now check back in the main telescope to make sure it hasn't moved. Then switch to a high-power eyepiece in the main telescope, and repeat the operation until the finder is locked in position with perfect aim.

Why, you ask, is the treetop upside down or oriented at some other weird angle? The answer is that this is an *astronomical* telescope, and after all, there's no up or down in space. So it doesn't matter how the field is oriented. Turning the image right-side up would require extra optical parts, adding to the expense and complication of the instrument and probably degrading its performance slightly. Therefore, "image erecting" lenses are used only in terrestrial telescopes, those intended for looking at things on Earth.

Figuring Out Your Mount

Next let's turn to the mounting. As noted in the previous chapter, telescope mounts come in two basic types: equatorial and altazimuth. An equatorial mount allows the telescope to swing only in the directions of celestial north-south and east-west. The altazimuth goes up and down (moving in *altitude*) and side to side (*azimuth*).

The equatorial mount. If this is what you have, find its polar axis (the rotating shaft that's more toward the base and has the setting circle showing right ascension). This shaft needs to aim upward at an angle that equals your latitude – about 40° or 45° in the northern United States and southern Canada, about 30° in the South. The telescope's instructions should tell how to make this adjustment. It only needs to be done once, then you can forget it.

With that done, take the telescope outside and place it so that the polar axis points roughly to where you know Polaris, the North Star, will be after dark. The telescope's motion around this axis now traces the paths taken by celestial bodies across the sky as the Earth turns.

Rotate the telescope around its polar axis so its aim sweeps from the eastern horizon across the sky to the west, to visualize nightly star paths. At first the mount's motions will seem awkward and unpredictable. But remember that no matter where the telescope is pointed, it will move only toward or away from Polaris (celestial north-south) and at right angles to this direction (celestial east-west). The orientation of these directions varies in different parts of the sky, but with some practice swinging the telescope around in daytime you'll get used to them.

The altazimuth mount. If your mounting just moves up-down and side to side, at least it has the virtue of simplicity. There's nothing tricky about pointing it. You will, however, have trouble aiming the scope at something very close to straight up, so avoid that part of the sky.

The Fine Art of Observing

The challenge of astronomy is that we must view most of the universe from *extremely* far away. When you're trying to see something well on Earth your instinct is to move closer for a better look. But when it comes to distant stars and galaxies, we're stuck where we are. So, ever since the dawn of telescopic astronomy, the art of observing has been the art of using your eye to the utmost of its ability.

Viewing tips. When looking through the telescope, focus and refocus with care. A good observer is always fiddling with the focus, trying to get it just a hair sharper. Many people find it best to keep both eyes open, since squinting strains the working eye. You can cover the "off" eye with one hand.

Don't expect to see right away everything an astronomical object has to offer. The first look always shows less than comes out with continued scrutiny. This is true whether your subject is a dim galaxy that can hardly be distinguished from the blackness of space, or detail on the Moon or a planet where the light is almost blindingly bright.

One reason it takes time to see detail is the unsteadiness of the Earth's atmosphere. Celestial objects constantly shimmer and boil when viewed at high power, due to weak but ever-present heat waves in the air around and above us. The severity of this shimmering – called the *atmospheric seeing* – varies from night to night and sometimes from minute to minute. As you watch an object quiver and churn, unsuspected detail will flicker into view during quick moments of stability when the view sharpens up, only to fade out again before you know it. The skilled observer learns to remember these good moments and ignore the rest. The quality of the atmospheric seeing is most important when viewing bright objects at high power, but it can influence the visibility of faint ones too.

The main reason it takes time to see detail, however, has to do not with the atmosphere but with the eye and mind. Wringing everything possible out of very distant views means learning new visual skills that involve active, concentrated effort. You'll discover that the eye's picture of a difficult object builds up rather slowly. First one detail is noticed and fixed, and you think there's nothing more to be seen. But after a few minutes another detail becomes evident, then another.

To convince yourself of this, look at a piece of sky with the naked eye and try to spot faint stars. Some will be visible right away; others take a few seconds to come out. When no more appear, most people would quit trying. But keep at it for a few minutes. Chances are some more will glimmer into view in places you would have sworn were blank. After a while you're seeing at least half a magnitude fainter than at first.

The planet Mars is another classic example of this effect. For the beginner taking a first look with a small telescope, Mars ranks as the most disappointing object in the sky. It's just a tiny, featureless, orange fuzzball. The beginner steps aside to let an experienced Mars observer look in the eyepiece. Silence. "There's the north polar cap.... That big dark area in the south must be Mare Erythraeum. Okay, I've got Sinus Meridiani.... There's a cloud patch on the western limb...." The beginner looks again. Nothing but a fuzzball. Well, maybe there *is* a bit of brightness at the north edge crawling around in the poor seeing, and the fuzziness isn't a *perfectly* uniform orange, but these hardly seem like things worth noticing. Nevertheless, the next time the beginner looks he or she won't be quite a beginner, and the bright spot and dark area will come into view more readily.

An excellent way to train yourself to see better is to make sketches. These don't have to be works of art; the idea is just to record details in your notebook more directly than you can with words. Star fields require no artistic talent whatsoever, but by sketching a field that contains a faint asteroid or outer planet, you can identify the intruder by checking back in the next few days or weeks and seeing which one changes position.

For practice sketching planets, try drawing the Moon with the naked eye. If you have reasonably sharp or well-corrected vision, the Moon shows more detail to the naked eye than any planet will in a telescope! Make a semicircle a couple of inches in diameter by tracing some round object and then draw in the terminator exactly as you see it on the Moon. Carefully add the major dark areas with pencil shading, then look for finer markings. By now you'll be seeing much more detail on the Moon's face than you ever thought possible without optical aid.

"The lesson is clear," wrote the British author James Muirden in *The Amateur Astronomer's Handbook,* long a classic:

> No opportunity should be lost to train the eye to work with the telescope; to observe the same object with different powers so as to see the effect of magnification; to try to see faint stars; and to draw planetary markings. In the beginning, to be sure, this may all seem to be wasted effort; the observing book will fill up with valueless sketches and brief notes of failure. But this apparently empty labor is absolutely essential; for, as the weeks pass, a steady change will be taking place. Objects considered difficult or impossible to see will now be discerned at first glance, and fainter specters will have taken their place. Indeed, these former features will now be so glaringly obvious that the observer may suppose that some radical improvement has occurred in the observing conditions. But the credit belongs entirely to the eye....

Life's Little Comforts

Naturally, this sort of concentration will be spoiled by any undue discomfort or inconvenience at the telescope. You'll need a table right at hand to hold charts, red flashlight, eyepieces, notebook, pencil, and other gear. The perfect solution for me has been a cheap cardboard card table with fold-up metal legs. It's big, very light, and easy to carry and store. I got it for $4 in a secondhand shop almost 20 years ago.

Nothing ruins your ability to see like having to twist and strain to look through the eyepiece. A rotating tube, which can turn in its cradle to orient the eyepiece more where you prefer, is therefore a nice plus in a small reflector and almost mandatory in a large equatorially mounted one. If you can find or make an adjustable-height observing chair, your telescope may start showing new worlds. I've used an assortment of seats from a milk crate to a stepladder.

Any jerkiness and backlash in the mount's motions can also spell doom, especially if you lack a clock drive. Make sure the telescope is balanced properly by adjusting any counterweights. Don't be afraid to take a mount apart and lubricate it, or return it to the manufacturer if it's unsatisfactory. The mount I bought for my 6-inch reflector years ago was originally quite jerky. After trying various lubricants, I settled on candle wax rubbed onto all the bearing surfaces. The mount's "clamps" were merely bolts that tightened head-on against the shafts; I epoxied small pieces of leather to the bolt ends, impregnated these with graphite and a little oil, and thus gained adjustable tension. The improvement was enormous. At high power I could follow the stars with a smooth, continuous motion just by pressing the side of my nose against the eyepiece.

In wintertime, you can either heed the astronomer's standard advice to dress for 20° to 30° F colder than the actual temperature, or you can learn the hard way. As for the summer, it remains a mystery how successful observations were performed before the invention of mosquito repellent.

In short: Anything that makes your observing easier, surer, or more relaxed, no matter how much trouble it takes beforehand, is well worth the effort.

"The Salvage Scope" is what Joe Monju calls his 12.5-inch altazimuth reflector that celebrates the junkyard look. He built it around an oil barrel and old auto parts.

Star-Hopping: Using a Map at the Telescope

By the time you set out with a telescope, you should know the constellations well enough to find your way around the sky. The all-sky maps on pages 16 to 27 will get you started, and they'll point the way to the star-hops mapped in detail later in this book. However, it's still an excellent idea to get a more thorough naked-eye sky guide, such as H. A. Rey's *The Stars: A New Way To See Them*. See the Recommended Reading list in the back of the book.

In addition to a constellation guide, an amateur astronomer needs a more detailed sky atlas in order to locate much of anything. Most of the charts later in this book are adapted from Wil Tirion's *Sky Atlas 2000.0,* one of the best all-purpose map sets currently available.

The maps in an atlas like Tirion's may look terribly complex at first. But step back for a minute and look at only the brighter stars; they form the same familiar constellation patterns. Suppose, for instance, you've learned Gemini from the all-sky maps in this book, where its stars are connected to form two stick figures holding hands. These same stick figures appear on chart 5 of the *Sky Atlas 2000.0* – but at a larger scale and almost lost in a wealth of detail. Part of this area of the Tirion map appears on page 86.

Directions and Distances

First get familiar with directions on the map. East, you'll notice, is *left* of north on sky maps, not to the right like on maps of the ground. The reason is simple: You look down at the ground but up at the sky. (If you looked up through the bottom of a land map of, say, the United States – as if you were at the center of a transparent Earth – it too would have east left when north was up.) One trick for keeping east and west straight on a map is remembering that right ascension *increases to the east.* If hours of right ascension are printed on the map they'll set you straight.

The next step is to learn the map's scale. You have to know how much of what's printed on the map appears in your finderscope before you can use the map to find anything! First determine the size of your finderscope's field. Locate two stars that just fit into its edges (try pairs in the Big Dipper or Cassiopeia). Then see how many degrees apart they are on your atlas map by referring to the declination scale along the sides, or by checking the Big Dipper diagram on page 29. That's the diameter of your finder's field.

Now do the same to find the field diameter of the main telescope's lowest-power eyepiece using a more detailed atlas map (ones of the Big Dipper are on pages 90 and 97). It will probably be only about 1° or so – the area your little fingernail covers at arm's length. This is so small that it may be hard to get pointed at a star pair on your map to measure the field size. Here's another way. Aim at any star within about 10° of the celestial equator – in Orion's Belt, for example. Center the star. Then turn off the telescope's clock drive (if any) and time how long the star takes to drift from the center to the field's edge. The time in seconds, divided by 120, equals the *diameter* of the field in degrees.

Now, using the scale on the margin of your atlas charts, make little rings out of wire – or draw circles on clear plastic – corresponding to your field sizes. An example is shown in the photograph below. By sliding these circles across the charts, you can see exactly what star patterns will pass through your field of view when you sweep across the sky. Beginners are always surprised at how tiny the view really is. Keep these little tools with the charts; you'll need them whenever you observe.

Now we're ready to go on our first deep-sky hunt.

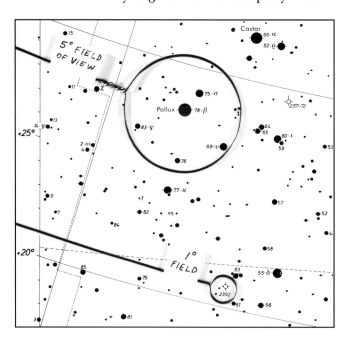

How much of a chart appears in your eyepiece? You'll be lost until you know. Handy aids like these tell at a glance. The large wire ring shows the 5° field of the finderscope on the author's 6-inch reflector. The small ring shows the 1° field of the telescope's 50-power eyepiece. Note the tiny size of the telescopic field, even on a large-scale chart like Wil Tirion's Sky Atlas 2000.0. *Examining the sky at 50 power is like examining the chart with a microscope.*

A Practice Star-Hop

Any observing session should begin with some indoor planning. Let's use Gemini for a dry run. If you know the constellations, you can find its two bright stars, Castor and Pollux, in the sky. These will be our starting point.

A couple of inches south of Pollux on the chart shown above is the planetary nebula NGC 2392, indicated by a little open circle with four spikes. This looks like a likely item to check out. In *Burnham's Celestial Handbook* it's described as a small, round glow of 8th magnitude, which is bright enough to show in most telescopes. So far so good. The next step is to plan how to get there by star-hopping. This just means following a trail of stars to move the telescope from a place we know, such as Pollux, to some place we don't, such as the location of the nebula. The trick is not to get lost on the way. Follow each step on the picture above.

Take the wire ring that corresponds to your finder's field and center it on Pollux. Several fainter stars are in the circle, just as they would be if you were looking through the finderscope at the sky. The bright star closest to Pollux is 75 or Sigma (σ) Geminorum, to the north of Pollux in the direction of Castor (which is out of the field of view). Near the southwest edge of the field is the star 69 or Upsilon (υ) Geminorum. It forms a long right triangle with Pollux and 75, with Pollux at the right angle. This triangle confirms 69's identity in the sky, where there's no convenient label next to it.

Shift the wire ring to center on 69; this corresponds to moving the telescope. Two new pairs of stars have entered the west edge of the field a little north of center: 64, 65, 60, and 59, the four of them forming a distinctive pattern. Shift the ring to center on 60. The fainter 59 just to its southwest will confirm you've got the right one.

Star 57 is now just on the south edge of the field. Shift south by half the width of the field so 57 is centered; bright Delta (δ) is now waiting just outside to the south. Shift south again an equal amount; δ quickly appears and can be centered just after 57 leaves to the north. See how δ forms an equilateral triangle with 56 and 63, to its south and east? With 63 identified – aided by two fainter stars on either side of it – we're less than 1° from our prey. Note the flat triangle that 63 and 61 form with the nebula. The shape of the triangle allows us to target the correct position even if the nebula is invisible, as it may be in the finder. The two faint stars just southeast of the nebula will help confirm the exact spot.

From Map to Sky: Know Your Directions

If we do this outdoors at night and move the telescope to match each step on the map, NGC 2392 should now be visible in the main eyepiece: a small, dim, eerie round glow quite unlike the pointlike stars, grayish green in color and with a very faint star at its exact center – a prize worthy of the rather complicated chase.

The star-hopping route may seem like a lot of trouble to the beginner, whose impulse is just to sweep from Pollux "about the right distance *that* way." But most deep-sky objects are many times dimmer than the faintest stars on the chart and won't catch your attention even if, by luck, your tiny telescopic field happens to sweep across them. The only way to succeed is to know exactly where you are at all times. If you suspect you're lost, go back and start over. Have patience. You'll speed up later when practice increases your skill.

The biggest pitfall in going from map to sky is keeping directions straight. Remember that in the sky, celestial north is not up but *toward Polaris,* no matter how cockeyed this direction may be in the eyepiece. To find north as seen in the eyepiece, just nudge the telescope a bit toward Polaris. New stars will enter from the field's *north side,* showing you where this is. Turn the map around accordingly, so north on the map points in this direction. This north-nudging trick will become such a habit at the telescope that you'll forget you're doing it. If you have an equatorial mount, turn the eyepiece of the finderscope so the crosshairs line up with the telescope's motion as you sweep north-south or east-west. The crosshairs will now mark the four cardinal directions no matter where you point the scope.

Okay, you've found north in the eyepiece. East and west can be a bit trickier, depending on your telescope. East is 90° *counterclockwise* from north if you're looking at a "correct" or right-reading image, just like on a map. A correct image is given by an optical system that has an even number of mirrors. Examples are a Newtonian reflector, which has two mirrors, or a straight-through refractor, which has zero. But east is 90° *clockwise* from north in a mirror image, which is what you see when light is reflected an odd number of times. A mirror image is very hard to compare with a correct-image map. Note that this is *not* the same as the image merely being turned upside down. In that case you could simply turn the map upside down too. A mirror image cannot be made correct no matter how you turn it.

The usual culprit is a star diagonal on a refractor or Schmidt-Cassegrain telescope. To get a correct image you can simply take out the diagonal and reinsert the eyepiece to view straight through. This is especially important to do to your finderscope, if it came with a diagonal. Alternatively, you can photocopy your map, turn the photocopy over, and shine a flashlight up through the paper from beneath to view a mirror image of the printing through the paper.

Better yet, photocopy maps onto clear acetate Viewgraph sheets, turn the Viewgraphs over, and tape them to a red background.

Some amateurs who insist on using their star diagonals while star-hopping have resorted to propping up a small mirror on their chart table and viewing their maps in the mirror. This way you see what you get. Or you can buy a diagonal that is made with an Amici prism, which employs two reflections instead of an ordinary diagonal's one.

When star-hopping, *always* think in terms of celestial north, south, east, and west – never up, down, left, or right, or you'll quickly get lost in trackless wastes of space. Once you get the hang of it you'll always be mumbling as you turn from map to scope: "From that bright one in the north of the kite shape… half a finder field east to the pair in the skinny triangle…then a quarter finder field south to the one at the west end of the flat triangle…." Triangles are the most basic units of star-hop patterns, and you'll be seeing a lot of them.

Secrets of Deep-Sky Observing

Okay, you're pretty sure you've got the telescope aimed at the position of the object of your desire. The crosshairs of your finder are on its exact location according to your map. Now what can you hope to see?

If it's a bright star it will be obvious and beautiful but contain no detail. A star as seen in a telescope is a tiny blaze of light looking about the same as a star does to the naked eye, only brighter.

More interesting but generally more difficult are *deep-sky objects*. This term covers the vast variety of nebulae, star clusters, galaxies, and anything else beyond the solar system that appears *extended:* having a visible size, rather than just being a starlike point. Hundreds, possibly thousands of these ghostly glows and subtle spatterings are within reach of a modest telescope.

Once you're precisely aimed you may see, with luck, a very dim, shapeless, glowing smudge floating among the stars. While finding it may bring a thrill of accomplishment, many novices are let down by the sight. "Is *that* all there is…to *galaxies?* It's nothing like the pictures in the books!"

You've just come up against the fact that the human eye cannot perform as well as a camera does at low light levels. Your real-life view of a galaxy will never match the spectacular photos so common in books and magazines. But here lies the challenge. Many deep-sky objects *do* show a surprising amount of detail when studied long and well.

A telescope serves a different function on deep-sky objects than on the Moon, planets, or scenes on Earth. In those cases, its main purpose is to magnify distant detail. With deep-sky objects, on the other hand, a telescope's main purpose is to collect a lot of light. The issue is not that they're too *small* to see without optical aid. It's that they're too *dim*.

Accordingly, deep-sky observing involves its own techniques. All are aimed at helping the eye to see in near-total darkness. Here are some pointers.

Sky brightness. The single most important factor in deep-sky observing is light pollution. Its worst effect is on dim, extended objects of just the sort we're considering. A dark sky is even more important than telescope size; a small instrument in the country will show faint nebulae and galaxies better than a large telescope in a city. If you live in a badly light-polluted area, take pleasure in what you *can* see – but don't blame yourself or your telescope for mediocre results. Plan to bring the telescope on getaways to the country.

Dark adaptation. The eye takes time to adjust to the dark. Your eyes' pupils expand to nearly their full nighttime size within seconds of when you step out into the dark, but the most important part of dark adaptation involves chemical changes in the retina that require many minutes.

After the first 15 minutes in total darkness you might think your night vision is fully developed, but no. Tests show that your eyes gain about another two magnitudes of sensitivity – in other words, a factor of *six* in how faint you can see – during the next 15 minutes. Thereafter, dark adaptation improves very slightly for 90 minutes more. So don't expect to see faint objects at their best until a half hour or more into an observing session.

In practice, complete darkness is unattainable. You need some light to see what you're doing. Astronomers have long used a dim red flashlight because red light has less effect on night vision. The reason is that in near-darkness you see with the "rod" cells in your retina, and these are blind to the far red end of the spectrum. When you see red light your "cone" cells are at work; these are the receptors responsible for normal daytime color vision. (You have three types of cones – red, green, and blue – but only one type of rod, which is insensitive to red.) The idea is to use the red cones for reading charts and finding eyepieces, while protecting the rods for the most delicate work at the eyepiece.

 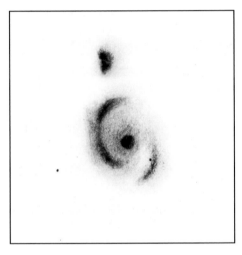

The majestic Whirlpool galaxy, M51 in Canes Venatici. Spiral structure is perhaps more easily seen here than in any other galaxy but still requires many minutes of study. All drawings in this chapter were made by Roger N. Clark using an 8-inch f/11.5 Cassegrain telescope and powers from 82× to 188×. Clark made the drawing at right under a very dark sky when stars of magnitude 14.3 could be seen at the zenith with his telescope. Compare its details to the photgraph at left. The scale is 5 arc minutes per inch. North is up in all illustrations in this chapter.

Red paper rubber-banded over the front of a flashlight provides a dim, diffuse glow. In a two-battery flashlight, install a bulb rated for three batteries. Its light will be dim and somewhat reddened, and the batteries will last longer. Much better than the traditional flashlight and red filter, however, is a red LED (light-emitting diode) flashlight. Its red is purer and deeper, so the division between rod and cone vision is more sharply drawn. LEDs also use much less current, so the batteries last for years. Many LED flashlights for astronomers are now available.

One more trick for preserving dark adaptation is to observe with one eye and read charts with the other. Keep the observing eye closed or covered with an eye patch when not in use.

Averted vision: When you look directly at something, its image falls on the *fovea centralis* of your retina. This spot is packed with bright-light receptors, the cone cells, and gives sharp resolution under strong illumination. But the fovea is fairly blind in dim light. So to see something faint, you have to look slightly away from it. Doing so moves the image off the fovea and onto parts of the retina that have more rod cells.

To see how dramatically this works, stare right at a star. It will disappear even if it's fairly bright. Look away a little; there it is again. Practice concentrating your attention on something a little off to one side of where your eye is aimed. This technique is called *averted vision.* You'll be doing it almost all the time when deep-sky observing.

Your eye is most sensitive to a faint object when it lies 8° to 16° from the center of vision in the direction of your nose. Almost as good a position is 6° to 12° above your center of view. Avoid placing the object very far toward the ear side of your center of vision. There it may fall on the retina's blind spot and vanish altogether. In practice, finding how far to avert your vision is a matter of trial and error. Not enough and you don't get the full benefit; too much and you lose resolving power, the ability to see details.

Wiggling the scope. Your peripheral vision is highly sensitive to motion. Under certain conditions, wiggling the telescope makes a big, dim ghost of a galaxy or nebula snap into view by averted vision. When the wiggling stops it disappears again into the vague uncertainty of the sky background.

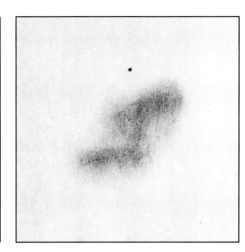

The Crab nebula, M1, in Taurus. The sketch at right records about as much detail as visual observers can usually perceive. This photograph and drawing are reproduced at a scale of 3.6 arc minutes per inch. To see M1 as large as it would appear in a 100-power eyepiece, hold the page 10 inches from your eye. Photograph by Evered Kreimer.

But under other conditions, especially involving faint objects that appear tiny, just the opposite technique seems to work. According to Colorado astronomer Roger N. Clark in his book *Visual Astronomy of the Deep Sky*, some studies indicate that the eye can actually build up an image over time almost like photographic film – if the image is held perfectly still. In bright light the eye's integration time, or "exposure time," is only about $1/10$ second. But in the dark, claims Clark, it's a different story. A faint image may build up toward visibility for as long as *six seconds* if you can keep it at the same spot on your retina for that long. Doing so is quite contrary to instinct, because in bright light fixating on something tends to make it *less* visible. Long exposure times could be one reason why an experienced observer sees deep-sky objects a beginner misses; the veteran has learned, unconsciously, when to keep the eye still. It also may help to explain why bodily comfort is so essential for seeing faint objects. Fatigue and muscle strain increase eye motion.

Using high powers. Conventional wisdom holds that low power works best for deep-sky viewing. After all, low power concentrates an extended object's light into a small area and thus increases its apparent surface brightness (the illumination of a given area on the retina). But as Clark proved after digging through laboratory vision studies, this assumption is usually false. High powers should do better on many faint deep-sky objects. The reason is subtle but key to understanding how low-light vision works, so we'll go into some detail. The essential point is that the eye, unlike a camera or other purely mechanical lens system, loses *resolution* in dim light. This is why you can't read a newspaper at night – even though you can *see* the newspaper and your eye lens theoretically resolves all the letters just as sharply as in daylight.

Studies show that the eye can resolve detail as fine as about 1 arc minute in bright light but can't make out features smaller than about 20 or 30 arc minutes across when the illumination is about as dim as the dark-sky background in a telescope. This is almost the size of the Moon as seen with the naked eye. So details in a very faint object can be viewed only if they are magnified to such a large apparent size – which can require using an extremely high power!

The explanation lies in how nature has adapted the visual system to cope with night. Photographic film records light passively, but the nerve system in the retina contains a great deal of computing power. In dim light, the retina compares signals from adjacent areas. A faint source covering only a small area – such as a small galaxy in the eyepiece – may be completely invisible at the conscious level. But it is being recorded in the retina, as evidenced by the fact that a larger galaxy with the same low surface brightness is visible easily. In effect, when rod cells see a doubtful trace of light they ask other rods nearby if they're seeing it too. If the answer is yes, the signal is passed along up the optic nerve to the brain. If it's no, the signal is disregarded.

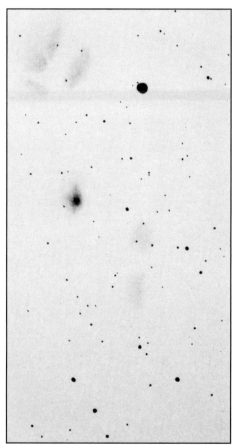

The famous region around Zeta Orionis, the southernmost star in Orion's Belt. Zeta is at upper right; the nebula to its left, divided by dust lanes, is NGC 2024. The bright reflection nebula surrounding the star near center is NGC 2023, while the dark Horsehead nebula, a supreme visual test, is to its lower right. North is up here, and the scale is 17 arc minutes per inch, much less magnified than the other photos and drawings in this chapter.

When an image is magnified by high power, its surface brightness does grow weaker. But the total number of photons of light entering the eye remains the same. (A photon is the fundamental particle of light. Most people can detect as few as 50 to 150 photons per second.) It doesn't really matter that these photons are spread over a wider area; the retinal image-processing system will cope with them – at least within certain limits. A tradeoff is needed to reach the optimum power for low-light perception: enough angular size but not *too* drastic a reduction in surface brightness.

What does all this mean for deep-sky observers? Simply that it's wise to try a wide range of powers on any object. You may be surprised by how much more you'll see with one than another.

One more point: There is a folk belief among observers that a telescope of long focal length (high f/ratio) gives a cleaner, higher-contrast view of dim objects than a short focal-length scope. But f/ratio is not the issue. A long-focus telescope is simply more likely to be used at high power! (It's also more likely to have high-quality optics, because they're easier to manufacture.)

Color. Deep-sky objects sometimes disappoint beginners not only by their frequent lack of obvious detail but also by the absence of the brilliant colors recorded in photographs. In order to see color, we must view something with a surface brightness great enough to stimulate the retina's cone cells – and the list of deep-sky objects this bright is short. The great Orion nebula M42 qualifies (some people can make out the pastel yellow or orange in parts of its brightest region), as do some small but high-surface-brightness planetary nebulae. The ability to see color in dim objects varies greatly from person to person, and surprises may occur.

Averted vision is *not* the way to look for color. The cones are thickest in the fovea, so stare right at your object. In this case, the lowest useful power should work best.

Heavy breathing. When you pour all your concentration into examining a deep-sky object at the very limit of vision, does it get even harder to see after 10 or 15 seconds while the sky background brightens a little into a murky gray? Diagnosis: you're holding your breath without realizing it. Low oxygen kills night vision fast. An old variable-star observer's trick is to breathe heavily for 15 seconds or so before trying for the very dimmest targets. And keep breathing deeply while you're looking.

Other tips. Night vision is impaired by alcohol, nicotine, and low blood sugar, so don't drink, smoke, or go hungry while deep-sky observing. Bring a snack. A shortage of vitamin A reduces night vision, but if you've got enough of it, taking more won't do any good. Virtually no one who eats a normal diet manages to get vitamin A deficiency any more. So don't expect that eating carrots will improve your eyesight.

 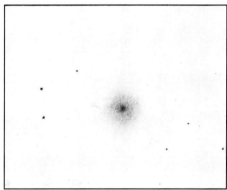

A typical galaxy with no spiral structure visible to the eye. M74 in Pisces is often considered the most difficult Messier object to find, because only the small nucleus is visible at first and it's often mistaken for a faint star. The surrounding glow comes out with careful attention. The scale is 5' per inch. Photograph courtesy Lick Observatory.

Prolonged exposure to bright sunlight reduces your ability to dark adapt for a couple of days, so wear dark glasses at the beach. Make sure the label on the dark glasses says they block ultraviolet light; some cheap ones don't. Over the years ultraviolet daylight ages both your eye lens and retina, reducing sensitivity. So if you wear eyeglasses outdoors, ask your optometrist about getting an ultraviolet-filter coating applied to your lenses. This option is so cheap and easy that everyone buying glasses ought to consider it.

Taking time. Most of all, be patient. If at first you don't see anything at the correct spot, keep looking. Then look some more. You'll be surprised at how much more glimmers into view with prolonged scrutiny – another faint little star here and there, and just possibly the object of your desire. After you glimpse your quarry once or twice, you'll glimpse it more and more often. Where at first you thought there was nothing but blank sky, after a few minutes you may be able to see it nearly continuously – what astronomers call "steadily holding" an object.

In the long run you can be sure your observing skills will improve with practice. Pushing your vision to its limit is a talent that can only be learned with time. "You must not expect to *see at sight*," wrote the 18th-century observer William Herschel, often considered the founder of modern astronomy. "Seeing is in some respects an art which must be learned. Many a night have I been practicing to see, and it would be strange if one did not acquire a certain dexterity by such constant practice."

STAR-HOP

1
ONE

A Binocular Tour of Orion's Belt

Betelgeuse

North

δ

ε η

ζ

M42

Rigel

Early December – 10 p.m.
Late December – 9 p.m.
Early January – 8 p.m.
Late January – Dusk

Sirius

Orion climbs the southeastern sky on December and January evenings, sparkling brightly for all to see. The circle indicates the binocular-size field of view magnified in the close-up on the next page.

Whether you're a newcomer to astronomy or a 50-year veteran, a pair of binoculars should be an essential part of your gear. They're simple, portable, and endlessly useful. They take you about halfway from the naked-eye view to what you can see in a 6- to 10-inch telescope, but at much less than half the price, weight, and trouble. And they're perfect for learning the techniques of serious sky hunting. Used with a good star atlas and reference books, binoculars will show enough to keep you busy forever.

To grasp the truth of this, take a pair of binoculars out on a winter's night and examine Orion's Belt, the row of three naked-eye stars in the middle of the constellation, and Orion's Sword, the row of fainter stars hanging down below it. Most long-time observers have looked in on this piece of celestial scenery dozens or hundreds of times – and still miss a lot, being unaware of all that's here.

That's what deep-sky reference books are for. For this chapter we've gone through these books and made a list of 10 cosmic sights in the single binocular field of view that is mapped below. The large numbers next to objects on the map refer to the following numbered sections.

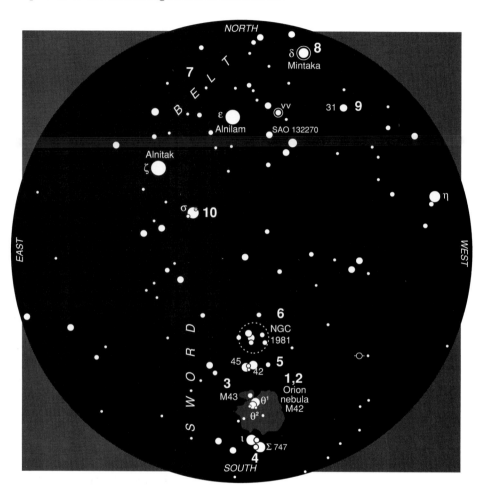

Turn an ordinary pair of 7-power binoculars on Orion's Belt and this is the field you'll see. The bigger the binoculars' aperture, the brighter the view with more stars discernible. Yet even a small household pair will show many of the celestial sights described on these pages. Bold numbers refer to sections in the text. The circle is 7° in diameter, and stars are shown to magnitude 8.5. As with all the sky maps in this book, north is up and east is to the left.

1. M42, THE GREAT NEBULA IN ORION

M42 is likely to catch your eye as soon as you aim at Orion's Belt and Sword. At first glance the nebula will probably look like just a small blur surrounding a few stars. But as with fine wine, an appreciation of M42 can only be developed by savoring its riches slowly.

Support your binoculars on something sturdy – if not a tripod then a car roof, wall, or fence post – and take a long second look. How much you'll see depends on the binoculars' aperture, the sky darkness, and also on having a careful, critical eye.

Even in the city, look for signs of shape and variety in the glowing luminosity. In the country you may be able to make out an intricate fluorescent region spanning the width of two full moons. Deep-sky author Philip Harrington describes it as looking like a cupped hand reaching toward the bunch of young, hot stars buried within. M42 is one of those rare objects that, no matter how often viewed, always holds some subtle aspect you've never noticed before.

2. THETA[1] (θ^1) AND THETA[2] (θ^2) ORIONIS

Fix your gaze on the northern edge of the nebula. There, in the brightest patch of soft, turquoise-gray cloud, is set this pair of brilliant stellar diamonds. Even the lowest-power opera glass used in the middle of a city should have little trouble resolving these 5th-magnitude suns, for they are separated by 135 arc seconds.

Theta[1], the one on the northwest, is the famous Trapezium multiple star. When viewed in a telescope this seemingly single point of light becomes a tight foursome. But this sight is beyond binoculars.

Theta[2], on the other hand, is an easily split binocular double. Its 5.2- and 6.5-magnitude components are parted by 52″. Both shine bluish white, contrasting nicely against the surrounding nebulosity.

3. M43

Shift a trace northeast, just past the edge of M42, to the little 7th-magnitude star there. Do you see a small, detached, nebulous puff surrounding it? If so you've spotted M43. In reality this is not a separate nebula but an extension of M42; it only appears isolated because a belt of dark nebulosity is silhouetted between them. M43 can be seen in 7×50 glasses in a dark sky, but most observers overlook it. In fact, while the big nebula was discovered in 1610, the fainter glow of M43 was not recognized until 1731.

4. IOTA (ι) ORIONIS AND STRUVE 747

A half degree south of M42 lies this easy and attractive pair marking the southern tip of Orion's Sword.

First take a careful look at Struve 747 (Σ747), the fainter, southwestern star of the two. With a sharp eye and steadily held binoculars you should be able to pick out the 5.7-magnitude companion from the 4.8-magnitude primary star. This attractive stellar duet is separated by 36″, with the secondary star toward the southwest – blue-white diamonds against the dark backdrop.

Iota Orionis, on the other hand, is a three-sun system. But the companions to the 3rd-magnitude primary star are magnitudes 7 and 11 and separated from it by 11″ and 50″, respectively, making them impossible to hunt down through ordinary binoculars. They do make an attractive sight in a telescope.

5. 42 AND 45 ORIONIS

Pass northward back over the Orion nebula and the same distance farther on to the upper star in Orion's Sword. Once again binoculars reveal what the eye alone cannot: that here are not one but two closely set suns. They form a wide double through binoculars. If you have keen color perception, you might discern that the eastern star (45 Orionis) glows with the palest yellow tint, while 42 appears perfectly white.

Surrounding 42 and 45 Orionis is another detached tuft of the vast Orion nebula network. It accounts for three entries in the *New General Catalogue of Nebulae and Clusters of Stars:* NGC 1973, 1975, and 1977. Of these only NGC 1977 can be seen through binoculars, and then only in the darkest sky.

6. NGC 1981

A fraction of a degree north of 42 and 45 Orionis, at the very top of the Sword, is another bevy of stellar beauties that is plain through binoculars. This is NGC 1981, a coarse open cluster of about 20 suns. Most observers will spot six right away, with another few yielding to a concentrated search. Many telescopists miss the beauty of this little-known cluster because of its relative sparseness and large size. However, discerning binocular users will immediately recognize the charm of NGC 1981, especially amid such grand surroundings.

7. COLLINDER 70

You've never heard of the open cluster Collinder 70? Maybe not, but if you've looked at Orion you've seen it. Collinder 70's three brightest members form Orion's Belt, and another several dozen stars brighter than 9th magnitude are visible in 7×50 binoculars on clear nights. In all, 100 suns spanning about 3° belong to this large association. Most shine with tints of pale blue and white, though some gleam with delicate shades of yellow. Collinder 70 is a delightful stellar family through low-power, wide-angle binoculars and is sure to become a seasonal favorite.

Look in particular for the little loop of 6th-magnitude stars curling west and south of Alnilam, the middle star of Orion's Belt. Sheltered in the loop's center is the little orange-red star SAO 132270, magnitude 5.9, spectral type *K*5 III, a speck of topaz among diamonds.

A telescopic view of the great Orion nebula, M42, framed in a 1.7°-wide field of view. Just above (north of) the nebula's brightest part is small, comma-shaped M43. The two bright stars at bottom are Iota Orionis and the double Struve 747. Near top, NGC 1973-5-7 surrounds the stars 42 and 45 Orionis. In a dark enough sky, binoculars show at least a hint of all these features. Adapted from a color photograph by Akira Fujii.

8. MINTAKA, DELTA (δ) ORIONIS

Delta Orionis, the northwesternmost star in the Belt, is a challenging double perfect for binoculars. Good, steadily mounted glasses will unveil the 6th-magnitude companion northeast of the 2nd-magnitude primary. Although their separation is a reasonably wide 53″, the disparity in magnitude makes this a difficult test for lens quality.

9. 31 ORIONIS

Slide about a degree southwest of Mintaka to pick up this next item. Another *K*5 star, 4.7-magnitude 31 Orionis gleams with a distinctive golden orange tint, in sharp contrast to the many blue and white stars throughout the region.

10. SIGMA (σ) ORIONIS

Finally, slide down the Belt to the easternmost star, Alnitak or Zeta (ζ) Orionis. Then take a sharp turn southwestward for the short trip to Sigma. Well known to double-star observers, Sigma Orionis is one of the finest multiple stars in the winter night. No fewer than five suns belong to the system, though binoculars will show only the 4.0-magnitude primary paired with a 6.5-magnitude companion 43″ to the northeast. Brace the binoculars well and look carefully; the difference of 2.5 magnitudes between the stars equals a factor of 10 difference in light.

Ten points of interest in one binocular field of view. Imagine how many more are waiting all over the sky.

STAR-HOP

2

TWO

Clusters in the Heart of Auriga

Frosty evenings of late autumn find the brilliant star Capella climbing the eastern sky. On the coldest nights of winter it shines high overhead. Capella is by far the brightest star in Auriga the Charioteer, one of the landmark constellations of the cold months. Auriga straddles the winter Milky Way and fairly bursts with telescopic riches – if you know how and where to hunt them out.

Among deep-sky observers Auriga is best known for three big open star clusters: M36, M37, and M38. They show as hazy glows in binoculars and fine splashes of stardust in a telescope. But there's lots more here too. If you're willing to step off the well-worn tourist path, all sorts of hidden treasures await discovery. In this hop, we'll take a walk through the byways of this interesting region.

The picture on the next page sets the scene in the eastern evening sky; note the times and dates in the picture's lower left. Auriga can be found elsewhere in the sky at other times and dates by using the all-sky charts on pages 16 to 27.

The tilted black box shows the area covered by the more detailed guide map on page 66, which shows stars as faint as magnitude 8.0. On this guide map, black circles highlight our points of interest. The circles are 2° in diameter. This is quite a bit smaller than the view in a finderscope and about twice the width of a typical main telescope's low-power field of view. The black rectangle on the guide map shows the area covered by the still more detailed chart on page 68, which shows stars to magnitude 9.5.

Of our 15 highlighted sights, some can be seen well in binoculars while others will challenge large amateur telescopes.

1. CAPELLA, ALPHA (α) AURIGAE

Let's start easy. At magnitude 0, Capella is the sixth brightest star other than the Sun. Its pale yellow color is plainly visible to the naked eye and beautiful in any optical instrument.

While we're here, use Capella to make sure your finderscope is properly aligned with the main telescope. First center the star in the main telescope's eyepiece, then adjust the finder's alignment screws to center the star in the finder's crosshairs. Check back in the main telescope to make sure it hasn't moved. Switch to your highest-power eyepiece and repeat for fine tuning. Taking care of this now will save a lot of grief later.

Capella is the brightest star of spectral type G (the Sun's spectral type) visible from midnorthern latitudes – not counting the Sun itself, of course. Capella is a trace yellower than the Sun, having a *color index* of 0.8 compared to the Sun's 0.6. Color index is defined as a star's magnitude measured through a standard blue filter minus its magnitude through a "visual" filter (which is pale yellowish tan). The higher the color index, the more a star's color is toward the red end of the spectrum. The bluest stars, pale blue-white, have color indexes of –0.2 to 0.0. White is about color index 0.2, yellow 0.6 to 1.0, orange roughly 1.0 to 1.5, and orange-red greater than 1.5.

Located 45 light-years away, Capella is actually a double star – a binary consisting of two giant stars about 90 and 70 times as bright as the Sun. They're too close together to be resolved in virtually any telescope; Capella's double nature was only discovered spectroscopically in 1899. The larger and brighter component is about 13 times as large as the Sun; the other is about 7 times the Sun's size. They orbit each other every 3½ months as far apart as the Sun is from Venus.

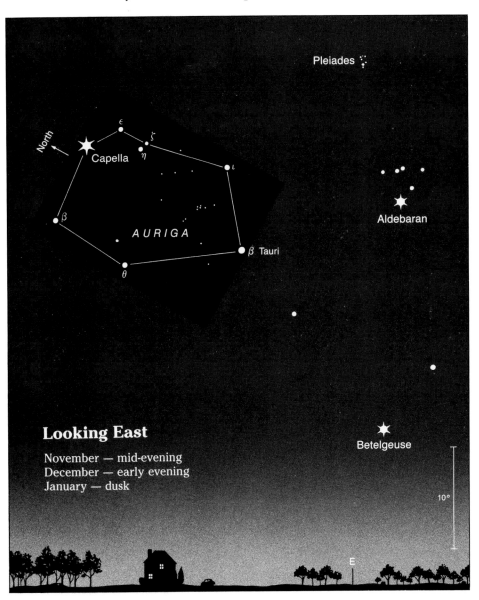

The view looking east in the evenings of late fall and early winter. The darker box surrounding the constellation Auriga shows the sky area covered by the guide map on the next page.

2. EPSILON (ε) AURIGAE

This 3rd-magnitude star is a little more than 3° southwest of Capella, as shown on the chart on the next page. It's the first stepping-stone to jump to in this star-hop.

Epsilon is visible to the naked eye, so you could simply aim your finderscope at it by eyeball judgment. But try instead to identify it by looking only in your finderscope, starting from bright Capella, to check that you can use the finder to move a specified direction and distance. Any trouble? If so, it would be a good idea to go back and review the section on sky distances and directions starting on page 28.

Epsilon Aurigae is a white, type *F*0 supergiant several thousand light-years away. It is a dullish, off-white color in my 6-inch reflector. Every 27 years it undergoes a partial eclipse by a gigantic, invisible dark body orbiting it. The most recent eclipse lasted from 1982 to 1984; the next is due to begin in 2009. The eclipsing object is believed to be a huge, opaque disk or cloud orbiting around an unseen smaller star that circles Epsilon.

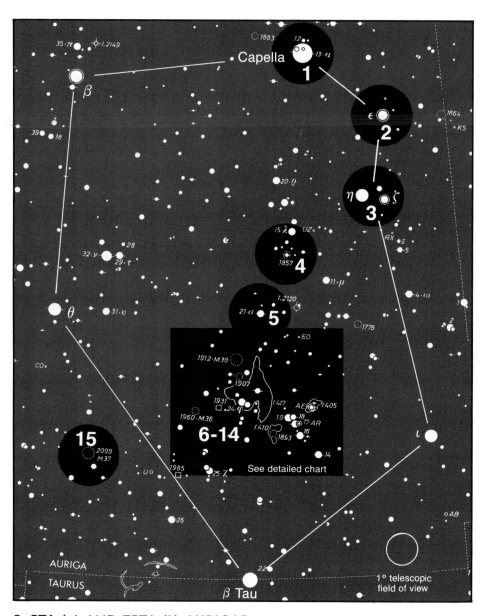

The central part of Auriga is sprinkled with star clusters (small dotted circles), nebulae (solid outlines and little squares), and double and multiple stars (star dots with horizontal lines through them). This chart, adapted from Wil Tirion's Sky Atlas 2000.0, *plots stars to as faint as magnitude 8.0 (the smallest dots). The black circles highlighting objects are 2° in diameter, and the black box shows the field of the more detailed map on the page 68. The large numbers refer to objects described in the text.*

3. ETA (η) AND ZETA (ζ) AURIGAE

This pair of stars is a nice study in color contrasts. Find them a little less than 3° south of Epsilon. Eta, the brighter of the two, is spectral type *B*3 and slightly bluish. In fact it is about as blue as a star can get, with a color index of −0.2. Zeta, on the other hand, is an orange giant of spectral type *K*4 and color index 1.2.

I find the color contrast plainest in binoculars or a finder. In my 6-inch reflector at 46 power Eta and Zeta are wonderful jewels, but their sheer brilliance seems to wash out some of their color. Both stars are several hundred light-years away. As a quick check that you know the field diameters of your finderscope and your main telescope's low-power eyepiece, Zeta is 2.7° from Epsilon, 0.8° from Eta, and 0.4° from the 6th-magnitude star just north of a line between Zeta and Eta.

Six of the objects described in the text are captured in this wide-field photograph from Hans Vehrenberg's Atlas of Deep-Sky Splendors. *At upper right is the big, rich star cluster M38, below it is the smaller cluster NGC 1907, and at bottom right is the Stock 8 - IC 417 complex next to Phi Aurigae. The small extended object at bottom center is NGC 1931, and M36 is in the lower-left corner. The bright star at the right edge just below center is the wide double Struve 698, barely resolved here. The field is 2.2° high.*

4. NGC 1857

Here we take our first leap into the dark. NGC 1857 is a hazy little open star cluster discovered by William Herschel two centuries ago. As can be seen on the guide map on the previous page, a good route for finding it is to shift about 2° east (left on the map) from Eta to pick up the north-south row of 5th- and 6th-magnitude stars from Rho (ρ) to Lambda (λ) Aurigae. Follow the row south to the little upside-down Y of 7th- and 8th-magnitude stars with NGC 1857 between its arms.

The cluster contains about 40 faint stars in an area just 6' across. In the 6-inch reflector it appears as a weak but definite glow hiding at the edge of a much larger, very loose group of brighter stars. It gives the impression of being far behind them, like something glowing deep underwater below bright specks floating on the surface. A 7th-magnitude orange star, plotted on the guide map, is almost on top of it.

This impression of depth is real. NGC 1857 is believed to be 6,000 light-years away, much farther than most field stars. The dozen or so bright ones, which generally lie a little to the north, form a very loose open cluster that goes by the name Czernik 20.

5. SIGMA (σ) AURIGAE

This double star is easy to find but hard to resolve. Use the chart to hop to it 2° south-southeast of NGC 1857. Sigma displays a strong fire-orange color, as might be expected from its spectral type of *K*4 III and color index of 1.4. The primary star shines at magnitude 5.0; a companion glimmers at 11th or 12th magnitude. The companion probably lies about 9″ to Sigma's south-southeast, but the last available published measurement of the pair is from 1922, so consider this value uncertain.

You might think a 9″ double star should be easy to resolve in any telescope. But it's a very different story when the components are so dissimilar in brightness. I had only occasional, doubtful glimpses of the companion in my 6-inch reflector at 200×.

If you have a large telescope or a very dark sky, you might take a slight detour to try for the dim and difficult planetary nebula IC 2120 just 1.3° west of Sigma. It is supposed to have a smooth disk 47″ in diameter. However, I can't see a trace of it with the 6-inch through moderate suburban light pollution.

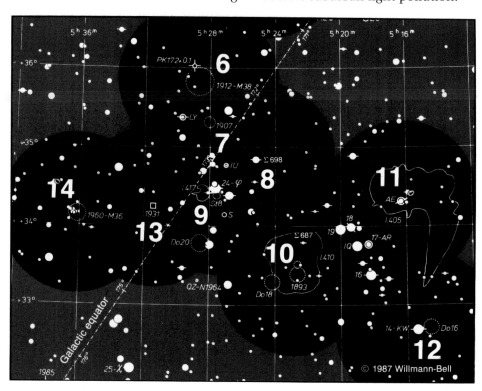

A close-up of Auriga's richest region, adapted from the highly detailed sky atlas Uranometria 2000.0. Stars are plotted to about magnitude 9.5. The grid boxes are 1° high.

6. M38

Shift almost 2° southeast from Sigma Aurigae, and you'll sweep into this big, bright showpiece of an open cluster. M38 is a rich swarm of some 100 stars of about magnitude 10 and fainter. The cluster is 20′ in diameter and looks rather squarish in the 6-inch at 46×, with clumps of stars in its corners. Gazing at it I get occasional glimpses of an even larger, richer background of countless extremely faint stars. Take the time to see if this remote wealth flickers into view.

7. NGC 1907

From here on you can switch to the more detailed guide map above, which is plotted at a larger scale and shows stars to about magnitude 9.5. Our next few objects are close enough together, and this map shows stars faint enough, so that you can probably star-hop your way around with your main telescope's lowest-power eyepiece and ignore the finder altogether.

Just ½° south of M38 is a smaller, fainter, but more compact companion cluster. NGC 1907 contains 30 stars in an area 7′ across. It lies at about the same distance as M38, 4,500 light-years, and may be physically related to it. In the 6-inch at 50× it appears as an eerie, partially resolved glow.

8. STRUVE 698

Next hop your way 0.7° southwest to this 7th-magnitude double star. It's a real eye-catcher, golden yellow and smoky gray-blue, with a wide separation of 31″. Over a century ago Rev. Thomas W. Webb, in his *Celestial Objects for Common Telescopes,* went out of his way to note the pair as "beautiful." The stars are magnitudes 6.6 and 8.7. Both are cataloged as spectral class *K*, so the bluish hue of the secondary must be a contrast illusion caused by the bright orange primary. Can you convince yourself that the secondary is really orange?

9. STOCK 8 AND IC 417

The map on the previous page, adapted from *Uranometria 2000.0,* places the cluster Stock 8 incorrectly. It does not lie due south of Phi (φ) Aurigae as shown but southeast of it in the midst of the nebula IC 417.

The photograph below illustrates the situation. Stock 8 is a small gathering of about 40 faint stars 5′ in diameter. I see no sign of the nebulosity in the 6-inch, but if your sky conditions are better maybe you can.

Phi Aurigae is the brightest star for some distance around. It is the most prominent of a nameless bunch of field stars about ⅓° in diameter. Another bunch of similar size lies ⅓° to its north.

A close-up photo of the small cluster Stock 8 surrounded by the nebula IC 417 next to bright Phi Aurigae. Martin Germano of Thousand Oaks, California, used an 8-inch f/5 reflector for this 60-minute exposure on hypersensitized Kodak 2415 film.

10. NGC 1893 AND IC 410

Here are another, larger cluster and nebula. NGC 1893 appears as a bold, irregular spray of stars in the 6-inch, very elongated north-south. There was no sign of the nebula IC 410, which appears on the left-hand photograph on the next page, much less the dark intrusion looming into the nebula from the southwest. The cluster is estimated to be a mere 1 million years old, compared to tens or hundreds of millions of years for most open clusters. It contains about 60 stars.

A half degree north of NGC 1893 is a tiny triple star in the form of a narrow isosceles triangle. This is Struve 687. The triangle is about 50″ long and 18″ wide, with the western star slightly brighter than the other two.

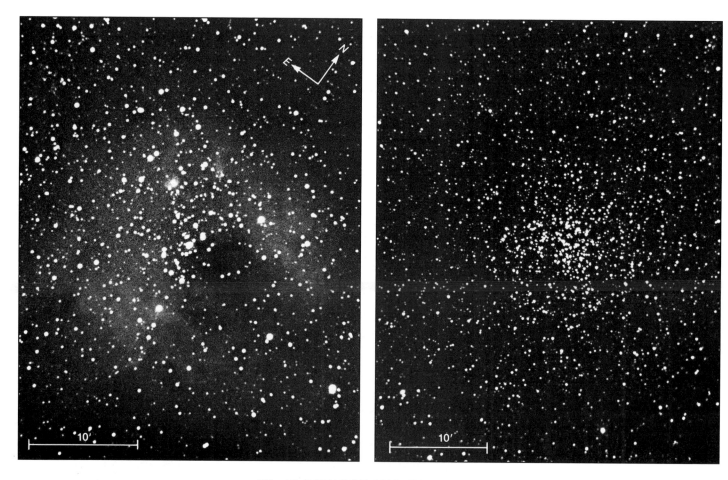

Left: The loose, scattered cluster NGC 1893 is all that can be seen here through light-polluted skies, but the big glowing nebula IC 410 embedded in the cluster may show under excellent conditions. Martin Germano used an 8-inch f/10 Schmidt-Cassegrain telescope and a 75-minute exposure on 103a-F film. North is toward upper right.

Right: M37 is the brightest, richest cluster in Auriga. Its somewhat triangular shape is captured in this 40-minute exposure by Germano on 103a-F film made with an 8-inch f/10 Schmidt-Cassegrain.

11. AE AURIGAE AND THE FLAMING STAR NEBULA

Hop less than a degree west to the prominent asterism of 16 through 19 Aurigae. This group is immediately recognizable in binoculars or a finder; I've always called it the Leaping Minnow. Continue northwest from there to find 6th-magnitude AE Aurigae.

This type *O* star is slightly variable in an irregular way. It illuminates the diffuse nebula IC 405, also known as the Flaming Star nebula. In moderately large amateur telescopes the "flames" appear as a large, vague glow toward the star's east and north about 20' across. To my surprise, the 6-inch seemed to show hints of it despite the light pollution. Quite a catch! Deep photographs reveal filamentary detail across the much larger area outlined on the chart. Using high power, look in particular for the narrow wisp ¼° north of AE. The photograph on the next page suggests that this is the most distinct piece of the nebula.

Unlike most *O* stars in nebulae, AE Aurigae was not born there but is just passing through – and fast. It is hurtling at about 80 miles per second directly away from the great star-forming region around Orion's Sword. Presumably it was expelled from there about 2.7 million years ago. AE Aurigae may have begun life in a tight, fast orbit around another star that blew apart as a supernova, leaving AE to hurtle away at its orbital velocity. We catch it lighting up the nebula for only a brief time, perhaps 20,000 years. After it has passed, the nebula will return to darkness.

12. KW AURIGAE AND DOLIDZE 16

Back to an easier target! A degree southwest of the Minnow's tail is the 5th-magnitude triple star 14 Aurigae. Two components are immediately obvious in the 6-inch at 46×; the third requires some close looking.

Component A, magnitude 5.1, varies by an unnoticeable 0.1 magnitude every two hours, earning it the variable-star designation KW Aurigae. Component C is the next brightest at magnitude 7.4; it lies 15″ southwest of A. Component B is the faintest at magnitude 11, a little spark about 10″ north of A.

AE Aurigae, the brightest star in this field, illuminates the large, dim Flaming Star nebula, IC 405, to its east and north. Preston Scott Justis used a 10-inch f/6 reflector for this 90-minute exposure on 103a-F film.

In addition, a 10th-magnitude star D is 180″ northwest. At that distance it is not likely to be a true member of the system.

Just west is a very sparse, irregular gathering of 10 stars known as Dolidze 16. It is listed as about 12′ across. In the 6-inch at 50× the cluster is evident once you look for it but is too poor and thin to call much attention to itself.

13. NGC 1931

We now make a long backtrack for our final three objects. Work eastward from the Leaping Minnow to Phi Aurigae, and from there almost 1° east-southeast to the little square marked "1931." NGC 1931 is a tiny but rather bright emission and reflection nebula surrounding a 9th-magnitude star. The star is quite obviously fuzzy in the 6-inch. At last, a nebula that shows well through light pollution! How much detail can you make out in it using your highest power? The star itself is triple and bears the designation ADS 4112. Its components A, B, and C are magnitudes 9, 10, and 11, respectively. B is 7″ west-southwest of A, and C is 10″ to A's northwest.

The bright little nebula NGC 1931 looks like a fuzzy star when observed at low powers. But with high power on a fairly large telescope, the star becomes triple and detail may be glimpsed within the nebula. Martin Germano used an 8-inch f/5 reflector for this 50-minute exposure on hypersensitized Kodak Technical Pan 2415 film.

14. M36

Here's a grand sight, after all the small and difficult treasures we've been hunting. M36 compares well with nearby M38, to which you might want to backtrack for another look. M36 has fewer stars than M38 and is hardly more than half the size, but its stars are brighter. Several of the brightest, including an equal-component double, are arranged in roughly parallel rows.

15. M37

And finally we end on the best object of the night. M37 combines the size and richness of M38 with the star brightness of M36. It is nearly 4° east-southeast of M36, so you'll have to return to the guide chart on page 66 to find it. M37 appears as a rich, somewhat triangular hive of stellar activity with a number of colored stars. The cluster comprises some 150 stars in an area 24′ across. Its distance, like that of the previous clusters, is about 4,500 light-years.

"Show objects" like this are so much bigger, better, and more rewarding when we come upon them after hunting for sights near a telescope's limits!

STAR-HOP
3
THREE

From Capella into Western Wilds

Many sky observers gravitate to familiar territory night after night. Bright constellations with lots of naked-eye stars naturally invite the telescope their way. But a constellation's naked-eye appeal tells little about its telescopic richness. Areas *between* constellations that seem blank and uninteresting to the eye are often full of big game.

Tonight let's explore a trail through some of this wilderness. We'll head northwest from Capella, the same bright starting point as for the previous chapter, into a blank-looking corner of Perseus. Here we'll find some unexpected riches. The map below, adapted from Wil Tirion's *Sky Atlas 2000.0*, will be our guide; it shows stars as faint as magnitude 8.0. The numbered

Capella is at far left on this chart. The numbered circles, 3° wide, highlight objects described in the text. The faintest stars are magnitude 8.0, easily visible in most finderscopes.

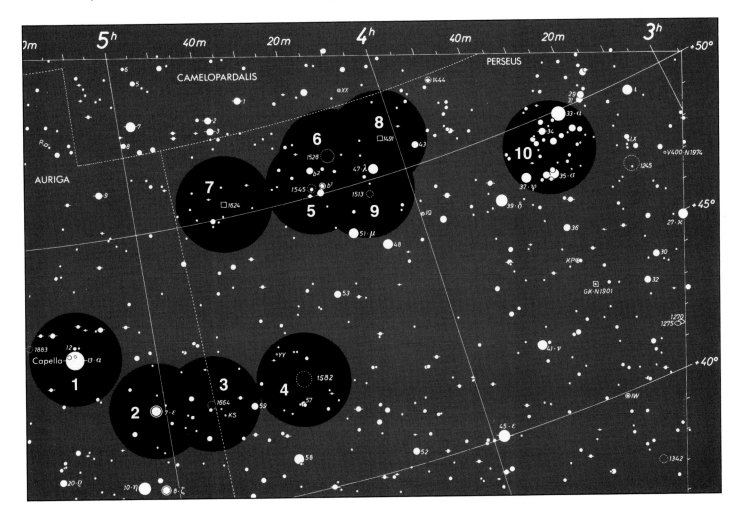

black circles on it are 3° in diameter, compared to 2° in the previous chapter. This is still small enough to fit easily into the field of view shown by most finderscopes.

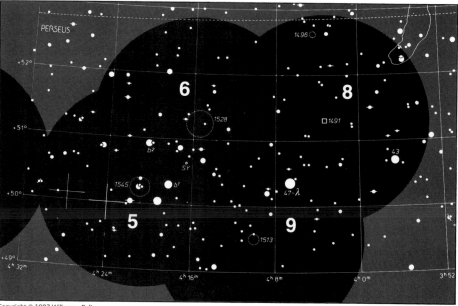

A close-up of part of the area mapped on the previous page, taken from the more detailed Uranometria 2000.0. The faintest stars are about magnitude 9.5.

1. CAPELLA

Capella can be spotted in twilight while you are setting up a telescope. It's described on page 64. You can use a bright star like this to judge the quality of what astronomers call the *seeing* – the tiny heat waves that are always rippling in the atmosphere, making stars twinkle to the naked eye and fuzz up into hazy, shimmering blobs when viewed at high power. The seeing sets a fundamental limit to how well a telescope can perform on a given night.

Try an experiment. Aim at Capella and turn it out of focus so the star becomes a large, round disk. The disk will contain fine concentric rings near its outer edge and, if you're using a reflector or Cassegrain-type telescope, a black circle in the middle. The out-of-focus star disk is, in effect, an image of the telescope's aperture. Is the disk crossed by wormlike dark ripples that slowly writhe and swirl around? This is a sign that the telescope tube contains currents of warm air. You've got a case of bad *tube seeing*. They'll go away when the telescope cools to the temperature of the surrounding air.

Faster ripples moving across the aperture may be caused by nearby sources of warmth such as a roof or pavement giving up the heat of the day, or your own body heat. Hold a hand in front of the telescope and you'll see swirls of warm air – poor *local seeing* – pouring off your fingers in the star disk. Asphalt pavement, rooftops, and especially chimneys during heating season are bad news when it comes to local seeing. Grass and trees are better surroundings for a telescope, since they absorb less heat in the day and give up less at night. If you can set up your telescope on some sort of height all the better; local seeing tends to hug the ground.

Very fast shimmering or flickering in the star disk is the signature of true atmospheric seeing at higher altitudes. There's not much you can do about it except hope for it to improve – which it may do from one minute to the next without warning.

Refocus Capella. Its yellow blaze looks like a miniature Sun – a reminder that Capella indeed resembles the Sun in temperature and spectral type (though not in size), as noted in the previous chapter.

2. EPSILON (ε) AURIGAE

Center this 3rd-magnitude star by swinging the telescope a little more than 3° southwest from Capella. It too is described in the previous chapter.

If you're not sure of directions in the eyepiece, now's the time to get them straight. Remember, north is the side where stars enter when you nudge the telescope toward Polaris. Stars *enter* from *east* when the clock drive is turned off or when you nudge the telescope eastward. If you've got an equatorial mount, turn the eyepiece of your finder so its crosshairs line up with these directions. (If you have a right-angle star diagonal in your finder, take it out if possible and view straight through. The diagonal gives a mirror image that cannot easily be compared to star patterns on a map.)

On a sky map, east is left when north is up. Right ascension *increases east*.

Also, be sure you know the size of your finder's field on the map. The 3.4° distance from Capella to Epsilon Aurigae can be used to judge this. Are the stars half a finder-field apart? Three-quarters? See page 14 for more on these basics if you need to.

3. NGC 1664

Hop exactly 2° west from Epsilon to arrive at our first deep-sky object. Don't expect it to jump out at you. NGC 1664 is a large, rather sparse open cluster, a loose sprinkling of about 40 stars 11th magnitude and fainter. It is roughly 4,000 light-years away.

The cluster appears sharply bordered on the north and west by three wide pairs of stars that form an arc encircling it. From its southeast side extends a long chain of stars, making the whole group look like a stingray with a long, curving tail. NGC 1664 is about 15′ across, half the diameter of the full Moon, so use your lowest power. This way you'll see it well framed by background sky. With too high a power a large cluster fills your field of view, and you can miss it by looking right through it.

Like most open clusters, NGC 1664 is young. Its stars are some 300 million years old, compared to the Sun's 4.6 billion.

4. NGC 1582

Because we are touring the Milky Way, this is going to be a night of open clusters. These are perhaps the most diverse class of visual deep-sky objects. They come in a wide variety of sizes, shapes, brightnesses, and degrees of richness. This next one, the enormous NGC 1582, is an extreme case of bigness and poorness.

To get to this cluster, shift the telescope 1½° west-southwest to 59 Persei, then a slightly greater distance in the same direction to the wide double star 57 Persei. This is a pair of *F* stars 2′ apart with a fainter third star farther away. From here go ¾° north-northwest to land in the midst of NGC 1582.

The cluster consists of only about 20 stars 9th magnitude and fainter dotting an area more than ½° across. In my 6-inch at 50× it appears as a huge, irregular, looping enhancement of the background star field with a big dark zone at its center. Despite its sparseness this is a real object, a swarm of stars born together and moving together through space. This would be much more obvious if we could view it in three dimensions, rather than seeing it projected flat on the sky along with all the background and foreground stars for thousands of light-years.

Consider the situation. A typical open cluster is 15 light-years in diameter. If we see all the field stars for, say, 5,000 light-years projected onto it, then a cluster that appears only 30 percent richer than the surrounding sky is actually something like 100 times denser in stars than space generally. So loose clusters are much more coherent than they appear.

5. NGC 1545

This next cluster is a big jump north-northwestward. Hop 3° to 53 Persei, then onward another 2° to pick up bright Mu (μ) and 48 Persei. Swing another 2° north-northeast from Mu to the little group of stars that includes b¹ and b² Persei. NGC 1545, just east of b¹, is a 15' clump of 20-odd stars that appears rather faint and sparse. It is dominated by a triangle of bright stars at its center and a wide double at its northern edge. The group is just about 2,500 light-years distant and is estimated to be 190 million years old.

North is up in this enlargement from a blue-light Palomar Observatory Sky Survey print showing b² Persei (lower left) and the open cluster NGC 1528. The field is ⅔° tall.

6. NGC 1528

NGC 1528 lies just 1¼° farther northwest. It is larger and richer, with a central portion that appears very elongated west-northwest to east-southeast. The west end has a big U-shaped dark bay outlined by seven bright stars. That, at least, is the impression the cluster gives visually in a 6-inch. Such distinctive features are less apparent on photographs. This cluster also is estimated to lie 2,500 light-years away, but measurement uncertainties could easily put 1,000 or more light-years between it and "nearby" NGC 1545.

7. NGC 1624

Let's take a short side trip to a rather difficult but intriguing little oddity. Backtrack to NGC 1545 and then go 3° due east. NGC 1624 is a small, round nebula only about 3' across, surrounding a tiny group of a dozen stars magnitude 12 and fainter. It lies in a dark, empty field – a dim, spooky glow deep in a forgotten corner of space. It gets better with prolonged viewing by averted vision. High powers help too. Only a couple of its stars were visible in my 6-inch at 50×, but a handful could be glimpsed at 200×.

The stars' ultraviolet light makes the nebula fluoresce. The group is almost too sparse to be called a cluster but has too many members to be considered a multiple star. Instead it may be an intermediate type of system known as a *trapezium* – a small, newborn clump of stars in chaotic, unstable orbits around each other. Eventually some will be expelled and the rest will settle into a hierarchy of stable binaries. Such groups are named for the original Trapezium, Theta¹ Orionis in the great Orion nebula.

8. NGC 1491

Let's try another nebula. Return west to NGC 1545, continue 2° farther west to bright Lambda (λ) Persei, and go 1° north-northwest from there. NGC 1491 is a slightly larger and more irregular dim glow than NGC 1624. It surrounds a clearly visible 11th-magnitude B0 star. The glowing gas is not too difficult, but you may want to use the detailed *Uranometria 2000.0* chart on page 74 to be positive you're at the right spot.

 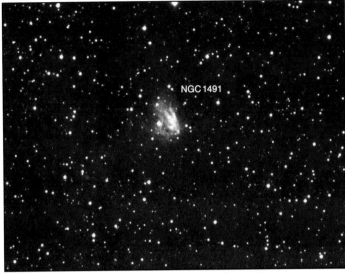

NGC 1624 (left) and NGC 1491 (right), from blue-light Palomar Observatory Sky Survey prints. Each field is just under ½° tall; north is up to match the charts. With a telescope, can you detect the two strong wisps just northwest of the star in NGC 1491?

9. NGC 1513

NGC 1513 is on the opposite (south) side of Lambda Persei. This mass of about 50 stars 11th magnitude and fainter is 10' across. At first it appeared small, dim, and poor in the 6-inch at 50×, but with averted vision it became much richer for fleeting moments. The cluster is estimated to be 2,700 light-years away and 430 million years old.

10. THE ALPHA PERSEI ASSOCIATION

Our tour ends with a big star-splattered finale. Moving 6° west-southwest we arrive in the midst of the bright stars between Alpha (α) and Delta (δ) Persei.

The Alpha Persei Association, also known as Perseus OB3 or Melotte 20, is a huge, loose grouping of young stars. Associations differ from open clusters in that they are much larger – up to several hundred light-years across instead of 10 or 20 for open clusters – and only weakly bound by gravity.

The Alpha Persei group is plain to the naked eye and best seen with binoculars. For the telescope it affords a wide realm of bright stars among which you can sweep lazily. There are about 100 true members of the group brighter than 11th magnitude. All are main-sequence stars except for Alpha Persei itself, an *F5* supergiant. Sunlike stars here are about magnitude 11. One bright yellow-orange star adds color, but it must lie in the foreground or background. The group is about 550 light-years distant, 50 light-years across, and 50 million years old.

A well-planned sky tour is far more rewarding than aimless poking around with a telescope. With references like *Burnham's Celestial Handbook* and *Sky Catalogue 2000.0*, Vol. 2 – the books most used in putting together this chapter – you can design your own tours on any quiet afternoon or cloudy night.

The Depths of Monoceros

The winter Milky Way is vague and dim to the naked eye, but it's every bit as rich in telescopic objects as the more renowned star clouds of summer. One of its most interesting areas is the obscure constellation Monoceros, the Unicorn, just east of bright Orion.

Our chosen area here is so small and crowded with things to hunt that the large-scale *Uranometria 2000.0* chart on the next page serves to cover it all. Stars are plotted to about as faint as magnitude 9.5. The white circles are only 1° in diameter this time, roughly the field of view in a typical amateur telescope's lowest-power eyepiece. This is exactly the size of the 45× view in my 6-inch f/8 reflector.

A 6-inch reflector on a German equatorial mount was once regarded as the ideal first "serious" scope for amateurs, and it deserves a comeback. It has enough aperture to keep you busy under the stars for decades, yet it's reasonably cheap and portable. You see a correct image (as opposed to a mirror image) in an eyepiece that's at a convenient height most of the time. With a focal ratio as high as f/8 it's low in coma, fairly forgiving of imperfect collimation, and unencumbered by a large central obstruction. So its images can rival a refractor's if the optics are well made.

I built mine at age 15 in 1966 and have been happy with it ever since. It now spends most of its time under wraps in a corner of the observatory that houses my12½-inch reflector. But when its big brother was spread all over the basement for five months undergoing an overhaul, the 6-inch had the observatory all to itself. And I found I had just about as much fun with it as with the 12½-inch. The old saying is really true: what you observe *with* is not nearly so important as how *much* you observe and how *well*.

The biggest part of observing well is planning what to do. A well-lit desk in the warm indoors is where to plan a night's sky hunting, using charts and reference books to create a program suited to the capabilities of your equipment. That's what I hope you'll find yourself doing by the time you've worked through this book.

1. XI (ξ) GEMINORUM

Our jumping-off point tonight will be this 3rd-magnitude star marking the southeastern foot of the Pollux twin in Gemini, as shown on the chart. Xi Gem is just 1° north of the Monoceros border. In the 6-inch it looks warm white, meaning white shaded with just a trace of yellow. This impression of color accords well with its spectral type of F5 IV.

That Roman numeral IV means the star is a subgiant probably just evolving off the main sequence. Here, then, is a star that was once very similar to our own, now living out the fate that awaits the Sun several billion years in the future. Xi's eons of aging have heated and swelled it until it now blazes 15 times brighter than the Sun (main-sequence stars become more luminous as they grow old). It will get much brighter still in the next few hundred million years as it evolves toward red-gianthood. Xi's measured parallax places it 65 light-years away.

Although Xi is marked on the *Uranometria* chart with the horizontal line signifying a double or multiple star, it is not listed as such in *Sky Catalogue 2000.0*, Volume 2, nor can I see any trace of a companion in the 6-inch.

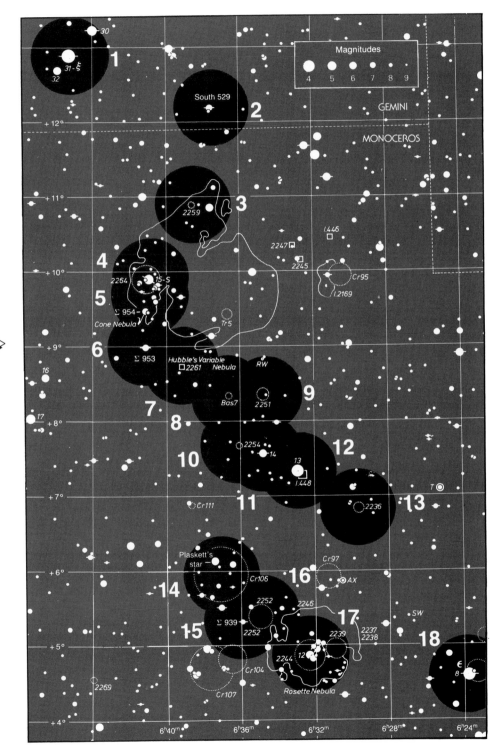

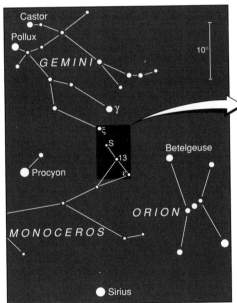

Monoceros the Unicorn occupies the region inside the "Winter Triangle" of Betelgeuse, Procyon, and Sirius. Although dim to the naked eye, it abounds with telescopic wonders. The small black box above shows the area covered by the large chart at right. The latter, from Uranometria 2000.0, *shows stars to about magnitude 9.5. Deep-sky objects are so close together in this region that once you get started, you may not need the finderscope – you'll be able to work your way from one to the next using the main telescope's lowest-power eyepiece.*

NGC 2259, the open star cluster at center, is composed of very faint stars that may not show in a light-polluted sky. But using a 10-inch telescope to view it in true darkness, Christian Luginbuhl and Brian Skiff describe NGC 2259 as "granular to partially resolved at 200×" in their Observing Handbook and Catalogue of Deep-Sky Objects. The cluster shows beautifully on this blue-light print from the Palomar Observatory Sky Survey. North is up and east is to the left, as on all charts and photographs in this book.

The Christmas Tree cluster. Note the nebula at the tree's northwest corner. Lowell Observatory photograph from Burnham's Celestial Handbook.

2. SOUTH 529

While carefully comparing the chart to the stars in your low-power eyepiece, shift your telescope 1⅓° west from Xi to pick up the 6th-magnitude star plotted amid a little bunch of 8th- and 9th-magnitude ones. From there go southwest 1° and you'll land on a 7th-magnitude star. This is South 529, an easy and colorful triple that I've never seen on any observing list.

The three components, magnitudes 7.6, 8.3, and 9.0, are arranged in a wobbly line about 140" long. Component A, the primary, is yellow with a spectral type of G5. Component C at the south end of the line appears bluish white to me despite its cataloged spectral type of F8. Star B between them is distinctly reddish. The colors were more apparent at 45× than at 110×.

Component A is a high-proper-motion star moving 1" southward every 3.3 years. Thus the line of three is getting shorter as the decades go by.

3. NGC 2259

Due south of South 529 by 1.3° is another 6th-magnitude star, this one orange. East of it by ¼° is the open star cluster NGC 2259. Darnley Wright of Scarborough, Ontario, who has spent many hours rummaging through this area, calls NGC 2259 "a rich cluster of about 25 stars." However, I couldn't see a trace of it in the 6-inch through my suburban light pollution (the naked-eye limiting magnitude is usually about 5.2). Perhaps you can do better. The 25 stars in this cluster are cataloged as being 13th or 14th magnitude and fainter, adding up to a hazy 11th-magnitude glow 4' across. An identifying mark is a pair of 12th-magnitude stars, only 7" apart, oriented east-west at the cluster's north edge.

4. S MONOCEROTIS

Swing 1° southeast to pick up 5th-magnitude S Monocerotis and you'll find yourself in a wonderful area for any telescope, one of the richest star-forming regions in the winter sky.

S Mon dominates this neighborhood. It's an extremely hot and luminous young star of spectral type O7. Its surface temperature of about 30,000° Kelvin renders it blue-white hot. With a color index of −0.25, this is about as blue a star as you'll ever see; they don't get bluer than this pale shade no matter how high the temperature goes.

In a telescope, a star's color shows best when its light isn't too brilliantly concentrated. Otherwise any hue washes out toward white. Try defocusing S Mon to spread its light over a larger area.

S Mon varies slowly and irregularly by a few tenths of a magnitude. It is also a rather difficult double star. The 7.5-magnitude companion is only 2.8" to the southwest, where it may be lost in the blazing skirts of the primary.

5. NGC 2264, THE CHRISTMAS TREE CLUSTER

This beautiful group extends ½° south from S Mon. It's a narrow, triangular outline of bright stars in the unmistakable shape of a fir tree with S Mon at its base. The tree is more brightly outlined in stars than the photo at left suggests – a grand sight in the 6-inch!

This whole region of sky is riddled with churning bright nebulae, but the only hint of them in the 6-inch through my light pollution is a large, very indefinite suggestion of a glow around the tree's northwestern lower bough. Dark nebulae, however, reveal their presence all over the place by the blank areas they create in the otherwise rich background of faint stars.

The star at the tip of the tree is a nice, wide double, Struve (Σ) 954, magnitudes 7.1 and 9.6, separated by 13". The secondary star is "above" the primary in the Christmas Tree's reference frame and set off from it at a jaunty angle.

Extending south from this pair is the awesome and famous Cone nebula, called "The Throne of God" in *Burnham's Celestial Handbook*. But despite the nebula's majestic appearance in photographs, its surface brightness is too low for it to show visually.

6. STRUVE 953

Continuing ½° south from the tip of the Christmas Tree we run into this beautifu double. Its stars are pale orange and bluish, magnitudes 7.2 and 7.7, and 7″ apart. They're easily separated at 45× with black space between. The colors hold up well at 110×.

7. NGC 2261, HUBBLE'S VARIABLE NEBULA

Shift another ½° south to pick up a row of 9th-magnitude stars; follow them west-northwest and you'll hit an object unique in the sky.

NGC 2261 is located 2′ southwest of an 11th-magnitude star and has a total magnitude of about 10. It looks like a little comet with a wide tail. This is a reflection nebula lit by the variable star R Monocerotis, which is buried in a tiny, bright patch just a few arc seconds across in the nebula's southern tip. The star, or starlike patch, generally remains around 12th magnitude. The rest of NGC 2261 extends to the north.

This object has a high surface brightness as nebulae go, so it shows through light pollution well. "Quite distinct and easy," I wrote in my notebook using the 6-inch at 110×. I can see irregularities in its east and west sides and a definite westward bend in the tail as it fades toward the north. This is exactly what photographs show. Try using high powers.

NGC 2261 earned its title as "variable" by the fact that on photographs it appears to change shape somewhat on a time scale of weeks to months. Evidently small, dense, dark clouds orbit close to R Mon and cast their moving shadows across the outer parts of the nebula.

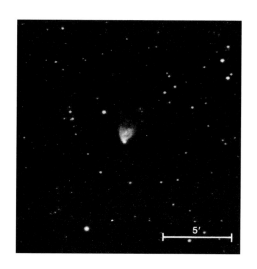

Hubble's Variable nebula, NGC 2261, is small but relatively bright. It has tricked more than one observer into imagining a comet discovery! Preston Scott Justis used a 10-inch f/6 reflector for this 9-minute exposure on 103a-O film.

8. BASEL 7

Continuing another ¾° southwestward we arrive at this obscure little cluster, pictured on the next page. It's a difficult one; locate its exact position carefully between the 9th-magnitude stars near it on the chart. I noted that it was "suspected pretty well" in the 6-inch at 45× and more definitely at 110×. "There's *something* there." Surprisingly, it didn't catch the attention of any of the 19th-century observers whose monumental lists became the *New General Catalogue (NGC)*. According to *Sky Catalogue 2000.0*, Volume 2, the cluster contains about 15 stars.

9. NGC 2251

This cluster is a beauty by comparison. It's a big, diagonal splash of stars, very elongated northwest to southeast. This assemblage is listed as having 30 stars magnitude 9.1 and fainter for a total brightness of 7.3. It is estimated to be 5,000 light-years away and 300 million years old.

About ⅓° south of NGC 2251 is an even bigger, brighter, but much looser group, well seen in the 6-inch at 45× even though there's nothing identified as a cluster here on charts. It too is very elongated, in this case east-west.

In fact all the stars around here seem to come in lines and shoals, like wave marks on a sandy beach. These star chains do not show well on photographs, which always make stars of different brightnesses look too much alike. Studies of star chains have never found them to be real, however; they are mere statistical flukes in the random star-scatter. But could the silhouetted dark nebulae that riddle this particular area help sculpt their appearance?

10. NGC 2254

This cluster is altogether different – a tiny, unresolved glow at 45×. At 110× it became clearer and partially resolved into tiny speckles. I suspected a crescent-shaped pattern of stars in it, which photographs confirm. The 50 stars here are all 12th magnitude and fainter. The cluster has a measured distance of 7,000 light-years; in this part of the sky we are peering far into the depths of the Milky Way.

Of these three dissimilar clusters, Basel 7 barely stands out from the background stars on this blue-light print from the Palomar Observatory Sky Survey. But visually it's more distinct. On the other hand, the nebula IC 448 around 13 Monocerotis is plain on the photograph but invisible to the eye.

11. 14 MONOCEROTIS

Just ⅓° farther west is this double star, magnitudes 6.5 and 10.7, separation 10″. After looking at so many faint subjects near the limit of vision, a 6th-magnitude star really dazzles the eye! Its companion is obvious at 110× – a pretty pair.

12. 13 MONOCEROTIS

This lone star is even more brilliant at magnitude 4.5. Its color is "cold white" (white with a trace of blue). Its grand brilliance is due to intrinsic luminosity, not nearness; this is a supergiant of type *A0* some 10,000 times more luminous than the Sun and 3,000 light-years away. The *Uranometria* chart indicates the faint nebula IC 448 next to it (also shown in the photograph on the previous page), but no trace appears in the 6-inch.

13. NGC 2236

Something funny – just a hint of abnormality – seemed to be going on around an 11th-magnitude star at the correct spot for this cluster when I used 45×. At 110× and 200×, a very dim swarm could just be resolved behind the star using averted vision. I had a sense of looking extraordinarily deep into the dark, and indeed, NGC 2236 has been measured to be fully 11,000 light-years out.

14. COLLINDER 106 AND PLASKETT'S STAR

Here's a cluster with an entirely different character. Collinder 106 is huge (more than $\frac{1}{2}°$ across) and extremely loose, but I had no trouble recognizing what it was when I swept over it at 45×. The cluster nearly filled the field. It was even visible in an 8×30 finderscope as a slight enhancement of the Milky Way. Looking through the finder, however, it was hard not to be distracted by the brighter, more dominant cluster NGC 2244 that had already entered the southwestern side of the finder's field, toward which we are gradually working our way.

The brightest star in Collinder 106 is 6th-magnitude SAO 114146, Plaskett's star, which has long occupied a niche in textbooks as the most massive star known in the galaxy. It is a spectroscopic binary consisting of two giant O stars orbiting each other every 14 days. Early quotes of 90 solar masses for each component resulted from misinterpretation of the star's spectrum; values of 60 and 40 suns are more likely. This still puts both components in the extremely rare category of stars near the top of the mass range that stars can theoretically have.

15. STRUVE 939

Only a few triple stars in the entire sky form a nearly equilateral triangle; this is one of them. The triangle, whose stars are 8th, 9th, and 10th magnitude, averages 35″ on a side. It's a lovely sight at 45×, a very compact little asterism.

16. NGC 2252

Even though it shows poorly on photographs, you should have no trouble recognizing this large, elongated, well-resolved cluster. It is triangular, I noted with the 6-inch, "like the narrow skull of a long-horned animal with its nose pointing northwest." It is cataloged as being 20′ across and containing 30 stars 9th magnitude and fainter.

17. NGC 2244 AND THE ROSETTE NEBULA

Here we arrive at our grand finale of star clusters. NGC 2244 is bright and easy in binoculars or a finder and lovely indeed in the 6-inch. Its six leading stars form a rectangular box shape that can be recognized at a glance in any instrument. Others scattered about give the impression that we have opened the door into a rich nest of suns.

And a nest it truly is – the stars are newborns that remain together in the nebula where they hatched. The cluster is at the heart of the Rosette nebula, NGC 2237-8, one of the most beautiful objects in the entire sky – on photographs. Visually, once again, the 6-inch showed no trace of nebulosity, nor has any other instrument I have tried from my location. The light pollution is to blame, of course. In a dark sky a very small aperture will show it, but it demands low power and a wide field. Through a nebula filter, the Rosette has even been seen with the naked eye

The cluster NGC 2244 in the dim Rosette nebula. If you have a dark sky and a rich-field instrument, use this as a finder chart for the nebula's brightest patches. This is a 90-minute exposure on 103a-F film by Preston Scott Justis using a 10-inch f/6 reflector.

¼°

18. EPSILON (ε) MONOCEROTIS

Let's have one last, brilliant object before closing up for the night. Epsilon Mon is a stunner of a double star, magnitudes 4.5 and 6.5, separation 9". It should show well even in a 2.4-inch. In the 6-inch it is a pair of glorious white blazes.

It's been a long evening; time to pack up and head for bed, memory replete with celestial sights that even as we settle down for sleep continue to float above the rooftops in the starry deeps.

STAR-HOP

5

FIVE

Among the Gemini Twins

Of all the bright winter constellations, Gemini lingers longest into spring. Darkness falls in March while Gemini is still high overhead, even as the rest of the winter panoply is lowering toward the west. The Twins remain well placed for telescopic observing through early May, though by then they are getting pretty low. The all-sky maps on pages 16 to 27 show where to find the pair of Gemini figures. They're holding hands with their feet in the Milky Way. The close-up guide map on the bottom of the next page, which includes their stick-figure heads and upper bodies, shows stars to magnitude 8.0.

1. CASTOR

Our starting point is one of the brightest and best-known double stars. That's not to say Castor is always easy to resolve cleanly. Its component stars, both white, are magnitudes 1.9 and 2.9. They were separated by 3.3" in 1993, on their way to widening to 4.0" in 2000 and 5.6" in 2010. In theory they're wide enough for almost any telescope to divide them easily. But so bright are the stars that atmospheric turbulence – poor seeing – can turn them into one big blur. In excellent seeing my 6-inch reflector at 200× showed them as two brilliant diffraction disks with black sky between even during the 1970s when they were closer than now. You may find that even on poor nights you can at least "elongate" Castor – see the blended blur extending distinctly toward the east-northeast.

Castor is changing character from decade to decade as the stars orbit each other. After generations of being separated by 5" or so, they closed to only 1.9" around 1969. Now Castor is widening toward a maximum separation of 7.3" to be achieved around 2085. It completes an orbit in 467 years, according to a recent determination by Swarthmore College double-star specialist Wulff D. Heintz.

How many observers know that Castor is an easy triple star? South of the bright pair by 71" is Castor C, an orange spark of magnitude 9.2. Its tint is plainly visible at all powers in the 6-inch, perhaps enhanced by contrast with the white stars. Castor C may orbit the AB pair in something like 37,000 years, according to Heintz. All three stars are themselves spectroscopic binaries, thus making Castor a sextuple. The components of Castor C are red dwarfs. They eclipse each other with an orbital period of only 19.5 hours, earning Castor C the variable-star designation YY Geminorum. The dimming at mideclipse is only 0.4 magnitude. The whole system is 45 light-years from Earth, the same distance as Capella.

2. POLLUX

Pollux is uninteresting by comparison. It's brighter and more colorful than Castor but single; faint companions that have been cataloged are mere background stars. Pollux is a typical orange giant of spectral type K0 III. "A beautiful pale orange-yellow," I noted with the 6-inch. Located 36 light-years from Earth, Pollux is 30 times more luminous than the Sun.

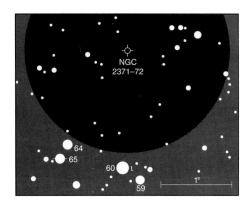

The double planetary nebula NGC 2371-72 is small and faint, so you may need this 9.5-magnitude chart to pinpoint its exact spot in a telescope.

3. NGC 2371-2372.

Off we step again into the deep sky. This little planetary nebula is no easy catch, at least not with a 6-inch from a light-polluted suburb. You'll need to zero in on the exact spot, which, as always, means precise attention to the use of maps.

To locate NGC 2371-72, start from Castor and move 4° south-southwest to the little asterism of Iota (ι), 59, 64, and 65 Geminorum. Backtrack a bit more than a degree to the little pair of 8th-magnitude stars. Now spot the other pair of 8th-magnitude stars to their west (right) on the map. Note the position of the nebula between the two pairs. That's the point to hit. If you still don't land on the position precisely enough to identify the dim little glow, use the larger-scale map at left, which shows stars to about magnitude 9.5. That should do the job. Compare it to what you see in the main telescope's lowest-power eyepiece.

NGC 2371-72 is a double nebula only about 50″ long. Under a dark, rural sky a 6-inch should show it as a faint, hazy area with a starlike spot, according to Christian Luginbuhl and Brian Skiff in their *Observing Handbook and Catalogue of Deep-Sky Objects*. Use high power. A 10-inch should show two distinct

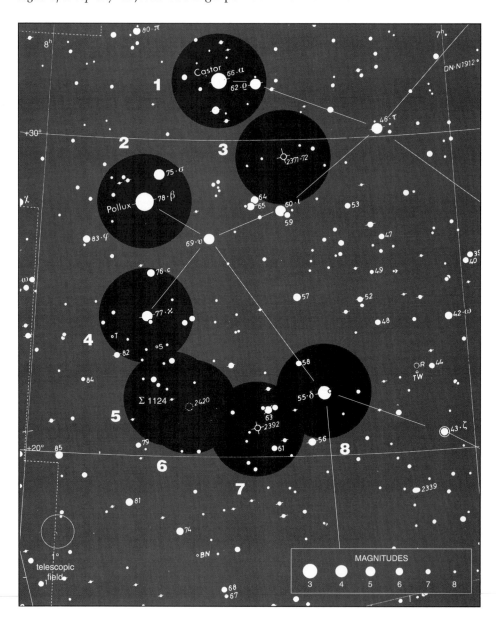

A guide map for sightseeing in one corner of Gemini. The numbered circles are 3° in diameter. Adapted from Sky Atlas 2000.0.

patches aligned northeast-southwest. The southwestern one (NGC 2371) is brighter and has a stellar center. The 14.9-magnitude central star lies between them. A nebula filter could be a big help with a planetary like this, if you've got a fairly large telescope that is troubled by a light-polluted sky.

4. KAPPA (κ) GEMINORUM

This star, the eastern hand of the Pollux figure and 150 light-years away, is an exquisite double if you can resolve it. The 3.6-magnitude primary is orange-yellow like Pollux. It has a tiny companion, about 9th magnitude, located 7″ west-southwest. Use your highest power, and don't give up if you fail to see it at first. Wait for moments of good seeing, just as if observing a planet.

5. STRUVE 1124

Here's an unexpected find! Star-hopping carefully southward from Kappa, you'll hit this beautiful, wide double star at the end of a 1°-long row of four. It's an eye-catcher in the 6-inch at 46×. The two white components are nearly equal at about 8th magnitude each. They're 19″ apart and oriented southeast-northwest.

There's more here too. Just a bit north of the pair is a longer, straight line of three fainter stars, oriented northeast-southwest, for a total of five. They look almost clusterlike.

6. NGC 2420

Jumping west-southwest by ⅔°, about the width of the lowest-power eyepiece field in many telescopes, we come to a genuine open cluster – large, rich, but rather faint. Although NGC 2420 has a total magnitude of 8.3, this light is spread out over an area some 10′ across. Its brightest individual stars are 11th magnitude. The 9.5-magnitude map at left shows the precise spot if you need it. Compare the map to the photograph below. I can make out NGC 2420 with the 6-inch at 46× even in bright moonlight.

The cluster is some 8,000 light-years away. Its age has been determined to be a remarkable 4 billion years, far older than most open clusters and nearly as old as the Sun.

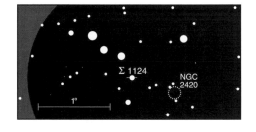

The open cluster NGC 2420 can be found even with small telescopes through light pollution if you know its exact location. Adapted from Uranometria 2000.0.

NGC 2420, a hazy glow in a 3-inch telescope, appears partially resolved into stars at high powers in an 8-inch. The cluster is fully resolved in this photograph by George R. Viscome of Lake Placid, New York. He used a 14.5-inch f/6 reflector for a 12-minute exposure on 3M 1000 color slide film. North is up, and the frame is 0.6° wide.

7. NGC 2392, THE ESKIMO NEBULA

Here's a fine little object! NGC 2392 is one of the brightest planetary nebulae in the sky. I can spy something odd here in an 8×50 finderscope. The 6-inch at 46× shows a round, sharp-edged disk about 45″ across with a very obvi-

The Eskimo, a bright planetary nebula, is one of the prettiest sights in Gemini. It looks green or blue-green to the eye; the similarly bright star just 1½' to its north is orange. Only the nebula's inner disk, not the fuzzy outer ring, generally shows to visual observers. Richard and Helen Lines used a 16-inch f/8 Newtonian reflector for this photgraph.

ous central star. The nebula is pale grayish green and 9th magnitude, making a lovely color contrast with the 8.3-magnitude orange star that lies just 1½' north of it. The larger your aperture the more definite and beautiful the colors.

Like other small planetary nebulae, NGC 2392 rewards high magnification. The central star is magnitude 10.5. Can you see a slightly darker patch just west of it? A 12-inch may show a complete dark ring about halfway from the center to the edge. Only photographs taken with large telescopes show the Eskimo face – a mottled visage with a bright nose in a parka hood.

8. DELTA (δ) GEMINORUM

We end with another challenging bright-faint double star. Delta Gem marks the waist of Pollux. Its 3.6-magnitude primary is an *F0* subgiant, a star somewhat hotter and brighter than the Sun ending billions of years of life on the main sequence and beginning to swell toward its final blaze of glory and death. The companion is an orange *K3* dwarf of magnitude 8.2 located 6″ to the bright star's southwest. Use your highest power.

Aside from color, Delta Gem looks similar to Kappa but should be a little easier to resolve. As with Kappa, keep trying even if you don't see the 8th-magnitude companion right away.

This pair is 55 light-years distant, making the bright star 9 times brighter than the Sun and the faint one 9 times dimmer.

STAR-HOP

6

SIX

A Springtime Galaxy Hunt

The Big Dipper, the best-known star pattern to naked-eye viewers, gives no sign of the faint wonders that lie hidden in and around it. To small-telescope users the Dipper is best known for the bright double star Mizar in the middle of its handle. But this part of the sky also contains scores of galaxies within reach of modest apertures.

Far behind the stars of the Dipper, roughly half a million times farther away, lies an outlying tendril of the gigantic Virgo supercluster of galaxies to which our Milky Way itself belongs. Also called the Local Supercluster, this great grouping – perhaps 100 million light-years across – is the nearest and most obvious piece of the large-scale cosmic structure, the filigreed network of matter that organizes the universe into great sheets and nodes of galaxy swarms separated by immense voids.

The secret to searching out the dim, distant riches in this part of the sky is, as always, having good charts – and skill in using them to pinpoint a difficult object's exact location in the eyepiece.

This chapter presents a tour through one small galaxy-strewn area just off the end of the Big Dipper's handle, in the constellation Canes Venatici. The black circles on the guide map on page 90 are 3° in diameter, and stars are plotted to magnitude 8.0.

1. ETA (η) URSAE MAJORIS

Our starting point is the star at the end of the Big Dipper's handle, also named Alkaid. It is 2nd magnitude, a bluish white main-sequence star of spectral type *B*3. With a color index of –0.2 it is nearly as blue as stars can ever get, though the hue is quite pale. The blue tint becomes more evident when the star is out of focus. Alkaid is estimated to be 300 times as luminous as the Sun and 140 light-years distant. Sight on it to make sure your finderscope is correctly aligned with the main telescope, a crucial adjustment for star-hop success.

2. M51, THE WHIRLPOOL GALAXY

This is one of the amateur showpieces of the sky. At any big star party you'll notice large telescopes aimed near the Big Dipper, and you can bet they're showing off what they can do on M51. The ability to locate it without charts is considered a star-party badge of honor.

For all that, M51 is not as grand a sight as its reputation and photographs imply. It is only one-fifteenth the diameter of the great Andromeda galaxy, M31, and only a hundredth as bright.

To find M51 start from Alkaid and move your telescope 2° westward – be sure you have the direction right! – to pick up the 5th-magnitude star 24 Canum Venaticorum. Now go 1½° southwest to hit a 7th-magnitude star.

From there go ⅔° south-southeast, and you're on top of M51 and its companion galaxy, NGC 5195. Another 7th-magnitude star lies just ⅓° to their east. Pay close attention to matching each little star pattern on the map with what you see in the finderscope.

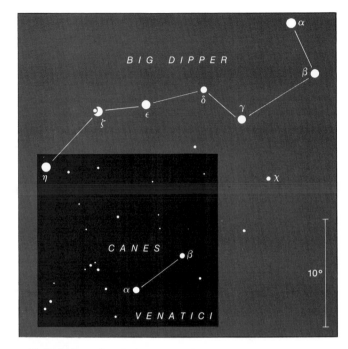

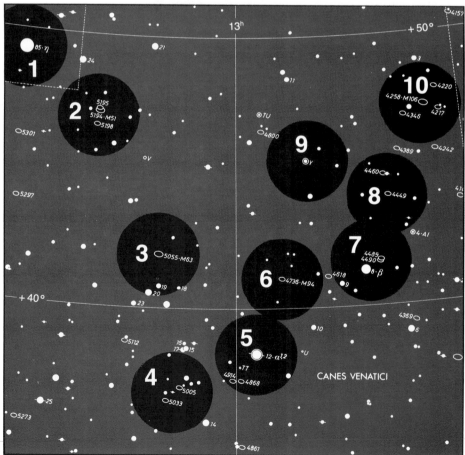

On the chart at upper right showing the Big Dipper, the black box shows the area covered by the detailed chart at right, adapted from Wil Tirion's Sky Atlas 2000.0. *The black circles are 3° in diameter.*

In my 6-inch reflector at 45 power under moderately light-polluted skies, M51 and its companion are a pair of hazy gray glows with brighter centers. They are only 4′ apart. Of the two, M51 looks much larger and rounder and its center is brighter.

M51 and its companion NGC 5195 have a lesser-known third galaxy, NGC 5198, ½° to their south. You can pinpoint its location in a telescope using this photograph from Hans Vehrenberg's Atlas of Deep-Sky Splendors. The streaks are satellite trails.

Keep looking, for in time you'll gradually perceive more detail. Try high powers on these galaxies, and patiently search their depths with averted vision for any dim secrets they harbor. At 200× the companion shows a bright, almost stellar nucleus that is definitely more concentrated than that of the main galaxy. Moreover, the companion seems to suffer a sharp cutoff in brightness just east of its nucleus, as if it is peering out from behind a dark dust cloud – an impression that photographs confirm. Not bad for a 6-inch scope in the suburbs.

An 8-inch telescope under a good sky begins to show traces of spiral or ring structure in M51. Indeed, this is the galaxy in which spiral structure was first noted by 19th-century visual observers. A 17-inch scope makes the spiral shape obvious.

A third galaxy, much smaller and fainter and usually overlooked by amateurs, lies just ½° south of M51. NGC 5198 forms the southeastern fourth corner of a little rectangle with three very faint stars. I couldn't swear I saw it at all in the 6-inch at 110×.

Despite its location, NGC 5198 is not a second companion of M51; its redshift suggests that it is about four times as distant. If M51 and NGC 5195 are about 30 million light-years away, NGC 5198 is roughly 120 million.

3. M63

Carefully comparing your finderscope view with the chart, swing $1\frac{1}{3}°$ south-southwest from M51 to pick up a 6th-magnitude star, then a little more than 2° farther the same way to hit an east-west pair. Continue 2° more to land on M63. It's just east-southeast of an 8.5-magnitude star.

M63 looks brighter than M51 in the 6-inch. It is very elongated nearly in the direction of the 8.5-magnitude star. Time and averted vision bring out a much larger, outer disk that is elongated in a somewhat different direction than the inner portion, a common occurrence in galaxies. The inner disk shows hints of a sharp brightness cutoff on its south side.

M63 is about 35 million light-years away. Its intricate spiral structure on observatory photographs has earned it the nickname the "Sunflower galaxy." It is a type Sb spiral a lot like our Milky Way, and its mass has been estimated at 115 billion Suns. To sky-observing creatures within this galaxy – surely there must be at least *some?* – the Milky Way is a nearly face-on spiral about as bright as M63 looks to us.

4. NGC 5005 AND 5033

Watching the chart, work your way south from M63 through three little asterisms. The first includes the stars 19, 20, and 23 Canum; the second 15, 16, and 17. The third, about $1\frac{1}{2}°$ farther south, is a faint, nameless little east-west star stream. Here lie the two galaxies NGC 5005 and 5033.

The former is easy in the 6-inch – very elongated northeast to southwest, with a central bulge and signs of a bright nucleus. This is the way a galaxy ought to look! There are hints of a sharper edge along its southeast.

NGC 5033 is quite a bit fainter but still not hard in the 6-inch. It looks more amorphous, with no sign of the beautiful spiral arms seen in the photograph below. Try high power on these galaxies to see if it reveals any more detail.

The spiral galaxy M63, about 35 million light-years distant, is probably a near-copy of the Milky Way. This frame is 0.3° wide. For this 45-minute exposure Bill Iburg used a cold camera on a 14-inch Schmidt-Cassegrain telescope at f/5.5 and Ektachrome 400 film pushed to ISO 800.

NGC 5033 (large spiral at lower left) and NGC 5005 (upper right) are ⅔° apart. Martin Germano used an 8-inch f/5 reflector for a 70-minute exposure on hypered Kodak 2415 film.

5. COR CAROLI

After searching out all these dim sights, the double star Cor Caroli (Alpha Canum Venaticorum) is a blaze of glory. Its two components, magnitudes 2.9

and 5.5, are 19″ apart – wide enough to separate in any telescope. At 45× in the 6-inch, the bright component looks white with possibly a touch of blue; the secondary is an odd tawny yellow. At 110× the secondary appears to have a sort of purple-brown tint, and at 280×, which magnifies the stars to fuzzy balls, the purple is undeniable. As with many doubles the colors are largely contrast illusions in the eye.

6. M94

Exactly 3° north-northwest of Cor Caroli is this fine 8th-magnitude galaxy. It's so bright you can probably hit it just by noting its exact location on the chart with respect to Alpha (α) and Beta (β) Canum.

M94 is rather small as well as bright, so it takes high power very well. It looks almost round. Its light increases steadily toward a brighter nucleus "much like an unresolved globular cluster," write Christian Luginbuhl and Brian Skiff in their *Observing Handbook and Catalogue of Deep-Sky Objects*. They note that a 12-inch telescope reveals patchy irregularities in the galaxy's outer parts.

7. NGC 4490 AND 4485

These colliding galaxies are easy to locate just ⅔° northwest of 3rd-magnitude Beta Canum. NGC 4490, with a total visual magnitude of 10, is the first you'll see. It's fairly easy in the 6-inch – a gray glow elongated northeast-southwest. Use averted vision to search for the much more difficult NGC 4485 located 3′.5 to its north-northwest. A larger telescope under a darker sky may show that the two are attached.

The 8th-magnitude spiral galaxy M94 is easy to spot, but what you're seeing is only its bright inner regions. The hazy, tightly wound outer spiral arms show up only with photography or with a large telescope in very dark skies.

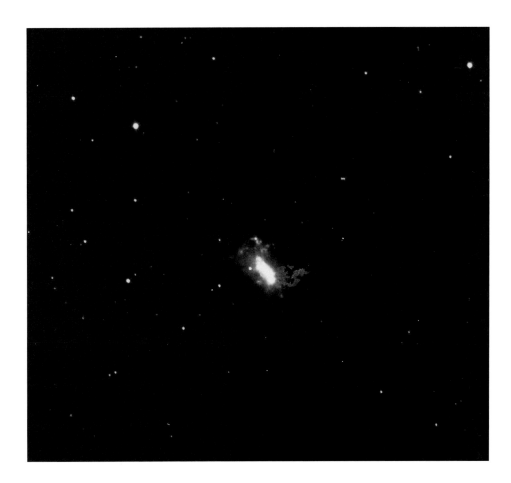

The irregular galaxy NGC 4449. Irregular galaxies have the same mixture of large nebulae and young, luminous blue stars that highlight the arms of spiral galaxies. However, they lack the population of old, yellower stars that form a spiral's inner hub. Preston Scott Justis used a 10-inch f/6 reflector for this 50-minute exposure on hypersensitized Kodak 2415 film.

8. NGC 4449

Another 2½° north brings us to our next way station among the island universes. NGC 4449 is a large irregular galaxy with a cataloged size of 5′ by 4′ and a total visual magnitude of 9.5. In the 6-inch it is a dim but easy patch of glow. This galaxy is a little nearer than the others we've been looking at, assuming its redshift can be trusted as an accurate distance indicator. If NGC 4490 and 4485 are 30 million light-years distant, NGC 4449 is only about 10 million.

North of NGC 4449 by 0.7° is the pretty double star Struve (Σ) 1645. Its two white components, magnitudes 7.4 and 8.0, are 10″ apart.

A mere 8′ north-northeast of this pair is very faint NGC 4460, which you're welcome to try looking for. It was totally invisible in the 6-inch.

9. Y CANUM VENATICORUM

Sweep 3° east from Struve 1645 with your finderscope and…*what's that?* You've hit Y Canum, "La Superba," one of the most colorful stars in the sky. It is a deep, rich orange, a carbon star of spectral type *N*8. It appears so red not just because its temperature is low but because the color of molecular carbon vapor (C_3) in its atmosphere is actually red. We see the star's surface through a red filter. The star's color index is tabulated as 2.5, but color index values this high begin to lose meaning for visual observers. Robert Burnham calls the tint "truly odd and vivid" in large telescopes. In the 6-inch it is a fiery coal. The color is even redder in a finder or binoculars.

Y Canum is one of the very largest stars known, with an estimated diameter of 10 astronomical units – about one billion miles – 1,200 times the diameter of the Sun. It is a semiregular variable, ranging from about visual magnitude 4.8 to 6.3 and back in roughly 5 months. Its color probably varies somewhat too.

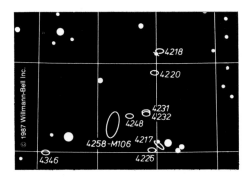

M106, one of the best and brightest galaxies in the northern sky, dwarfs its companions, most of which lie far in the background. This chart is from Uranometria 2000.0; the grid boxes are 1° tall.

This photograph from Hans Vehrenberg's Atlas of Deep-Sky Splendors *will aid in locating the many faint galaxies, identified by their NGC numbers, surrounding M106.*

10. M106 (NGC 4258)

We could wander on forever among the galaxies in this region of the sky. But for now we'll make just one more stop, working 5° northwest to reach the brightest galaxy we've looked at yet.

M106 is big and bold in the 6-inch, very elongated north-south, with hints of irregularities around its ends. I've even spotted it through thin clouds. A 6th-magnitude star ½° to the east-southeast makes it fairly simple to locate. I haven't sighted any of M106's companion galaxies, but hunting them down would be a good project for an 8-inch or larger telescope under dark skies. See the chart on the previous page.

M106 is a grand galaxy to contemplate as you try to imagine what is impossible to picture – that these misty little smudges are incredible swarms of hundreds of billions of suns, spanning tens of thousands of light-years from end to end. Each probably contains billions of planets harboring a near-infinity of wonders that would shatter the imagination. But we must be content to view them from extremely far away, privileged just to detect them as the merest wisps before packing up the telescope and retreating indoors.

STAR-HOP

7

SEVEN

Across the Big Dipper's Bowl

The Big Dipper is so well known, and it's such fertile ground for star-hopping, that we'll spend another chapter here – this time working across the Dipper's Bowl. Our target area is smaller than in the previous chapter, so we can use a more detailed, narrow-field map. The one at the bottom of the next page, adapted from two *Uranometria 2000.0* charts butted together, shows stars to about magnitude 9.5. This is about the faintest visible in a 50-millimeter finder under moderate suburban light pollution. The black circles are only 1° in diameter, about the size of the lowest-power view in many telescopes. As always, celestial north is up and east is to the left.

The celestial terrain for this chapter was originally scouted out by *Sky & Telescope* contributor Philip Harrington. Many of the remarks here are his.

1. MERAK AND COLLINDER 285

We'll start at the southwest corner of the Big Dipper's Bowl. This 2nd-magnitude white star is the rear of the two Pointers, the stars at the front of the bowl known to every skywatcher as pointing the way to Polaris. In a telescope Merak is a blaze of "cold white" light, white shaded just a trace toward blue. With a spectral type of A0 it is somewhat larger than the Sun, a lot hotter, and 45 times more luminous.

Before moving on, let's pause to look at the entire Dipper figure. Although you'd never guess it from a casual glance, five of its stars – all but the two on the ends – belong to the closest open cluster to our solar system. Nicknamed the Ursa Major Moving Cluster and formally cataloged as Collinder 285, this sparse grouping probably holds only 17 stars within its weak gravitational grip. They're widely scattered across a large oval area of space roughly 18 light-years wide by 30 long. The cluster's proximity – it's only about 75 light-years from Earth – spreads the stars across more than 20° of our spring sky. Other members include Alcor (80 Ursae Majoris), 78 and 37 Ursae Majoris, and 21 Leonis Minoris. Additional, more widely separated stars that suspiciously share the same space motion include Sirius, Alpha Ophiuchi, Beta Aurigae, Alpha Coronae Borealis, and about 100 fainter stars.

2. THE BROKEN ENGAGEMENT RING

One of the most enjoyable things about deep-sky observing is bumping into unexpected little star patterns (asterisms) scattered throughout the sky. Here's an example. Finding it will also help in getting oriented for the journey to come.

From Merak, sweep 1.5° due west to pick up a pair of 6th- and 7th-magnitude stars aligned north-south 0.4° apart. Got them? Once again, little maneuvers like this are the key to star-hop success. Measure the distance by the size of your finderscope's field of view; 1.5° is probably about a third of its diameter. It's also about twice the width of the field in a typical eyepiece that gives 60× on your telescope.

As for directions, nudge the telescope a little toward Polaris; the north edge of the field is where new stars enter from. East is 90° counterclockwise from north if your telescope gives a correct image, one that matches the map. East is 90° *clockwise* from north in a mirror image, which is usually caused by using a star diagonal. West, of course, is opposite east.

Once you've got the two stars, center your finder's crosshairs on the fainter, southern one and take a look in the main telescope. A low-power eyepiece shows the star to be the brightest of seven suns forming a broken oval about ¼° in diameter. The overall effect is a bit like a ring, with the bright star representing the diamond. From the shape it's in, however, the ring seems to have been through quite a battle. That's why Phil Harrington named it the Broken Engagement Ring.

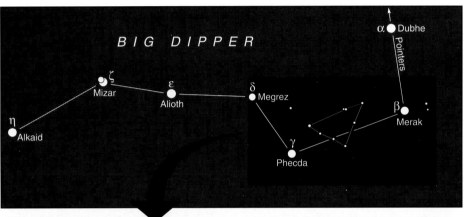

The bowl of the Big Dipper is rich in galaxies and other objects suitable for backyard telescopes. On the map at right, the black box shows the area covered by the larger and more detailed chart below, adapted from Uranometria 2000.0. *The circles are 1° in diameter.*

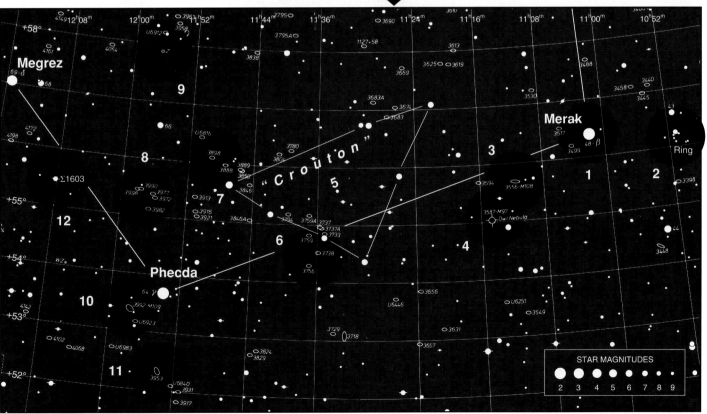

3. M108

Now we push off into the deep to our first galaxy. Go back to Merak and shift ¾° east-southeast to pick up the 7th-magnitude star charted at that point. From there, note the little pattern of 8th- and 9th-magnitude stars running about 0.6° farther southeast. When dealing with patterns this small and faint, it's best to use the main telescope's lowest-power eyepiece instead of the finder. The last two stars of the chain are only ⅙° apart and point almost due east. Go this same distance farther east and you're smack on top of our first deep-sky object.

M108 (the edge-on galaxy at top right) and M97 (the planetary nebula at bottom left) are only 0.8° apart, bringing them within the same low-power field of view in many telescopes. Martin Germano took this 20-minute exposure with an 8-inch f/5 reflector on 103a-F film.

M108 is a wide-armed spiral galaxy of type Sc tilted nearly edge on to our line of sight. Its 10th-magnitude glow appears decidedly cigar-shaped. A 6-inch telescope shows M108 as a long splinter of dim grayness behind an attractive field of faint stars. A slow, concentrated scan with medium power reveals some bright knots along its length. But don't be fooled by the brightest knot of all, seen near the galaxy's center. That's a faint Milky Way star superimposed in the foreground.

Bigger telescopes show more of M108's irregularities, and its overall length grows to about 8′ by 2′ in 10-inch and larger instruments. That's under good skies. Light pollution, of course, determines what you can see of galaxies every bit as much as aperture does.

4. THE OWL NEBULA, M97

From M108 it's just two short hops to one of the Dipper's most famous – and infamous – residents: M97, the Owl nebula. Go ½° southeast to an 8th-magnitude star, then a similar distance farther south-southeast, and there you are.

The Owl is a planetary nebula, an expanding shell of gas jettisoned by an aging giant becoming a white dwarf. Photographs show a round disk highlighted by two strange dark ovals on either side of its center (see the photo on the previous page). In 1848 their likeness to owl eyes led the deep-sky surveyor Lord Rosse to give the nebula its nickname, which has stuck ever since.

M97 stands out clearly enough in deep photographs, but it is well known among amateur astronomers as one of the most difficult Messier objects to see visually. Although rated at 10th magnitude, the Owl suffers from low surface brightness (light per unit area), making it tough to pick out against the background sky. Narrow-band light-pollution filters, such as Lumicon's UHC or Orion's UltraBlock, increase its visibility, especially from suburban locations.

A 6-inch telescope under a fairly dark sky shows M97 as a very dim, perfect circle with a uniform texture. It may come into view better if you wiggle the scope a little. Under excellent rural skies the Owl's eyes can just be glimpsed. From such locales an 8-inch begins to add a little more personality to M97 by accentuating its diffuse edges and the two eyes.

Many deep-sky observers enjoy the sport of trying to spot the central stars of planetary nebulae. In the case of the Owl, the central star shines weakly at 14th magnitude, making it a difficult catch in anything less than a 12-inch telescope at high power.

5. THE DIPPER'S SUNKEN CROUTON

Looking back in the finderscope, sweep from Merak to Phecda, the other star forming the bottom of the Dipper's bowl. They're 8° apart, probably a good deal wider than your finder's field. Along the way you'll cross a large triangle of 6th-magnitude stars inside the Dipper's bowl, measuring nearly 4° from end to end. It's outlined on the map. The triangle is especially easy to see in binoculars, but it's hardly a well-known part of the Big Dipper. Perhaps it's a lump of something in whatever the Dipper is dipping – a crouton in soup? This triangle will be the key to finding our next several objects.

6. NGC 3738 AND NGC 3756

These two faint island universes lie near the Crouton's southern point. Move one star northeast from that point along the triangle's edge, then shift ¼° southeast. There lies NGC 3738.

Although its location is easy enough to find, the galaxy proves a tough catch with a 6-inch telescope. Take your time and use averted vision. A couple of 10th- and 11th-magnitude stars lie just to its east. Look for a round, uniform disk of about 12th magnitude no more than 1′ across, with no central brightening. The galaxy's indistinct stellar nucleus takes at least an 8-inch telescope to be seen.

Now turn your attention another ⅓° southeast, moving down a short arc of faint stars. Just beyond the arc's end the spiral NGC 3756 awaits your visit. Like its neighbor to the north, NGC 3756 shows only a round, uniform disk of dim grayness. Most deep-sky reference books list it as slightly brighter than NGC 3738, but it actually seems to look a little fainter.

5′

M109, a barred spiral galaxy, is easily found less than 1° southeast of Phecda in the bottom of the Dipper's bowl. Its pinwheel arms are recorded beautifully here, but they are very elusive visually. Kim Zussman used a 14½-inch f/8 Cassegrain reflector for this 2-hour exposure on hypered Kodak 2415 Technical Pan film.

7. NGC 3898

Looking in the finderscope, move northeastward along the Crouton's edge to its easternmost star. Continuing farther in this direction brings you to 66 Ursae Majoris. A third of the way there you'll encounter the spiral galaxy NGC 3898. It's just east of a slender rectangle of faint stars too dim to show on the chart (or in a finder; switch to the main eyepiece).

Through a 4-inch refractor at 42× in the suburbs, NGC 3898 appears like a small, oval piece of extragalactic cotton. With a little concentrated effort, a faint stellar heart can be made out embedded within it.

8. NGC 3998, 3990, AND 3982

Check back in the finderscope again to 66 UMa and the eastern star of the Crouton. A tight gang of five galaxies is plotted on our map near the point forming an equilateral triangle with them to their south and east. The brightest of the batch is NGC 3998. It stands out surprisingly well in a 4-inch refractor as an 11th-magnitude oval patch of fuzz punctuated by a pinpoint nucleus. It's just east of the midway point between two faint field stars.

If you're using an 8-inch or larger telescope, you just might spy a second, smaller smudge exactly halfway between those two stars. If so, you have found NGC 3990. It appears about a magnitude fainter and much smaller than its neighbor.

To the south-southwest of NGC 3990 and 3998 by 0.4° lies another challenging spiral. Although it glows at only magnitude 11.7, NGC 3982 stands out fairly well in 4- to 6-inch telescopes. With a low-power eyepiece, a 4-inch refractor reveals a blur about 1' in diameter and slightly oval.

9. Z URSAE MAJORIS

Take a break from galaxy hunting to look at this semiregular variable star. Cycling from about magnitude 6.5 to 8.3 and back every six months or so, Z Ursae Majoris is bright enough to be followed in just about all amateur telescopes and binoculars. Its spectral type is *M5*. Look for its pale orange light about 1¼° due north of 66 Ursae Majoris and just south of a crooked little right triangle formed by four 8th- and 9th-magnitude stars.

The American Association of Variable Star Observers recommends Z Ursae Majoris as a perfect star for anyone new to observing variables. Many veteran variable-star observers began their careers by monitoring it. How about you?

10. M109

Swing several degrees back south to center on 2nd-magnitude Phecda. Compare what you see around it to the busy little patterns on the chart. Note the north-south row of four 8th- and 9th-magnitude stars roughly ⅔° to Phecda's southeast, and take aim at the second one from the north. Just northeast of here lies M109, a barred spiral galaxy.

Once spotted, M109 shows a nebulous pear-shaped core surrounded by the dim, nondescript glow of the galaxy's spiral arms. Most backyard telescopes also show a faint star lying close to the galactic core, especially at high power. Many observers excitedly mistake this for a possible supernova, but it's just a dim member of our own Milky Way.

Photographs, such as the one on the previous page, show M109 as a barred spiral with two distinct arms curving away from an elongated hub. Although the arms photograph well, they are difficult to confirm visually. Large amateur telescopes hint at the galaxy's spiral structure, but only on exceptionally dark and transparent nights.

11. NGC 3953

Extending that little line of four stars its own length south-southwestward brings you to an easy-to-spot spiral, NGC 3953. At 10th magnitude it's visible in good skies in telescopes as small as 3 inches. A 4-inch refractor shows it as distinctly oval and drawing toward a brighter center. Several faint, low-contrast patches of nebulosity might also be glimpsed within it using averted vision through 8-inch and larger telescopes.

Near M109 lies the similar-looking barred spiral NGC 3953. Preston Scott Justis took this 70-minute exposure with a 10-inch f/6 reflector on 103a-F film.

12. STRUVE 1603

Shifting back to the finderscope, sweep back and forth from Phecda to Megrez, Delta (δ) Ursae Majoris; these two stars form the back side of the Dipper's bowl. Three-fifths of the way from Megrez to Phecda and just a trace east you'll find a 7th-magnitude star. That's Struve 1603, an attractive double for any aperture. Even the smallest backyard telescope resolves it into an east-west pair of pearly white points separated by 22″. The brighter primary star shines at magnitude 7.8, while its companion glows half a magnitude fainter.

STAR-HOP

8

EIGHT

At the Head of Ophiuchus

Two giants float head to head among the evening constellations in the warm months of the year – Hercules, the legendary hero, and Ophiuchus, the Serpent Holder. Their Alpha (α) stars, just 5° apart, traditionally mark each figure's head. Alpha Herculis is named Rasalgethi, from the Arabic for Head of the Kneeler. Alpha Ophiuchi is Rasalhague, Head of the Serpent Collector.

These two stars can be found 30° southwest of Vega. This is to Vega's right when it is partway up the eastern sky as it is on evenings in June. The diagram below shows this scene. Later in the night or in the season, when Vega is overhead, the two heads are below it in the southwest.

Alpha Herculis and Alpha Ophiuchi mark the beginning of the telescopic sky tour on the 8th-magnitude guide map on the next page.

1. ALPHA HERCULIS

Alpha Herculis is both a spectacular double star and one of the brightest red semiregular variables in the sky. Its total light varies between 3rd and 4th magnitude slowly and fairly irregularly, with a 6-year cycle of 0.5 magnitude underlying more random variations. To estimate the star's brightness with the naked eye, compare it to the row of Beta (β), Delta (δ), Lambda (λ), and Mu (μ) Herculis, whose magnitudes are marked on the small map at left.

If you have sharp or well-corrected vision, the orange color of Alpha Herculis (the color astronomers call "red") is just visible to the naked eye. The slightest optical aid makes plain the strong tint of this *M*5 star.

A small telescope reveals a 5.4-magnitude companion star hiding 4.7″ to the east (at position angle 105°) in the fringes of the red giant's glare. The pair is easiest to resolve when the brighter star is near minimum light and the magnitude difference is least.

The companion, Alpha Herculis B, is a *G*5 giant and therefore ought to look yellow. But in my 6-inch reflector it looks gray-blue. Mary Proctor, author of *Evenings with the Stars* (1924), called it "emerald" as seen in a large refractor. William Henry Smyth, who also used a refractor, termed the companion "emerald, or bluish green" in his *Cycle of Celestial Objects* (also known as the *Bedford Catalogue)*, published in 1844. He also noted "two distant stars of 10th and 12th magnitude" in the field "which are remarkable for their lilac tinge." No doubt these are contrast effects with the primary star's orange. Perhaps chromatic aberration in these early observers' refractors played a role too. What color do the stars appear to you?

Alpha Herculis is estimated to be 600 light-years away. If this distance is correct the red giant is one of the largest known – more than 5 astronomical units (a.u.) in diameter, big enough to fill the solar system out to the asteroid belt. If the Sun were a yellow-white pea, Alpha Herculis would be a fuzzy orange ball about 10 feet wide.

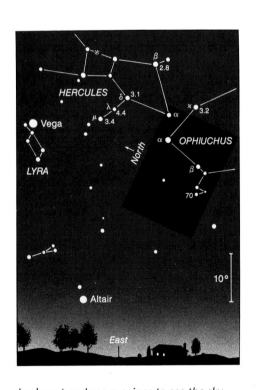

Look east on June evenings to see the sky sparkling with Lyra, Hercules, and Ophiuchus. The tilted black box shows the area covered by the guide map on the next page. Celestial north is to the upper left.

Alpha Herculis B lies at least 800 a.u. from A – a third of a mile away in our scale model – and may orbit it in 3,000 or 4,000 years. B is a spectroscopic binary consisting of G and F giants in a 52-day orbit, a pair rather like Capella. In the same scale model it would be represented by a golf ball and a tennis ball circling each other roughly a foot apart.

2. ALPHA OPHIUCHI

Alpha Ophiuchi, at magnitude 2.1, is the brighter of the two head stars. It lies 5° east-southeast of Alpha Herculis and is a very different kind of object. In our scale model it would be only a small marble, slightly flattened due to fast rotation and shining dazzling white. Alpha Ophiuchi is an A5 main-sequence star 50 light-years away, twice as luminous as Sirius and 40 times as bright as the Sun. Its wide spectral lines show that it is rotating very rapidly.

In the same low-power telescopic field, 0.6° north of Alpha Oph, is a wide pair of 7th-magnitude stars. The western and brighter of the two is 54 Ophiuchi, a wide, unequal double star. Its components shine at magnitudes 6.7 and 11.6. Their separation is 21.5", and the position angle is 72° (meaning the faint star is east-northeast of the bright one). "A most delicate double star, on the crown of the Serpent-bearer's head," wrote Smyth, "pale straw-colour [and] blue."

The bright star is a yellow G5 subgiant. The faint one, easy to see with averted vision at 100× in my 6-inch, is a dwarf about 1/20 as luminous as the Sun. The system is 160 light-years distant, judging by the bright star's presumed luminosity.

Alpha Herculis and Alpha Ophiuchi are at upper right on this chart adapted from Sky Atlas 2000.0. North is up and east is to the left. The circles are 3° wide. The faintest stars are magnitude 8.0, easily visible in most finders. The size of a 1° field, typical of an amateur telescope's lowest power, is at bottom right.

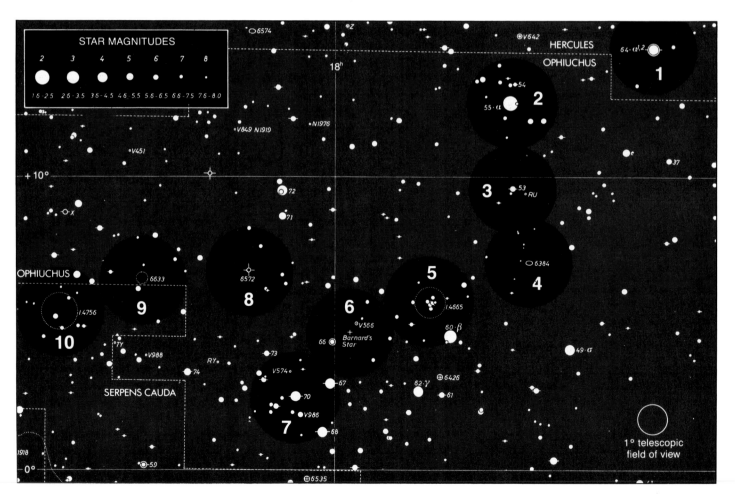

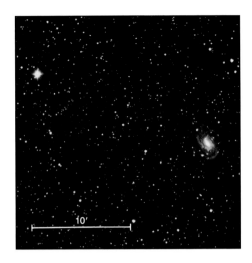

The spiral galaxy NGC 6384, one of the most distant objects visible in amateur telescopes, is a near-copy of the Milky Way. Its spiral arms show very well in this blue-light image from the Palomar Observatory Sky Survey, but in amateur telescopes only the hazy nucleus is likely to be detectable. The star at upper left is 8th magnitude. North is up and east is to the left.

IC 4665 near Beta Ophiuchi is a beautiful star cluster for binoculars. Reproduced from a Palomar Sky Survey blue print.

3. 53 OPHIUCHI

Shift 3° south from Alpha Oph to pick up this 6th-magnitude stepping-stone on our way southward. It's a very wide double star with components of magnitudes 5.8 and 8.5 separated by 41″. The position angle is 191°. To me they look white and purplish.

4. NGC 6384

Star-hop carefully another 2½° south to find this dim, out-of-the-way little galaxy, a challenge in any but the darkest sky. On a night with slight haze I could barely suspect it in my 6-inch – a glow so dim that it might have existed only in the imagination, on that deep-sky observer's borderland where outer and inner space merge. How hard it is to appreciate what this ghost of a smudge really is! It is a type Sb giant spiral galaxy very much like our own, an entire grand Milky Way containing hundreds of billions of stars.

The radial velocity of NGC 6384 suggests it is 50 to 100 million light-years distant, nearly a million times farther than the typical field stars around it in the eyepiece. If those foreground stars were dust motes floating near enough for you to reach out and touch, NGC 6384 would be a vast dust storm some 100 miles away. Nowhere in human experience does reality so far surpass appearance than in the case of a galaxy viewed in a backyard telescope.

5. IC 4665

Back to the comforting confines of our own Milky Way. Swing about 4° southeast to pick up 3rd-magnitude Beta Ophiuchi, the Serpent Holder's shoulder. From there go 1½° northeast and you're in the midst of the huge, loose open star cluster IC 4665.

This big, beautiful object deserves to be in the Messier catalogue, but it didn't even get into the *NGC*. Binoculars or a finderscope show it best – as a well resolved swarm of stars about ⅔° across. There are about 30 stars in the cluster 7th magnitude and fainter. The whole group has a total magnitude of 4.2, so in theory it should be visible to the naked eye. But I can't see it in my sky, which has a limiting magnitude of about 5.2. Magnitude usually tells little about the visibility of an object so big and diffuse.

The cluster's inner group of bright stars spells the ragged word "HI" when southwest is up. The greeting is not obvious in the eyepiece until you notice it; then it looks almost shockingly impertinent. (Warning: anyone who sends this to the tabloids as proof of alien skywriting earns 100 years of bad karma.)

At high powers the cluster loses its identity, the stars being so few and far apart. IC 4665 is thought to be about 1,400 light-years distant and its stars 35 million years old.

6. BARNARD'S STAR

Our next stop represents another huge jump closer. This 9.5-magnitude red dwarf is the closest star to the Sun after the Alpha Centauri system. At a distance of 6.0 light-years, it is *the* closest star visible from the midnorthern latitudes of most of North America. To locate it use the finder chart on the next page.

In 1916 Edward Emerson Barnard discovered that this insignificant-looking star has an extremely rapid motion across the sky. Even today, its proper motion of 10.31″ per year (1° in 350 years) remains the greatest known for any star.

Barnard's star, spectral type *M4*, is a good example of the faint but abundant red dwarfs that populate space almost unnoticed. At absolute visual magnitude 13.2 it is only ¹⁄₂₃₀₀ as luminous as the Sun. If the Sun were placed next to Bar-

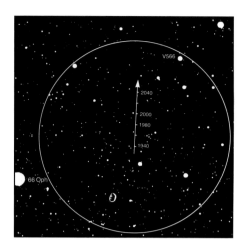

Barnard's star, which holds the all-sky record for fast proper motion, is also the nearest star (after the Sun) visible from midnorthern latitudes. Use this chart to locate the position of the 9.5-magnitude red dwarf for the current year. The circle is 1° in diameter; the bright stars V566 and 66 Ophiuchi are also plotted. Adapted from Burnham's Celestial Handbook.

nard's star it would blaze at magnitude 1.1, as bright as Deneb! And Deneb itself seen at the same distance would be magnitude –11, as bright as the gibbous Moon three days after first quarter.

While looking at the tiny orange spark of Barnard's star, try to imagine these comparisons. They are a reminder of something that's easy to forget: the word "star" covers an extremely diverse range of objects.

7. 70 OPHIUCHI

Here is another cool dwarf star – actually a pair of them – though not nearly as dim as Barnard's star in either apparent or absolute magnitude.

Note the V-shaped asterism formed by 66, 67, 68, 70, and 73 Ophiuchi. In a dark sky it is easily visible to the naked eye. This is "Taurus Poniatovii," the Bull of Poniatowski, invented in 1777 by the Abbé Poczobut to honor King Stanislaus Poniatowski of Poland. The V shape reminded Poczobut of the Hyades in Taurus, so we got a faint bull for summer skies as a counterpart to the one of winter. His eastern eye is 70 Ophiuchi.

In a fine telescope during good seeing 70 Ophiuchi is a very interesting double. In 1989 its components, magnitudes 4.2 and 6.0, were separated by only 1.5″. This is the closest they ever appear in their 88-year orbit. In 1995 the stars are 2.5″ apart.

70 Ophiuchi is one of the fastest-changing binary stars in the sky for small telescopes. The most noticeable change is in its position angle. In June 1989, the faint star was at position angle 233° from the bright star – southwest of it. The position angle decreased by 15° per year to reach 180° by 1993, placing the faint star due south of the bright one. In 2000 the separation will be 3.8″ and the position angle 148°; in 2005, 4.9″ and 138°. By 2010 the pair will widen to 6″.

Both stars are orange dwarfs, types $K0$ and $K4$, 16 light-years away. They give off only 40 and 8 percent as much light as the Sun, respectively, and range from 11 to 33 a.u. apart as they orbit. This should leave plenty of room for earthlike planets in stable orbits close to either star. The system was long suspected of having an invisible, low-mass third component – a giant planet – but recent work indicates it does not.

8. NGC 6572

A careful star-hop nearly 5° north-northeast brings us to this exquisite mite of a planetary nebula. Perhaps the best route is to backtrack to 66 Oph, then pick up the scattered row of stars 2° to its north and work along them eastward.

NGC 6572 is a minute, bright oval, about 9th magnitude and 8″ across. It is easily mistaken for a star at low power. As you sweep for it, be alert not just for its tiny disk but for its unstarlike color. Some observers see it as green; others insist it is blue.

Once you've identified the nebula, use high power to examine its disk. The high surface brightness – about 100 times that of the Ring nebula in Lyra – should make this NGC object visible through even the worst big-city light pollution.

The nebula's central star has been called everything from brighter than 10th magnitude to as faint as 13.6. No doubt the uncertainty results from the difficulty of judging a star's brightness against a glowing nebular background. *Sky & Telescope* columnist Walter Scott Houston has seen the central star with his 4-inch refractor. Other observers have failed with 10-inch telescopes. Use your very highest power when searching for it.

NGC 6572 is some 2,000 light-years away – close for a planetary – and about 5,000 a.u. (¹⁄₁₂ of a light-year) in diameter.

The loose open cluster NGC 6633, from a Palomar Sky Survey blue print.

9. NGC 6633

NGC 6633 is another bright, loose cluster that might have qualified as a Messier object. Its 30 or so stars, magnitude 8 and dimmer, seem to form an arc centered on a 6th-magnitude star ⅓° to the southeast. The combined light of the cluster stars adds up to magnitude 4.6, making this a sparkly haze in binoculars or a finder. NGC 6633 is about 1,000 light-years away and 660 million years old.

10. IC 4756

To find our last object for the night, we cross into Serpens Cauda. Here is a very large, poor cluster with about 80 stars of 9th magnitude and fainter spread over nearly 1°. The challenge with an object like this is telling it from a random enhancement of the star field. It can be made out nicely in 10×50 binoculars, but a rich-field telescope with a 3° field of view might do best. The cluster is about 1,300 light-years distant and 600 million years old.

All evening we have been working eastward as the sky rotates westward. If you've taken an hour and a half to walk through our tour – certainly a reasonable time to linger over 10 objects – you are pointing at about the same altitude above the horizon as when you began. More wonders lie short hops farther east off the chart. The exquisite 4th-magnitude double star Theta Serpentis is only 4° east-southeast of our last object, and other sights are farther on through the riches of the summer Milky Way. But the hour grows late. These things will go unobserved in their glory, waiting for another night.

STAR-HOP

9

NINE

Up from Antares

Summer brings some of the sky's greatest splendors into view. The Milky Way rises in a huge arc spanning the eastern evening sky all the way from the northeast to the south. Leading this wide parade on its southern flank is the orange-red star Antares, a fiery topaz among the bluish white diamonds of Scorpius.

Antares highlights a unique bit of sky that never rises high for those of us at midnorthern latitudes. For best results you'll need to catch it when it's near the meridian in the south – in June around midnight local daylight saving time, or soon after dusk in early July.

Binoculars will show some of tonight's chosen sights, a small telescope will reveal others even through city light pollution, and a few will challenge large apertures under the most pristine dark skies. The guide map on the next page, again adapted from *Sky Atlas 2000.0,* shows stars to magnitude 8.0. The black circles this time are only 2° wide, much smaller than a typical finderscope's field of view but about twice the field of a low-power eyepiece on an average amateur telescope. North is a little to the right of up; east is a little above left.

1. ANTARES

This 1st-magnitude orange-red supergiant twinkles balefully in the south during the evenings of early summer. With a declination of –26°, it never climbs higher than 24° above the southern horizon for viewers at latitude 40° north (the latitude of Philadelphia, Pittsburgh, Indianapolis, Denver, and northern California). Seen from south of there, Antares culminates higher, like all southern stars; farther north, less high. You may need to tote your scope around to find an open view toward the south so low down.

Antares is rivaled only by Betelgeuse as the most colorful 1st-magnitude star. Indeed, *Sky Catalogue 2000.0,* Volume 1, lists Antares and Betelgeuse as almost identically red with color indexes of +1.83 and +1.85, respectively. But to me Antares looks a trace redder – perhaps because it's often seen through the same low-altitude summer haze that reddens summer sunsets and the June Moon.

The star is several hundred light-years away; various sources give 230, 330, and 520 light-years, typical scatter for a star too far to measure by trigonometric parallax. It is a member of the great Scorpius-Centaurus Association of luminous young stars that enriches this whole region of the sky.

Antares is a famous but difficult double star; it has a 5.4-magnitude companion 2.7″ to its west. This separation might seem wide enough to make the pair easy to resolve, but Antares is so bright that its light generally overwhelms the fainter star. The poor seeing near the horizon doesn't help either.

The companion is usually called green, no doubt due to color contrast with Antares. Its spectral type is *B*3. "When seeing conditions are good, it appears quite plainly in a 6-inch telescope as a little spark of glittering emerald," writes Robert Burnham, Jr., in his *Celestial Handbook.* But I've never definitely seen it in my 6-inch reflector despite often trying.

Don't be misled by atmospheric dispersion! When any bright star is low in the sky, its image is drawn out into a tiny spectrum with red at the bottom

© 1987 Willmann-Bell

A close-up of the region around Antares, from Uranometria 2000.0. *Stars are plotted to about magnitude 9.5 The grid boxes are 1° high and 4 minutes of right ascension wide.*

and blue-green on top. This "green flash" atop Antares can easily be mistaken for evidence of its companion star. Remember that the companion is due *west*. Some say it is easier to see during twilight when Antares's glare is suppressed. Try using a blue filter, which will dim Antares much more than the companion.

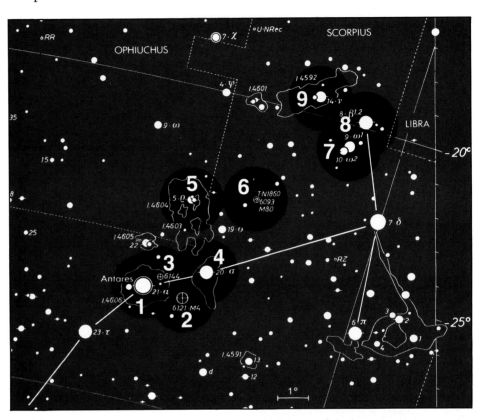

The region around bright Antares in Scorpius is dotted with interesting double stars, globular star clusters (circles with crosses), and very dim nebulae (outlined by solid lines). The objects with large white numbers are described in the text. This chart from Sky Atlas 2000.0 shows stars to as faint as magnitude 8.0. The black circles are 2° in diameter.

2. THE GLOBULAR CLUSTER M4

Swing your telescope 1.3° west of Antares, measuring the distance by the size of your eyepiece field of view. Here you will run into one of the sky's grand globular star clusters.

Under fine conditions Messier 4 can be seen with the naked eye. In binoculars it is a dim, hazy glow nestled under a line from Antares to nearby Sigma (σ) Scorpii. In a telescope M4, pictured on page 111, is one of the easiest globulars to resolve into stars, since it is one of the closest to Earth – about 7,000 light-years from us compared to 23,000 for the more famous M13 in Hercules. M4 and M13 are about equal in total apparent brightness at magnitude 5.9, but they look quite dissimilar. M4 appears bigger (more than ⅓° in diameter when its outlying stars are glimpsed), generally dimmer, and composed of more easily visible stars less densely packed.

Running across it roughly north-south is an odd bar of light, a chain of stars that presumably fell into this alignment at random. The bar is easy in my 6-inch at 45 power. It gives M4 a look like no other globular. At 200× some weaker star chains glimmer in and out of view around the cluster's edges. Take your time; so fine a piece of cosmic jewelry deserves long contemplation.

3. THE GLOBULAR CLUSTER NGC 6144

Here's a much harder target! Backtrack to Antares and look just 0.6° to its northwest. Get Antares out of your field of view or its glare may overwhelm the

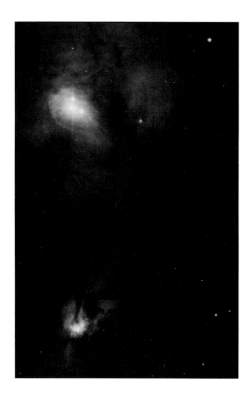

A very deep photograph of Antares and some of its reflection nebulosity (left) and NGC 6144 (top). In a small telescope, deep-sky objects are much less apparent than moderately bright stars that merely appear as tiny points on a photograph. From a European Southern Observatory sky survey plate taken in blue light with the ESO 1-meter Schmidt camera.

Rho Ophiuchi (top) amid the very dim nebula IC 4604. At bottom, IC 4603 surrounds an 8th-magnitude star. From the same ESO blue plate as the photo above.

little 9th-magnitude globular hidden here. NGC 6144 is inherently about as luminous as M4 but some 20,000 light-years behind it.

Using my 6-inch at 95× through 5th-magnitude suburban light pollution, I can barely make out NGC 6144 as a tiny, dim patch about 6' north-northeast of a 9th-magnitude star. The *Webb Society Deep-Sky Observer's Handbook*, Volume 3, "Open and Globular Clusters," calls it very difficult in a 12-inch scope, but *Sky & Telescope* columnist Walter Scott Houston has seen it well in a 4-inch. Sky conditions no doubt have a great effect on it, so if at first you don't succeed, try again another night. Use the detailed chart on page 108 if you have trouble locating the cluster; the chart, adapted from *Uranometria 2000.0*, shows stars as faint as about magnitude 9.5.

4. SIGMA (σ) SCORPII

Back to an easy object. This 3rd-magnitude star is a wide, unequal double for small telescopes, with an 8.5-magnitude companion 20" due west of the primary. The companion is readily visible in the 6-inch. E. J. Hartung in his *Astronomical Objects for Southern Telescopes* says the pair is well shown in even a 3-inch, "a fine sight in a field sprinkled with a few stars."

To me the components look yellowish white and blue. The bright one is a giant of spectral type *B1*; the companion is a main-sequence star around *B9*. They form a real binary, sharing the same proper motion across the sky.

The bright star itself is a triple too close to resolve. Its brightest member is a gently pulsing variable star of the Beta Canis Majoris type. The combined light of the triple rises and falls by about 0.1 magnitude every 6 hours, too slight a change to see.

5. THE RHO (ρ) OPHIUCHI REGION

Just north of Antares is a uniquely weird zone of space. Here are some of the most eerie, inky dark nebulae in the sky, lit up in spots by embedded stars. Color photographs of the Rho Ophiuchi complex made with giant Schmidt cameras show phantasmagoric blazes of blue, white, and red splashed over with smoky brown and black. Antares lights up a huge zone of red and yellow reflection nebulae, Sigma Scorpii is surrounded by an emission nebula, and Rho Ophiuchi itself illuminates a complex nest of swirling clouds in blue.

Unfortunately little or none of this can be detected by eye, at least from northerly latitudes. No bright nebulae can be seen with the 6-inch. Hartung refers to a "bluish luminous haze" around Rho Ophiuchi, the nebula IC 4604, but Burnham calls the nebula "too faint to be studied visually." You might try for the small reflection nebula IC 4603 around the 8th-magnitude star 1° due south of Rho.

More interesting are the area's gigantic dark nebulae. They are evident in rich-field binoculars on a dark night if you know what you're looking for. Sweep the region east of Rho Ophiuchi and notice the large areas totally barren of faint background stars. You are seeing the silhouettes of enormous black clouds against the more distant Milky Way. Dark lanes stretching east from the Rho Ophiuchi region appear "like black tentacles obscuring the starry background," writes Burnham. At least that's how they look on photographs. How well can you distinguish them with a wide-field instrument visually?

Even using an ordinary narrow-field telescope, you'll find areas utterly starless and black. It was here that William Herschel, unaware of the existence of dark nebulae, declared that he had found a veritable hole in the heavens to the nothingness beyond.

Rho Ophiuchi itself is the brightest of a neat little triangle of stars 4' long. Rho is a delicate binary with components of magnitudes 5.3 and 6.0 separated by about 3"; the fainter is north-northwest of the brighter. The bright component is spectral type *B*2 but looks yellow to me, perhaps reddened by the interstellar dust that lies so thick here.

As the night and season grow later, the brighter Milky Way farther east in Sagittarius rises into view, and here dark nebulae stand out more prominently. In fact the whole center line of the Milky Way is riddled with them, as you can see with the naked eye on a truly dark night.

Two dissimilar globular clusters near Antares, M80 (left) and M4 (right). M4 has the greater total brightness, but its stars are so spread out that its surface brightness is much less. Also, this photo of M4 was underexposed to show the north-south "bar" of stars. M4 Photo by S. J. Warkoczewski using a 16⅜-inch f/6 reflector; 25-minute exposure on ISO 50 Ektachrome. M80 photo by Martin Germano with an 8-inch Schmidt-Cassegrain; 30-minute exposure on 103a-F film.

6. THE GLOBULAR CLUSTER M80

The cloud complex around Rho Ophiuchi and Antares ends abruptly on its west and south, allowing us to look past its edge to stars and clusters many times farther beyond.

M80 lies exactly midway between Antares and Beta (β) Scorpii. At 7th magnitude it is not as bright as M22, but it's so small and condensed that it was more obvious in the 6-inch through the light pollution. M80 is remarkably concentrated, brightening rapidly from its edge to a very tight core. William Herschel in 1785 called it "the richest and most condensed mass of stars which the firmament can offer to the contemplation of the astronomer." That may be so in a large telescope, but the 6-inch only provides hints of resolution into stars even at 200×. M80 looks more like a 7th-magnitude comet head, though pale white instead of a comet's icy blue-green.

A nova, now known as T Scorpii, appeared inside the cluster in May 1860. It reached 7th magnitude, as bright as the rest of the cluster's hundreds of thousands of stars combined.

7. OMEGA[1] AND OMEGA[2] (ω^1 AND ω^2) SCORPII

This wide double is plainly resolved with no optical aid as a tiny pair of "eyes" looking akilter down at the Earth. It is a beautiful sight in binoculars, as is the whole field for several degrees around. Omega[1] and Omega[2] are 15′ apart, magnitudes 4.0 and 4.3, spectral types *B*1 and *G*2, respectively – blue-white and yellow-white. The color difference can be seen in binoculars or a finder.

This is not a true binary but just a chance alignment of stars. Omega[2] is estimated to be 175 light years from us, Omega[1] five times as far. How hard it is to picture this when looking at them!

8. BETA (β) SCORPII, GRAFFIAS

Here's a bright and glorious double star for any telescope at all. Swing 1° north of Omega. Beta's components are blue-white B stars, magnitudes 2.6 and 4.9, separated by 13.6″. The position angle is 21°, meaning the fainter star is north-northeast of the brighter.

In my 6-inch reflector Beta Scorpii looks white and purplish, a beautiful pair of blazes. As with Sigma Scorpii, the bright component is a triple star unresolvable in amateur telescopes.

9. NU (ν) SCORPII

We end with the southern sky's answer to the Double-Double in Lyra. The quadruple star Nu Scorpii is, however, more challenging than Epsilon Lyrae.

Find it 1.6° east of Beta. The smallest telescope or even good, tripod-mounted binoculars will separate Nu's AB pair of stars from the fainter CD pair 41″ to the north-northwest. The 6-inch reflector splits C and D well at 200×. They are 2.3″ apart, magnitudes 6.4 and 7.8.

The AB pair is much more difficult to resolve, with magnitudes listed in *Sky Catalogue 2000.0* as 4.3 and 6.8. A separation of 1.2″ was measured in 1967; possibly the pair is widening slightly. Close, unequal double stars like this are much harder to separate than pairs with similar brightnesses. Star B is almost due north of A.

Now from the tiny and brilliant to the huge and dim: Nu Scorpii is embedded in a very faint, degrees-long nebula known as IC 4592, a target for big scopes at low power in superdark skies. The nebula, part of the Rho Ophiuchi complex, was discovered photographically by E. E. Barnard in 1895. The *Webb Society Handbook* volume on nebulae describes it as "seen very faintly" around Nu Scorpii in an 8½-inch telescope, "extending farthest to the southwest and northeast; possibly a dark lane to the southeast." That sounds promising; a big Dobsonian might show a lot more.

These nine highlighted objects can easily be covered by two fingers at arm's length. Compare this little area to the sky's wide expanse and you'll appreciate the riches awaiting telescope users who take the time, using charts and books, to prepare lists of what to see.

STAR-HOP

10

TEN

Plumbing the Depths of Lyra

No constellation of the summer night is more familiar than Lyra with its brilliant, zero-magnitude star Vega. Lyra also contains the famous Ring nebula M57 and the Double-Double star Epsilon (ε) Lyrae, both easy to find, as well as several other bright, well-known doubles. But there's more to this little piece of territory than most observers realize. Tonight let's work through Lyra more thoroughly than is usually done, going a little deeper and pushing a modest telescope closer to its limits.

1. VEGA, ALPHA (α) LYRAE

There's no problem locating this first object! Vega is the brightest star high in the east as darkness falls on June and July evenings. It's overhead in August and early September, and high in the west during the early fall.

Extending from Vega is the distinctive little constellation pattern of Lyra – a nearly equilateral triangle with Vega at one corner and a parallelogram attached to another corner. All the stars of this design but Vega are 3rd or 4th magnitude.

Vega is essentially tied with Arcturus (shining off to Vega's west) as the brightest star of the summer sky. Compare their colors. Vega looks white to slightly bluish, in definite contrast to the pale yellow-orange of Arcturus. Vega looks so bright is because it's nearby, only 26 light-years from Earth. Otherwise it's very ordinary as naked-eye stars go. It's a main-sequence star of spectral type $A0$, hotter, whiter, and somewhat larger than the Sun. It probably has about three times the Sun's mass.

It may also have planets. In 1983 Vega became the first star beyond the Sun definitely discovered to have solid matter orbiting it. The solids are millimeter-size sand grains whose infrared emission was discovered by the Infrared Astronomical Satellite (IRAS). But larger pieces of rubble are almost certainly mixed in with the grains, perhaps supplying enough material to make a proper solar system. However, Vegan planets would be an unpromising place to search for advanced life. The star is burning its fuel so fast that it cannot be more than about a billion years old. Any life there would have had to get off to a much faster start than it did on Earth in order to have evolved beyond the bacteria and mudworm stage by now.

In my 6-inch reflector Vega is a dazzling blaze of cold-white light – white with a trace of blue. The blue tint is highlighted in an ordinary achromatic refractor, which gives all bright objects a slight blue fringe when the rest of the light is in focus. Seen through the 40-inch Yerkes refractor, Vega's "vivid blue blazes and the twirlings of the diffraction rings which surround the great star make it appear a marvel of beauty," wrote the celestial guidebook author Mary Proctor 70 years ago. Other writers of the time called Vega "the arc-light of the skies" for its intensity and color.

The companions of Vega. Although most people think of it as single, Vega is cataloged as a multiple star with four faint companions widely separated from it.

The two brightest, components B and E, are both about 9th magnitude. Vega E is currently 90″ northeast of Vega; Vega B is about 75″ due south. Can you make them out from the primary's dazzling glare? They may require a 6-inch or larger scope and high power. All the companions have proved to be mere background stars that do not share Vega's proper motion across the sky.

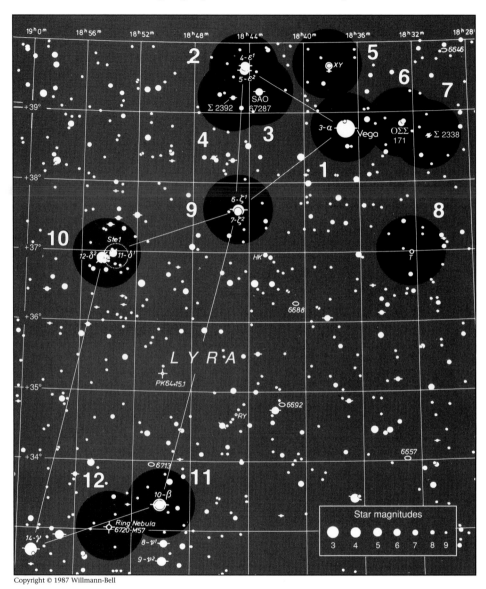

A close-up chart of the region around Vega, adapted from Uranometria 2000.0. *The black circles are 1° in diameter; compare their size with your telescope's lowest-power field of view. Stars are plotted to as faint as about magnitude 9.5. The five small ovals are galaxies with their NGC numbers; all are 13th or 14th magnitude.*

2. EPSILON (ε) LYRAE

This is the famous Double-Double, a 4th-magnitude showpiece less than 2° northeast of Vega. Even the smallest finderscope or shirt-pocket opera glass resolves Epsilon Lyrae into a wide pair of stars of equal brightness. In fact I *think* I can resolve them with the naked eye (I have 20/15 vision with glasses). Larger binoculars make quick work of them. The pair is separated by 208″, about five times the apparent diameter of Jupiter but less than a third the separation of Mizar and Alcor in the Big Dipper. At 45× in my 6-inch reflector, each of the two stars looks single. But at 115× each becomes a tiny pair of white dots with diffraction rings practically overlapping.

The southern pair, Epsilon², is slightly easier to resolve. Its components are nearly equal in brightness, magnitudes 5.2 and 5.5, and are currently 2.3″ apart.

They're oriented east-west. Epsilon[1] is a bit harder because its stars are unequal, magnitudes 5.0 and 6.1, even though they're a little more widely separated at 2.6″. The fainter component of Epsilon[1] is north of the brighter, so that the two pairs are set at right angles to each other. They'll change a bit in coming years.

Just east of the point midway between the two pairs lies a much fainter star, Epsilon Lyrae I ("eye"). It's listed as magnitude 9.4 and is easy in the 6-inch scope at all powers – but I can't recall ever noticing it before specifically looking for it after I found it in a double-star list.

3. SAO 67287

This unassuming 6.4-magnitude star is just 0.4° southwest of Epsilon in the same low-power field of view. It is marked as double on the *Uranometria* chart, and sure enough, the 6-inch scope very easily reveals it to be a wide pair, orange and faint purple. The companion, 60″ south of the primary, is cataloged as magnitude 10.4. The primary is spectral type *K*5 and is listed as being a spectroscopic binary.

4. STRUVE 2392

Moving a scant 0.4° east-southeast, still in the field of Epsilon Lyrae, we come to this virtually unknown triple star. Two components, magnitudes 8.5 and 9.6, are wide and easy in the 6-inch. The third is quite close to the brighter star, perhaps 3″ to its northwest, and as faint as magnitude 10.4. It was just a little beyond the abilities of the 6-inch even at 200×, but it shows clearly in my 12½-inch reflector at only 110×.

5. XY LYRAE

This orange variable star is noteworthy in binoculars, lying just north of a line from Vega to Epsilon Lyrae. It is a red giant, type *M*4 or *M*5, that changes brightness by about a half magnitude slowly and (as far as is known) irregularly. Once you've recognized it, XY Lyrae becomes a familiar part of Lyra as seen in binoculars. Its color shows nicely in both binoculars and the 6-inch.

6. OΣΣ 171

Here's another little-known binocular object that, once found, becomes a familiar part of the scenery. This wide double star is just 0.8° west of Vega. The magnitudes are 6.9 and 8.2, separation 145″. The fainter star is northwest of the brighter; it's not always obvious at first glance in 10×50 binoculars but pops right out with averted vision.

The stars are types *F*8 and *G*5. If we assume they are main-sequence dwarfs, which seems likely considering their moderately large proper motions, then we are looking at two stars that, unlike most, are fairly similar to the Sun. One is a little hotter and brighter than the Sun, the other a bit cooler and fainter. But either could pass for our home star if you weren't too choosy, and either could have attractive planets.

As main-sequence stars, their brightnesses would put them about 100 light-years away. Despite their similar distances, however, their different proper motions give them away as just an optical pairing, not a true binary star whose members stay close together in space.

7. STRUVE 2338

Inching your scope just another ½° southwest, you'll hit this neat triple star. All three are about 9th magnitude; they're wide and easy at low power in the 6-inch, forming a narrow triangle 13″ wide and 75″ long. The star at the point of the triangle (to the southwest) begins to show a trace of orange color in the 6-inch. The color is obvious in the 12½-inch.

8. T LYRAE

Some 2° due south of OΣΣ 171 is this deeply colored variable. To find it, use your telescope's lowest power to star-hop down the stream of 7th- to 9th-magnitude stars running southeast from OΣΣ 171 on the guide map on page 114, then southwestward from star to star to T. At each step of the way compare what's on the map carefully to what you see in the eyepiece, keeping in mind just how big your field of view appears on the map. If you get lost, go back and start over.

When you hit T you'll recognize it right away. This star is *red*, at least as stars go. It's a much deeper, more fiery color than XY Lyrae, providing an instructive comparison of how differently "red" giants can actually be colored. T, like XY, is an irregular variable; it ranges from about magnitude 7.8 to 9.6. The difference is that T is a carbon star. Tricarbon (C_3) vapor in its atmosphere acts as a red filter to color its light.

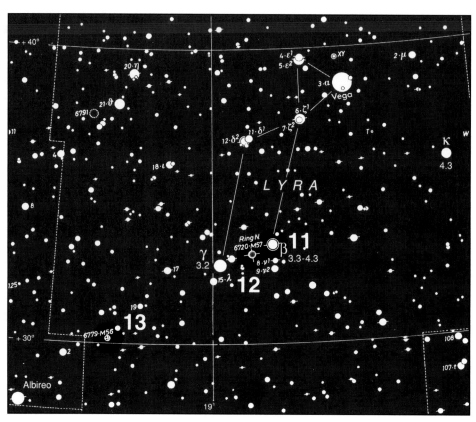

A wider-field chart of Lyra, showing stars to only magnitude 8.0. The black circles are still 1° in diameter. Visual magnitudes are given (with the decimal points omitted) for Gamma (γ) and Kappa (κ) Lyrae, for comparison with variable Beta (β). Adapted from Sky Atlas 2000.0.

9. ZETA (ζ) LYRAE

Now on to some bright and easy sights to wrap up the night. Everything we've looked at so far has been within only 2° of Vega in a region covering less than 2 percent of Lyra's area – and Lyra is a small constellation! By casting our nets wider we'll pick up some bigger fish.

Zeta Lyrae is still only 2° from Vega, but for my money it's the grandest double star yet tonight. Its two components, magnitudes 4.4 and 5.7, are 44″ apart – wide enough to be resolved in steadily held 10×50 binoculars as a gorgeous little duo, pale yellowish white and purplish white. The tints are also noticeable in the 6-inch. It's hard to believe that these colors are merely a contrast illusion, but measurements have shown that both stars are merely plain white. At any rate they make a lovely pair of blazing jewels.

10. DELTA (δ) LYRAE AND STEPHENSON 1

Here's an even more gorgeous binocular double – wide, easy, and genuinely colorful. Delta[2] Lyrae is a reddish orange *M*4 giant of about magnitude 4.3. Delta[1] is a bluish *B*2 star of magnitude 5.6. They are separated by a very wide 620″ or ⅙°, almost as much as Mizar and Alcor.

Between and around them is a loosely scattered star cluster known as Stephenson 1. It contains about 15 stars down to 10th magnitude or so. The cluster adds to the beauty of Delta in a small telescope, but for generations it has been strangely overlooked by amateur guidebooks and maps. The two stars of Delta are presumably its brightest members. The whole bunch is thought to be 1,000 light-years away.

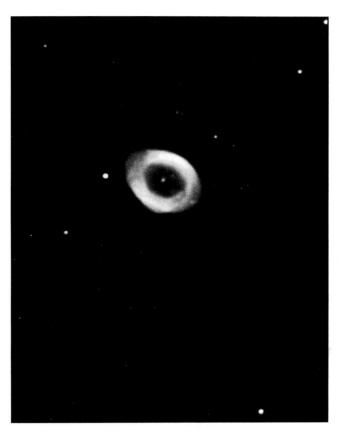

The Ring nebula as it might appear at high power in a very large telescope. The 15th-magnitude central star tends to be more conspicuous on photographs than visually because it is very blue. Kim Zussman took this 20-minute exposure with a Celestron 11-inch Schmidt-Cassegrain telescope on hypered Kodak Tech Pan 2415 film.

11. BETA (β) LYRAE

This was one of the first variable stars discovered – by John Goodricke in 1784, the same year he noticed the variability of Delta Cephei. Beta Lyrae is the prototype of the ellipsoidal eclipsing binaries, pairs of stars orbiting so closely that their mutual tides distort them into ellipse shapes. Beta Lyrae varies continuously between magnitude 3.3 and 4.3, with its dips to minimum light coming every 13 days – once per orbit.

Compare Beta to Gamma (γ) Lyrae, magnitude 3.2, and Kappa (κ), magnitude 4.3 (at the right edge of the chart on page 116). Don't use a telescope – just take a look with the naked eye whenever you see Lyra. Sooner or later you'll catch Beta deep in eclipse.

12. M57, THE RING NEBULA

At last we come to a showpiece deep-sky object, the textbook example of a planetary nebula. The Ring (shown above) is easy to spot as a little round smoke

The globular cluster M56 lies behind a rich scattering of Milky Way stars. It appears anywhere from 2' to 7' in diameter depending on the visibility of its scattered outermost stars. Martin Germano used an 8-inch f/10 Schmidt-Cassegrain for this 50-minute exposure on 103a-F film.

puff ⅖ of the way from Beta to Gamma Lyrae. With a visual magnitude measured at 8.8, it can be seen in a 2.4-inch refractor as a small disk with a darker center. In my 6-inch reflector at 45× the disk is clearly oval, the dark "doughnut hole" is plainly seen, and the ends of the oval look a trace dimmer than the sides. All these features become more evident at higher powers. Many planetary nebulae are unmistakably blue or green, but M57 looks gray to me.

The Ring is about 70″ in diameter. A 12th-magnitude star lies just off its east edge. The nebula's own central star, the one that blew off this gas shell, is 15th magnitude and beyond reach visually in nearly any amateur scope. This is especially true since the interior of the ring is not completely dark.

If M57 lies 2,000 light-years away, the shell we see is about ⅔ light-year in diameter. Planetary nebulae are very short-lived on a cosmic time scale; the Ring will probably be gone in a few tens of thousands of years.

13. M56

Our final item is the farthest afield. M56 is a globular star cluster just over halfway from Gamma Lyrae to Albireo, Beta Cygni. If you don't hit it on your first try by dead reckoning, star-hop to it carefully from either direction, step by step.

M56 is not viewed nearly as often as M57 even though it's brighter (magnitude 8.2) and larger (several arc minutes across). I can see something slightly unstarlike here in a finderscope, and when I turn to the 6-inch's eyepiece, sure enough, there's a fine fuzzy glow embedded in a rich Milky Way star field. A 10th-magnitude star is off the cluster's western edge. At 200× M56 shows tantalizing signs of breaking up into innumerable faint stars, like a sugar spill in dim moonlight. It has a three-dimensional look to me at 200× that's not apparent at 45×.

M56 is believed to be 30,000 light-years from Earth, making it by far the most distant object on tonight's list.

Before closing up, you can hardly skip Albireo just a little farther southeast, one of the grandest doubles in the sky. Albireo is also the starting point for the next chapter.

A Meander in the Summer Milky Way

Our jumping-off point this time is one of the best "show objects" in the summer and fall evening sky, the colorful double star Albireo or Beta (β) Cygni. Albireo shines at 2nd magnitude at the foot of the Northern Cross, near the middle of the bright Summer Triangle of Vega, Deneb, and Altair. The chart at left shows the scene in June as these stars ascend the eastern sky after dusk. Later in the night and later in the year they're high overhead, then finally in the west. The gray box highlights the area covered by the guide map on the next page, adapted from *Sky Atlas 2000.0.* Stars there are plotted to 8th magnitude and the white circles are 3° in diameter.

1. ALBIREO

Albireo is one of the most gorgeous double stars. The smallest telescope resolves it into sparkling jewels of topaz and sapphire 34″ apart. Even good 10-power binoculars held steadily will separate them. The pure, deep blue of the secondary star is largely an illusion. The star is actually very pale blue-white; the tint looks more intense because of the color contrast with the golden-yellow primary.

The stars' magnitudes are 3.1 and 5.1, their spectral types *K*3II and *B*8V. Both are thought to be about 400 light-years away, though there is some evidence that they may be unrelated, with the faint star much farther than the bright one.

2. STRUVE 2525

Just 1.2° southwest of Albireo is a 7.5-magnitude star that's indicated as double on the guide map by a horizontal line drawn through it. This is Struve (Σ) 2525, a very humble member of the double-star community compared to Albireo. But despite its dimness this pair has a special relevance for us earthlings. Its two components, magnitude 8.1 and 8.4, are stars of an intriguing type: they are both similar to our Sun. Either or both of them could have Earthlike planets.

The stars lie about 200 light-years away. They orbit each other every 1,000 years with an average separation of at least 120 astronomical units, three times the distance from the Sun to Pluto. Inhabitants of a planet circling either star would see the other star as a beacon blazing in their sky several times more brilliantly than the full Moon does in ours.

The stars of Σ2525 appear 2″ apart, the fainter one west-northwest of the brighter. You may find them surprisingly difficult to separate even in a fairly large telescope. Faint double stars are much harder to resolve than bright ones with the same separation. Use your highest magnification.

In July 1984 a nova appeared next to Σ2525 and reached 6th magnitude in early August. It attracted much attention because it was so easy to find near Albireo. By December 1987 it had faded to magnitude 15.

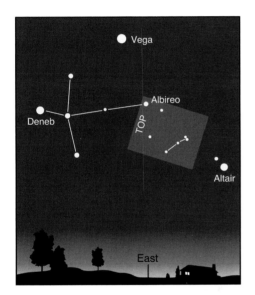

Albireo can be found in the middle of the triangle formed by Vega, Deneb, and Altair. On June evenings it's ascending the eastern sky as shown here. The gray box highlights the area covered by the guide map on the next page.

3. Z VULPECULAE

Shift the telescope 1⅓° farther southwest to center your finderscope on the 5th-magnitude star 3 Vulpeculae. Be careful not to get confused by the many fainter stars in this crowded field! Hop another ¾° south-southwest from there to a pair of 7th-magnitude stars just 3′ apart.

Normally these two are similarly bright. But the southeastern one, Z Vulpeculae, is an eclipsing binary that fades dramatically by about two magnitudes every 2.45 days. A complete eclipse takes only 10 hours, so chances are you'll have to look at this star several times before catching it in the act. Binoculars will suffice. Once you've located Z Vul, you can take a glance at it whenever Albireo is up.

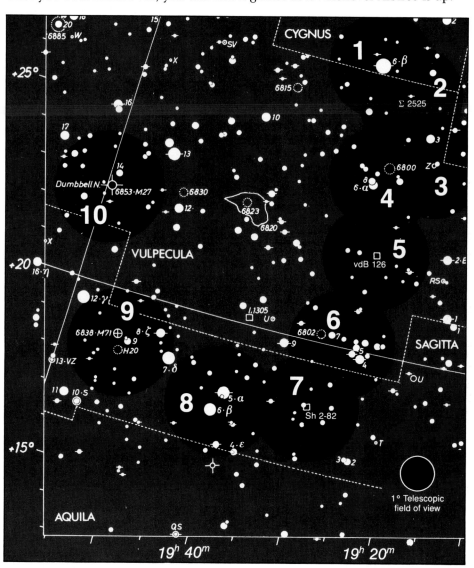

This guide map is adapted from a small corner of Chart 8 of Wil Tirion's Sky Atlas 2000.0. *The limiting magnitude is 8.0, and the circles are 3° in diameter.*

4. NGC 6800

Move 1⅓° east-southeast to our first deep-sky object of the night. NGC 6800 is a large, loose open cluster of about 25 stars that are 10th magnitude and fainter. The group spans some 15′, straggling far across a low-power field of view. It lies in a nice star field dominated by the wide pair Alpha (α) and 8 Vulpeculae ½° to the southeast. The cluster shows no concentration toward its center, but it is clearly a real object that stands out from the general star field.

Shift southeast to center on Alpha and 8 Vul. Both are reddish orange, spectral types *M*0 and *K*0, respectively. Now swing 2° due south to the next objects plotted on the guide map, a pair of 7th-magnitude stars lined up east-west. They lead to our next target, marked by a small square to their west.

Van den Bergh 126 is the bright nebulosity at right in this photograph. This field, from a blue plate taken with the Palomar 48-inch Schmidt camera, is ½° high and oriented to match the chart on the previous page. The two stars at upper left pointing nearly to the nebula appear on the chart.

Sharpless 2-82 is the nebula near the top. The field is 1° high. Several stars on this blue-light plate appear on the chart on the previous page, where the nebula is plotted just a trace too far south. From a Palomar Observatory Sky Survey print.

5. VAN DEN BERGH 126

This one's a real challenge! It's a small reflection nebula lit by an 8th-magnitude star. VdB 126 was overlooked by all the observers whose deep-sky discoveries were collected in the *New General Catalog of Nebulae and Clusters of Stars (NGC)* in 1888. Nor does it appear in the *NGC*'s supplementary *Index Catalogues (IC)* of 1895 and 1908. Nevertheless the nebula is rather bright, according to Beverly T. Lynds's 1965 catalog of nebulae. At least that's how she judged it on a red-sensitive photograph. Like many reflection nebulae it is very blue, implying that it should be even brighter visually than Lynds's description. I have detected no definite sign of it in a 6-inch reflector under suburban skies. Best of luck.

6. THE COATHANGER (BROCCHI'S CLUSTER, COLLINDER 399)

This one couldn't be easier. The Coathanger is a favorite binocular object, a very large, loose grouping of 5th- to 7th-magnitude stars including 4, 5, and 7 Vulpeculae. The Coathanger is upside down: its hook extends south from the middle of an east-west line of stars 1½° long. The whole thing is too big to fit in the field of most telescopes; a finder gives the best view.

Just off the east end of the Coathanger look for a nice little telescopic cluster, NGC 6802. This bunch of about 50 faint stars has a total magnitude of 9. It's enclosed in a box or four stars that include two wide pairs. In a small telescope it appears as a dim, barely resolved glow about 3' across. It is elongated into a bar shape oriented north-south. NGC 6802 is thought to be 3,000 light-years away and perhaps 1.7 billion years old.

7. SHARPLESS 2-82

Two degrees south of NGC 6802 lies another non-NGC challenge. This combination reflection and emission nebula, lit by an 11th-magnitude star, is 7' wide and irregularly round. It is termed moderately bright in the Lynds catalog, and its position is easy to find next to a 7th-magnitude star.

I wasn't expecting the 6-inch scope to show anything here – but much to my surprise, there was a faint but undeniable irregular glow around the star in the correct spot. Quite a find!

8. ALPHA AND BETA SAGITTAE

Back to easier targets. These two naked-eye stars form the feathers of the Arrow constellation, Sagitta. Binoculars or a finder show that both are yellow-orange. Can you detect any color difference between them? Alpha, type *G*0, has a color index of 0.78; Beta, type *G*8, 1.05. Color index is the magnitude difference between a star's brightness in blue and "visual" (yellowish) light. The larger the color index, the redder the star. Alpha and Beta Sagittae make an excellent test of your ability to discriminate star colors because they are close together and identically bright, magnitude 4.37. Both are giants some 600 light-years away.

9. M71 AND HARVARD 20

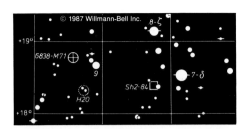

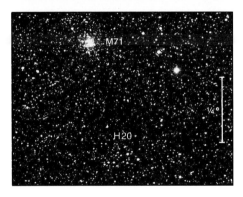

Moving east-northeast along the Arrow's shaft we come to this fine field. Presented at left is a more detailed chart of it adapted from *Uranometria 2000.0;* the grid's boxes are 1° tall.

M71 is a rich star cluster of the rare intermediate type between open clusters and globulars. In a very small instrument it is a 9th-magnitude glow some 7′ across. A larger telescope (or perhaps just a higher power) will resolve it into a swarm of tiny stars. Isaac Roberts, the pioneering 19th-century celestial photographer who discovered the spiral shape of the Andromeda galaxy M31, decided that M71 was a spiral too! The faint stars surrounding it, he wrote, are "arranged in remarkable curves and lines which are very suggestive of having been produced by the effects of spiral movements."

H20, which lies ½° to the south-southwest, is a poor thing by comparison. It's a 10′ smattering of about 20 stars magnitude 11 and fainter, highlighted on its western end by the pair of 9th-magnitude ones plotted on the *Uranometria 2000.0* chart. It hardly stands out from the background star field. You may need to step back and squint to see it on the photograph at left.

The field of M71 and H20 in Sagitta. Photograph by Hans Vehrenberg from his Atlas of Deep-Sky Splendors. *As on any photograph, bright and faint stars appear more similar here than they do in the real sky.*

M27, the Dumbbell nebula in Vulpecula, is the second-largest planetary nebula in apparent size and the most easily visible. It measures 5′ across its brightest diameter. Kim Zussman took this 60-minute exposure with an 11-inch f/10 Schmidt-Cassegrain telescope on hypersensitized Kodak Technical Pan 2415 film.

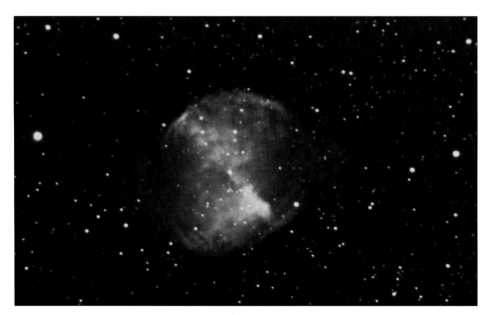

10. M27, THE DUMBBELL NEBULA

We've saved the best for last. From Gamma (γ) Sagittae, the point of the Arrow, star-hop your way 3.3° northward. The Dumbbell is a remarkable planetary nebula that appears about 8th magnitude and 8′ by 5′ in size. It is readily visible in 7×50 binoculars even under moderately light-polluted skies. In a 6-inch telescope it looks vaguely rectangular with a hint of mottling. In a 12-inch it is a huge, delicate, crumpled bubble with a 13th-magnitude star at its center and other faint stars scattered across it. A "magnificent and singular object," Admiral W. H. Smyth called it in his *Cycle of Celestial Objects (Bedford Catalogue).* M27 "is truly one of those splendid enigmas, which, according to Ricciolus, are proposed by God but never to be subject to human solution."

Smyth underestimated the future of astronomy. Today we know that M27 is the former outer layers of a red-giant star. The star puffed the material into space very recently on the cosmic time scale – perhaps a few tens of thousands of years ago – leaving the giant's tiny, intensely hot core in open view.

Most sky tourists are content to star-hop straight to M27 from Albireo, which is easily done via 10 and 13 Vulpeculae. But wasn't the scenic route more interesting?

STAR-HOP

12

TWELVE

Along the Northern Cross

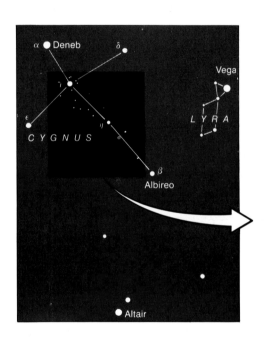

The richest part of the northern Milky Way lies between Gamma (γ) and Beta (β) Cygni. On the constellation map above, the black rectangle shows the area of the detailed chart at right. That chart, adapted from Sky Atlas 2000.0, plots many telescopic objects among stars to 8th magnitude. The circles are 2° in diameter.

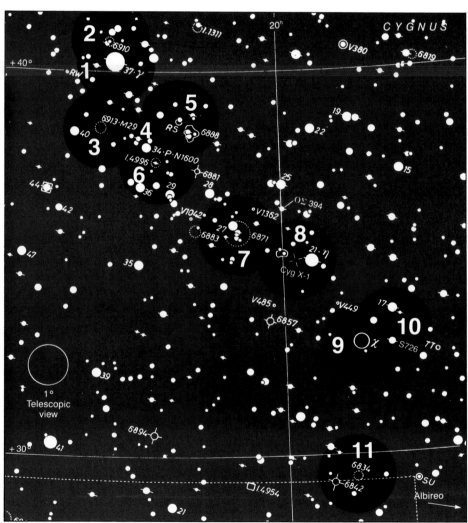

Cygnus the Swan has a reputation for being a fine constellation for the naked eye and binoculars but barren telescopically. But in fact Cygnus is loaded with telescopic riches. Granted, most of them are unspectacular, noteworthy more for their collective abundance than any individual glory. But even if they do take some seeking out, that only makes the chase more interesting.

This chapter will take us through the wondrously rich star field right in the center of the Cygnus Milky Way. Because this tour concentrates on stars and their varieties of congregation, it's especially appropriate for light-polluted areas. Even where light pollution blots out nebulae and galaxies, stars and clusters shine through fairly well – especially when you switch to high powers for closer inspection.

We'll start from Gamma Cygni, the centerpiece of the Northern Cross. The guide map goes to 8th magnitude, and the circles this time are 2° in diameter. Are you confident of celestial directions and distances in your finderscope? If not, refer back to the chapter "Finding Your Way in the Sky." In any case it helps to practice navigating before setting out on a lengthy voyage. Our first object provides a convenient little backwater to paddle around in and get a feel for which way is which.

1. GAMMA (γ) CYGNI

Gamma Cygni is the 2nd-magnitude star at the center of the Northern Cross. It's bright enough to have its own proper name, Sadr, from the Arabic for "Breast of the Hen." In my 6-inch reflector it blazes clear, pale yellow. A supergiant of type *F*8, it is located about 800 light-years away.

Gamma Cygni is surrounded by a little incomplete ring of 5th- and 6th-magnitude stars 2° across. The ring is quite plain in a finderscope or binoculars. On the chart, notice in particular the pair of stars about 1° north of Gamma and the wider pair 1° to its west-northwest. Identify them in your finderscope to check how your sense of scale and direction in the finder's view compares with what's on the map.

While you're at it, use Gamma to check that you've aligned the finder perfectly with the main telescope. The star should be centered in both views at once. This is especially important tonight because we'll be working through rich and confusing Milky Way fields where it will be necessary to stay carefully on course.

2. NGC 6910

Our first deep-sky object is just ½° north-northeast of Gamma. NGC 6910 is a small, loose open cluster of 10th-magnitude and fainter stars behind two much brighter orange ones. In my 6-inch at 50× the group is obvious the moment it's swept up. The brighter stars are arranged in straight lines that look for all the world like a stick-figure horse in profile pulling backward against a rope – perhaps a rocking horse, with the two bright orange stars for feet. It's facing northwest; a unique little pattern.

Continued use of averted vision with the 6-inch brings glimpses of many additional fainter stars swarming through the group. NGC 6910 is cataloged as having 50 stars in an area 8' across. Under darker skies than I enjoy, a 6-inch scope might show the fainter cluster members much better. I could see no trace, incidentally, of the many dim nebulae often charted around Gamma Cygni.

NGC 6910 is estimated to be 5,000 light-years away. It is composed of very hot, young stars thought to be only 10 million years old.

3. M29

Our next deep-sky object is bright enough to see in a finderscope. M29 is about 2° south-southeast of Gamma Cygni. Locate it by identifying the triangle formed by Gamma, 40, and 34 (also known as P) Cygni. Then examine the spot in this triangle where the chart shows M29 to be. As I mentioned before, triangles are the fundamental stepping stones of star-hopping.

M29 is arranged in another unique shape. Seven of its brightest stars form two small arcs bowing toward each other like the outline of a power plant's cooling tower. There are supposed to be 50 stars here, but I certainly don't see that many with the 6-inch. What *is* apparent, however, is that this whole region is heavily obscured with dark clouds – they blot out patches of the Milky Way background. Suspicious dark zones lie just east and north in particular.

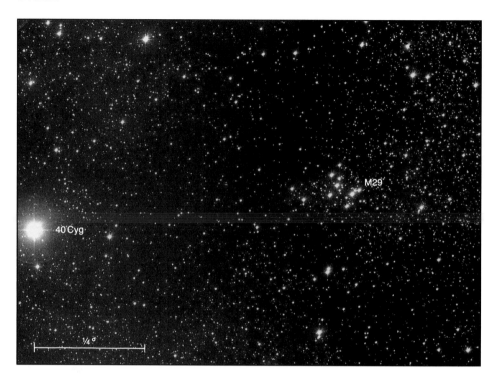

The loose open cluster M29 is visible in binoculars and finderscopes. This image is from a red-light print in the Palomar Observatory Sky Survey. North is up and east is to the left.

4. P CYGNI

This ordinary-looking 5th-magnitude star is actually one of the most luminous known, putting out an estimated 700,000 times the energy of the Sun (its absolute bolometric magnitude is –10). It lies some 7,000 light-years down the Cygnus Arm of the Milky Way, along whose length we look in this part of the sky – which is why this region is so full of stars.

In the year 1600, P Cygni was seen at 3rd magnitude, gaining it the title of Nova Cygni 1600. But it clearly has no connection to ordinary novae. For the next 115 years it fluctuated between magnitudes 3 and 6 or fainter. Then around 1715 it steadied at 5th magnitude and has remained there ever since. Photoelectric measurements reveal irregular variations of about 0.2 magnitude, too small to judge reliably by eye, on a time scale of roughly a month. Its main claim to fame this century has been its spectral lines, which show the prototype "P Cygni profile" – each broad emission line is flanked by a narrow blue-shifted absorption line, the telltale signature of a massive stellar wind.

5. RS CYGNI

Northwest of P by 1° is a pair of stars including this red long-period variable. It ranges from a maximum brightness of magnitude 7.2 to a minimum of 9.0. The other star, just 132″ to the north, is magnitude 7.1. Its white makes a beautiful color contrast with the orange-red of RS.

6. IC 4996

Go back to P Cygni and southwest ½°. Here is an open cluster that escaped the notice of all the 19th-century sky sweepers whose lists of objects became the *NGC*, the *New General Catalogue of Nebulae and Clusters of Stars.* But IC 4996 is not hard to see once you know to look for it. An 8th-magnitude triple star marks the spot. Use averted vision, and out of the dark background shimmers a spray of many more stars elongated north-south. IC 4996 is thought to be 5,000 light-years away.

7. NGC 6871

Work your way along the arc of 36, 29, and 28 Cygni, then jog southwest (the direction away from P and Gamma) to yellow-orange 27 Cygni. You're now at the north edge of a gorgeous field to explore. The whole area, covering more than ½°, appears as a big, elongated enhancement of the Milky Way. *Sky Catalogue 2000.0,* Volume 2, says the cluster has only 15 rather bright stars very loosely spread over 20'. But there's clearly a lot more going on here, perhaps in the cluster's background. Two bright pairs in the cluster's middle are each surrounded closely by many fainter stars, more and more of them the longer you look. Here's a place to use high power.

What a grand region! The whole area is worth poking through at leisure. It contains many double and multiple stars, some surprisingly colorful. Examples are the two 7th-magnitude stars charted ½° south of 25 Cygni. The northern one has a little arc of three just south-southwest of it; the grouplet displays unexpected color contrasts of white, orange, and blue. Farther south-southwest in the same telescopic field is OΣ 394, a 7th-and 10th-magnitude orange and blue pair with a separation of 11".

8. CYGNUS X-1

Our next object is invisible, but you can see the star it closely orbits. Cygnus X-1 is one of the most powerful X-ray sources in the sky and a first-rate candidate for a black hole. It orbits the 9th-magnitude blue supergiant HDE 226868, which can easily be found ½° east-northeast of yellow Eta (η) Cygni using the photograph at left.

This star is about 8,000 light-years away. Orbiting it every 5.6 days is the X-ray source, almost certainly a tiny, extremely hot accretion disk of gas spiraling toward a black hole of about 16 solar masses. The black hole itself seems to be immediately surrounded by an even smaller, hotter ball of electrons, positrons, and gamma rays in equilibrium with each other, and having a temperature of several billion degrees Kelvin. This ball is only about 300 miles in diameter; the hole itself, 30 miles.

HDE 226868 is a completely unremarkable star to look at. It's hard to imagine that, if you had X-ray eyes and the Earth's atmosphere were stripped away, this would be one of the most brilliant places in the sky.

9. CHI (χ) CYGNI

This red long-period variable star comes in and out of hiding. At maximum brightness Chi Cygni is visible to the naked eye as an extra star in the shaft of the Northern Cross, typically reaching 5th magnitude and occasionally 3rd. At its minimum of 13.4 you'll be hard put to detect it in a 6-inch scope. The star's average period is 13⅓ months. *Sky & Telescope* prints monthly predictions of the maxima of long-period variables in the Calendar Notes section of each issue.

Try to find Chi using the chart at left, which shows stars only to about 9th magnitude. Chi's red color helps identify it if you have a telescope large enough to show color at all in such a faint star. If the star is invisible, remember this scene. The next time Chi is the brightest in the field, you'll have a hard time believing there was once nothing here.

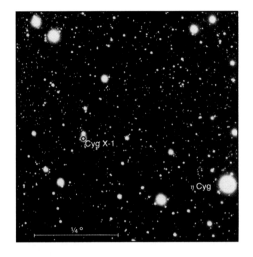

The X-ray source Cygnus X-1 orbits the 9th-magnitude star marked with a circle in this photograph from Burnham's Celestial Handbook.

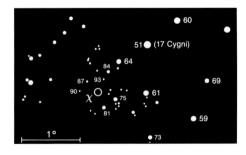

This map pinpoints the location of the wide-ranging red variable Chi Cygni. It's often many times fainter than any of the stars plotted. The two-digit numbers are visual magnitudes to the nearest tenth with the decimal point omitted, for estimating Chi's magnitude. Courtesy American Association of Variable Star Observers.

10. 17 CYGNI AND SOUTH 726

Within about a degree of Chi are these two very similar, wide doubles. Both primaries are bright yellow. The components of 17 Cygni, magnitudes 5 and 9, are separated by 26″ with the fainter one east-northeast of the brighter. South 726 (discovered by Sir James South in the early 19th century) has 6th- and 9th-magnitude components 30″ apart with the faint one south of the brighter.

11. NGC 6834

About 3½° south of Chi Cygni is another faint but interesting cluster. At first glance it displays a straight line of five stars oriented east-west. With averted vision a smattering of many additional faint stars appears behind it, apparently elongated in the same direction. I also thought I saw hints of a second cluster, smaller, fainter, and much more condensed, just off the southern edge.

The 13th-magnitude planetary nebula NGC 6842 close by was totally undetectable in the 6-inch scope from my light-polluted location. A 12-inch, however, will reportedly show it.

The cluster NGC 6834 can be seen in a 6-inch telescope; the interesting little planetary nebula NGC 6842 may require a larger aperture. From a red-light Palomar Observatory Sky Survey print.

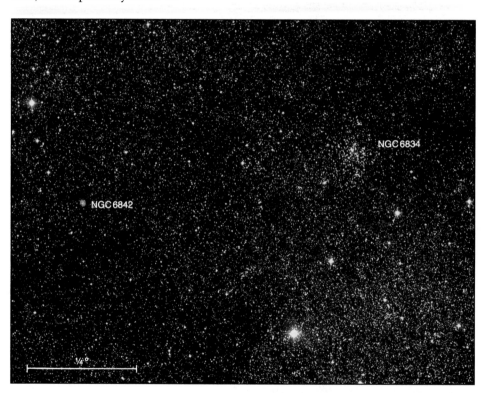

12. ALBIREO, BETA (β) CYGNI

To close out our tour, swing 5° west-southwest to the brilliant double star Albireo. It's the foot of the Northern Cross just off the lower right corner of our map. What an amazing double star this is after viewing so many fainter ones! It too follows the common color scheme of bright yellow and fainter blue. Albireo's components are magnitudes 3.1 and 5.1, separated by 34″ with the fainter to the northeast.

If you want to continue farther on to make this an all-nighter, Albireo begins the star-hop of the previous chapter. But don't rush things. Working through these 12 points of interest took me an hour and a half on my last run through, and that was moving at a steady clip. Take the time you need to get to know everything along the way. Take all the time in the world. The stars aren't going anywhere.

STAR-HOP

13

THIRTEEN

Deneb and the North America Nebula

To enjoy deep-sky astronomy you've got to enjoy maps. Hunting for faint things in space is like a celestial version of orienteering, the increasingly popular sport of crashing through trackless wilderness with a topographic map in one hand and compass in the other to locate hidden checkpoints faster than your competitors. Deep-sky orienteering is much quieter and less athletic, but the map work can be every bit as intense.

One area I always used to get lost in is the North America nebula region in Cygnus. Under a clear, dark sky the nebula is visible to the naked eye as an enhanced patch of the Milky Way just east of Deneb. Binoculars show it better. But if there's any light pollution it becomes challenging even in a telescope – especially because the nebula is bigger than a telescopic field of view, making it tricky to find your way around. Unless, that is, you use your map correctly. Then finding your way is easy.

This chapter's star-hopping project takes us on a trek through the North America nebula, then on to some other, little-known sights nearby in the Cygnus Milky Way. This is the third chapter in a row working though the rich Cygnus region.

Our orienteering map on the next page is adapted from *Uranometria 2000.0* showing stars as faint as about magnitude 9.5. The black circles are only 1° in diameter, about the size of a typical amateur telescope's lowest-power field of view. This map is so detailed, and the area is so rich in stars, that you'll probably be able to star-hop from point to point using just your main telescope. You'll need to rely on the finderscope only occasionally to reorient yourself when you get lost.

After setting up your telescope and chart table, be sure to take a few minutes to get your celestial bearings. Celestial north is up on the map and toward Polaris in the sky. Nudge your telescope toward Polaris while looking in the eyepiece, and notice where new stars enter from. That's north. Turn the map around accordingly. If your telescope has an even number of mirrors, the view will match the map. With an odd number of mirrors (including the one in a star diagonal), east and west will appear reversed; see page 51 for coping with a mirror image.

Also, check star patterns to compare the *size* of your low-power field to the black circles.

1. DENEB

Our starting point is the 1st-magnitude star in the tail (that's what *Deneb* means in Arabic) of Cygnus the Swan. It's the faintest corner of the Summer Triangle, which it forms with Vega and Altair.

A great white blaze in my 6-inch reflector, Deneb overpowers its Milky Way star field. Deneb is very far away for a 1st-magnitude star, about 1,600 light-years compared to Vega's 26 and Altair's 17. It looks so bright because at absolute visual magnitude –7.5 it shines with 80,000 times the light of the Sun. If the Sun were so distant it would glow at only magnitude 13½, the detectability limit of a 6-inch scope.

Deneb is a supergiant of spectral type *A*2Ia, not only hotter than the Sun but roughly 100 times its diameter. As with nearly all supergiants, it varies slightly in brightness in a more or less irregular way.

While you're here, use Deneb to check the alignment of your finderscope. A finder should be aligned well enough so that when you center a star on the crosshairs, it will be near the middle of the field in your highest-power eyepiece.

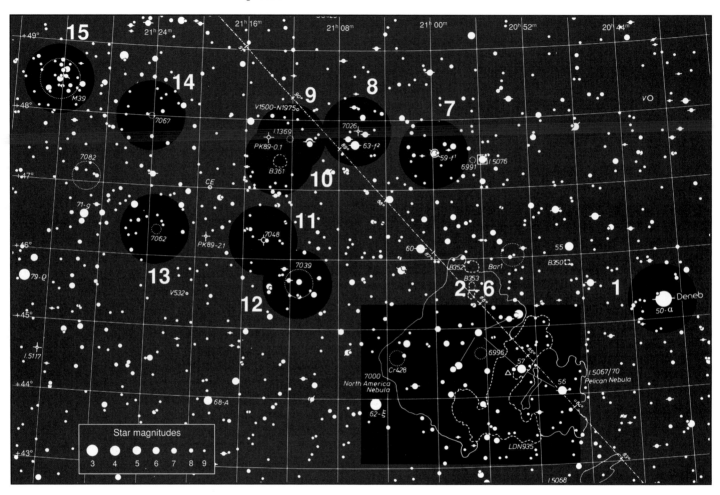

The crowded sky country east of Deneb, adapted from the Uranometria 2000.0 *atlas. The black circles are 1° in diameter; compare their size with your telescope's lowest-power field of view. Stars are plotted to about magnitude 9.5.*

2. THE "SCORPIUS" ASTERISM

Let's stop to check the lay of the land and plan the next move. The North America nebula is in the same finder field as Deneb, but it may appear so dim that you'll need to examine the exact positions of its edges to make a positive identification in a telescope. This means using stars like surveyor's benchmarks to keep track of exactly where you are.

The drawing on the next page shows a 6° finderscope field east of Deneb, including the nebula and several asterisms around it. One of them is the key to North America. I call it the "Scorpius" for its vague resemblance to that constellation. Swing 2° east from Deneb to spot it in your finder.

3. NGC 6997

Inside the Scorpius pattern, framed in a triangle of 5th- and 6th-magnitude stars, is this open star cluster (mislabeled 6996 on *Uranometria 2000.0* and in

Sky Catalogue 2000.0, Volume 2). Seen in my 6-inch reflector at 45× it's a large, faint sprinkling of stars in a fainter glow that shows tantalizing hints of resolution when viewed with averted vision. Like many open clusters it stands out better visually than on photographs.

NGC 6997 is about 10′ across and somewhat elongated southeast-northwest. It includes about 40 stars 11th magnitude and fainter. The cluster is about 1,500 light-years away, rather near as open clusters go. After I picked it out of the star field a couple of times, it became an immediately recognizable telescopic landmark whenever I swept across it thereafter.

A finderscope's view of the North America nebula region, with asterisms and points of interest marked. Compare it with the map on the previous page; the scale is the same. Stars are plotted to 6th or 7th magnitude; numbers next to some are their names in the Flamsteed numbering system (for example, 55 Cygni). Both maps are correct-reading images, with north up and east to the left.

4. NGC 7000, THE NORTH AMERICA NEBULA

Under my suburban light pollution the Cygnus Milky Way is only dimly visible with almost no detail except the Great Rift. The North America nebula is totally invisible to the naked eye and too mixed up with stars to be positively seen in binoculars. Nevertheless the 6-inch reveals its unmistakable presence.

I can only see the nebula's edges. Using the Scorpius asterism as your reference, try following North America's coast with the finder chart above. Bright stars are nicknamed with cities and regions they seem to represent. The nebula's most definite edges are the Atlantic seaboard and especially the Texas Gulf Coast; here the sky is dim reddish black on one side of the telescopic field, plainer gray-black on the other. Southern Mexico gives the impression of an irregular band of the reddishness with ordinary black on both sides. The coasts can be followed in greater detail by referring to the photograph on the next page. The two 7th-magnitude stars of Cuba are pale orange and blue.

Celestial north and south in the North America nebula correspond remarkably well to the same directions on land, but watch out for east and west. Because we're looking up at the sky from underneath, rather than down at the land from above, California is on the celestial *east* coast and Florida is in the nebula's celestial southwest!

The North America nebula, with the "Scorpius" asterism marked. This image is more subdued than the brilliant photos often printed in books, but it's just the right density for visually marking the nebula's individual features among the stars as seen through a telescope. Note the dark nebula B352 at top center. The field is 3° wide.

5. XI (ξ) CYGNI

Xi Cygni lying off the California coast is the brightest star (at magnitude 3.7) that we've hit since Deneb. It is noteworthy for its strikingly deep golden orange color. Xi Cygni is a supergiant with a spectral type of K4.5 and a color index of 1.65, which makes it almost as red as Antares or Betelgeuse.

6. COLLINDER 428

Collinder 428, in the Oregon of the North America nebula, is a large, loose, sparse cluster near a somewhat brighter star with an orangy color; the tint is barely discernible in the 6-inch scope. The cluster's 20 or so stars are scattered across about ¼°. Its total photographic magnitude is cataloged as 8.7, but such a figure means little for the visibility of a large, scattered object like this. It is about 1,600 light-years distant.

7. 59 CYGNI

When you're done with the North America region, backtrack to Deneb in your finder to start off on a new tack. Comparing the view with the round finder chart on page 131, follow the Arrowhead asterism northeastward to pick up the Northern Line. The second star of the line is 59 Cygni.

This is a quadruple star that reveals itself in stages. It looks like a pretty double at first glance in the 6-inch at 45×; the components are magnitudes 4½ and 9½ and 20″ apart. The fainter star is north of the primary, which is pale, diamond-colored blue. At 115× the 11th-magnitude third star begins to be glimpsed 38″ southwest of the primary; it's easier at 300×. I couldn't quite make out the 4th star, magnitude 11½ and 27″ southeast of the bright primary, but a look in a 12.5-inch scope at 180× confirmed that it's indeed there.

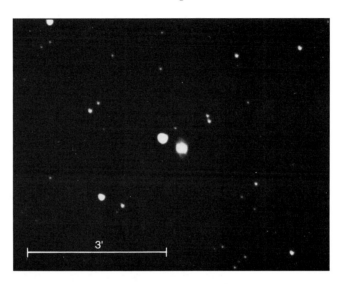

NGC 7026, the messy-looking "star" near center, is a planetary nebula only about 20″ in diameter. Visually it looks like a dim, gray-green glow next to an orange pinpoint. Martin Germano took this 6-minute exposure with a 14½-inch f/5 reflector on hypered Kodak TP 2415 film.

8. NGC 7026

Now for something different! NGC 7026 is a little planetary nebula whose position is easily located near 63 Cygni in the Northern Line. The 6-inch showed two faint stars of 10th and 11th magnitude next to each other at 45×, but even at first glance something looks funny. The fainter one shows itself as a tiny fuzzball, while the other focuses to a pinpoint. At 115× the nebula is easier and the sight beautiful – a dim, greenish gray ball next to a pale orange point. The higher the power the better; at 300× the nebula shows definite hints of asymmetry. It appears less than 20″ in diameter.

Photographs such as the one above come nowhere near conveying the loveliness of the sight. *Sky Catalogue 2000.0*, Volume 2, lists NGC 7026 as photographic magnitude 12.7, but it must be much brighter visually. If you used a nebula filter to try for North America, try using it here too.

9. IC 1369

Carefully following the chart, move ⅔° east to the fourth star of the Northern Line, a wide north-south pair in a finderscope. A little beyond is a faint star cluster that didn't even make the *NGC* list. I can barely see IC 1369 in the 6-inch as a faint glow, but averted vision gives hints of resolution into many extremely faint stars. Don't be misled by the brighter five-star, bow-tie asterism ¼° to its northeast, which distracted my attention at first.

IC 1369 is a compact group of about 40 stars 12th magnitude and fainter only 4′ across. It is believed to be 5,000 light-years away – no wonder it looks so faint! – and 1.3 billion years old.

NGC 7048 is a well-formed little planetary nebula, a nearly spherical bubble of gas expelled by a red-giant star as it became a white dwarf. The 18th-magnitude central star is beyond hope of amateur sightings. For this 55-minute exposure, Martin Germano used the same telescope and film as on the previous page.

10. BARNARD 361

Much of the Cygnus Milky Way is riddled with dark nebulae, opaque clouds of gas and dust that blot out the stars behind. The North America nebula is just a piece of this great gassy complex that happens to be lit up.

A well-defined and eerie dark nebula lies just south-southeast of IC 1369. It is outlined with dashes on the guide map. The 6-inch at 45× shows it as a big, dark hole in the Milky Way, its edges limned by rich star fields. Barnard 361 fills much of my eyepiece field; sweeping the scope around a little to get a larger view heightens its appearance as a spooky black blob. Of course, the darker your sky the better dark nebulae stand out.

11. NGC 7048

NGC 7048 is another planetary nebula. Following the little pairs of 9th-magnitude stars on the chart, work south from Barnard 361 to the 8th-magnitude star just east of the nebula. Right away I could make out a vague glow barely north-northwest of a little Y-shaped asterism. I couldn't see any real structure in this 60″ gas bubble, but try using very high powers. Its circular edges are very well defined in the photograph at left. Despite its dimness I found it unusually attractive in such a rich star field.

12. NGC 7039

Working another ¾° southwest, we find this large, faint, well-resolved sprinkling of stardust, elongated east-northeast to west-southwest. It is nearly ½° across; its 50 stars are magnitude 11 and fainter.

It's merely a vague glow in small amateur telescopes, but NGC 7062 is completely resolved into stars in this photograph by Lee Coombs of Atascadero, California, using a 10-inch f/5 reflector. This 10-minute exposure was on Kodak 103a-O film.

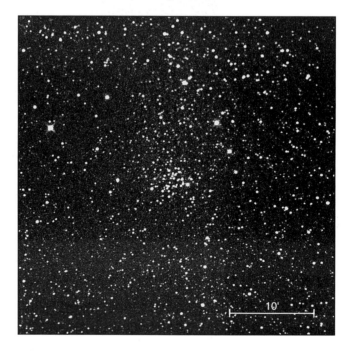

13. NGC 7062

Our next stop is farther east. The location of this faint cluster is easy to find with the chart by careful star-hopping at low power, but you may have to look carefully to see it once you get there. NGC 7062 is a small glow in the 6-inch, seemingly stretched between two faint stars marking its east and west edges. The cluster is about 7′ across. Despite its faintness it seemed to me eerily pretty.

14. NGC 7067

Some more hopping northward and we're at this very faint and small cluster, only 3' across, just west of a 9th-magnitude star. At first I only suspected it in the 6-inch, but it becomes more definite when I jiggle the telescope. It looks small and nebulous. This cluster is roughly 11,000 light-years deep in the Milky Way, which puts it about 30° around the curve of our galaxy from the position of the Sun. It is the most distant object we've looked at tonight.

The scattered stars of Messier 39 fade into the Milky Way background on photographs, but to the eye they stand out brilliantly. Binoculars give a fine view of this very open cluster. For this 10-minute exposure, Lee Coombs used the same setup as on the previous page.

15. M39

We end with a bang. Creep another 1° east-northeast and you hit M39, a big, nearly field-filling spangle of about 30 bright gems 8th magnitude and down. The cluster, only about 900 light-years away, is ½° across and triangular. None of its stars is strongly colored.

This fine object looks better in a finderscope than many of the dim little clusters look in big apertures. In fact M39 is easy to spot in a finder or binoculars starting from Deneb. Follow the Arrowhead to the Northern Line, then continue eastward beyond the line by about its own length to hit M39. That's how most people would locate it, missing everything along the way. The roundabout route is lots more fun.

STAR-HOP
14
FOURTEEN

A Walk Through Cassiopeia

The signature constellation of the northern sky in autumn and winter is Cassiopeia. It's one of the first constellations that anyone learns who starts out at this time of year. Right inside its familiar W (or M) pattern of five bright stars are a couple dozen telescopic sights. Cassiopeia lies in the middle of the Milky Way where stars are thick and deep-sky objects are abundant. There are so many here, in fact, that we will limit tonight's sky tour to 17 of them around the middle of the W. The guide map below once again shows stars to magnitude 8.0. The circles highlighting our points of interest are 2° across, less than half the field of view in a typical finderscope and about twice the field in a main telescope's lowest-power eyepiece.

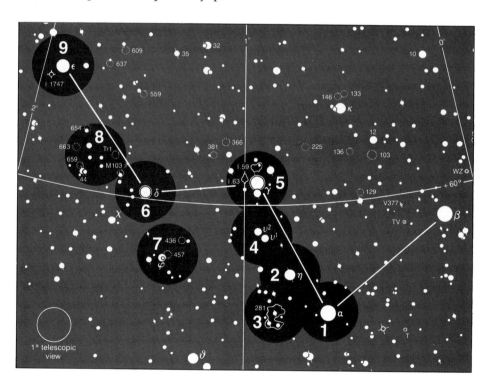

The familiar W shape of Cassiopeia holds swarms of telescopic star clusters and other interesting objects. The black circles, 2° in diameter, highlight the sights discussed in the text. North is up and east is to the left. Stars are plotted to magnitude 8.0; adapted from Wil Tirion's Sky Atlas 2000.0.

1. ALPHA (α) CASSIOPEIAE

Our starting point is the bright star in the sharpest point of the W. Alpha Cas is an orange giant, type *K*0, magnitude 2.2, estimated to be about 110 light-years away. If this distance is correct the star is 120 times as luminous as the Sun. It shows a rich, golden yellow color in my 6-inch reflector; its color index is 1.2. A 9th-magnitude companion star, Alpha Cas D, lies 1' west of it. This is just a chance optical alignment; there is no physical relationship between the two stars.

Hundreds of millions of years ago, Alpha Cas may have been a small main-sequence star very much like the Sun. But it used up the supply of hydrogen that kept it burning stably, and thus swelled to gianthood. When we look at Alpha Cas we are looking billions of years into our own solar system's future.

2. ETA (η) CASSIOPEIAE

Less than 2° northeast of Alpha (moving toward the middle of the W), we come to a much more sunlike star – except that Eta Cas is double. It is a beautiful object for small telescopes.

Eta's two components are magnitudes 3.4 and 7.5. They are widely separated by 12.5″. The bright one, Eta Cas A, is a main-sequence star of spectral type *F8* or *G0* – just a trace hotter and brighter than the Sun. The fainter component, Eta Cas B, is an orange-red dwarf variously listed as type *K4* or *M0*. It is only ¹⁄₄₀ as luminous as the Sun; like all red dwarfs it is thriftily hoarding its fuel for a long life. It will still be shining unchanged billions of years after its companion (and the Sun) have swelled up and burned out.

What colors do A and B appear to you? Their spectra indicate they are yellowish white and yellow-orange. Indeed, in my 6-inch reflector at 50×, I see them as yellow and brown (brown is merely dark orange.)

Eta Cas is a near neighbor, only 19 light-years away. The stars orbit each other every 480 years while ranging from 33 to 100 astronomical units apart. By comparison, Neptune is 30 a.u. from the Sun. An Earthlike planet of Eta Cas A would have a normal sun in its daytime sky and, for much of the year, an overwhelmingly brilliant star at night. The B component would vary between magnitudes –13 and –15.5 (2 and 20 full Moons) in a cycle of 480 years. During the months of each year when it was near conjunction with the primary sun, it would be plainly visible in daylight. During the months when it was near opposition there would never be a dark night.

3. NGC 281

This combination nebula and star cluster shows at least a little of itself in the smallest telescope, but its full extent challenges the largest. The first thing to find is the 7th-magnitude multiple star Burnham 1 at the cluster's heart, 1.7° east of Alpha Cas. The chart at left, adapted from *Uranometria 2000.0,* will help. It has twice the scale of our main chart (the grid squares are 1° high) and shows stars as faint as about magnitude 9.5. Burnham 1, also known as ADS 719, has two main components of magnitudes 7.8 and 8.8; the fainter star is 3.8″ southeast of the bright one. There is also a 9.3-magnitude component 8.9″ south of the bright star; it may catch your eye before the brighter but closer companion. A much more difficult fourth star, magnitude 9.8, is just 1.4″ to the brightest one's east.

This group is embedded in a much larger, sparse star cluster about 4′ across. In the 6-inch reflector at 95× I see occasional glimmers of scattered faint stars and also what seems like a little extra light among them. This may be the NGC 281 nebula, a great, mottled cloud of glowing hydrogen. According to the *Webb Society Deep-Sky Observer's Handbook,* Volume 2, an 8-inch telescope shows the sky around Burnham 1 "clearly bright," and in a 16-inch the nebula is a "large, easy object."

4. UPSILON[1] AND UPSILON[2] (υ[1] AND υ[2]) CASSIOPEIAE

This pair of 5th-magnitude stars, 18′ apart, is a stepping-stone on our way northeastward. Both are orange giants but have slightly different colors, with spectral types of *K2* and *G8* and color indexes of 1.2 and 1.0, respectively (meaning υ[1] is slightly redder). They test your ability to distinguish star colors. I can easily see the difference of tint in the 6-inch reflector.

A close-up of the area around Alpha (α) and Eta (η) Cassiopeiae and NGC 281, showing stars to about magnitude 9.5.

5. GAMMA (γ) CASSIOPEIAE AND ITS NEBULAE

Now we come to the center of the constellation's W. Gamma Cas is a tremendous, unstable blue-white *B*0 star about 700 light-years distant that pours out some 5,000 times the light of the Sun. Gamma Cas has shown substantial naked-eye brightness variations over the decades and in fact is the prototype of the "Gamma Cassiopeiae variables." These are rapidly rotating *B* stars evolving off the main sequence and occasionally flinging shells of gas from their equatorial regions into the surrounding space.

The elusive Gamma Cassiopeiae nebulae lie ⅓° north and northeast of the overwhelmingly brilliant star at the middle of Cassiopeia's W. They show up splendidly on this blue-light print from the National Geographic Society–Palomar Observatory Sky Survey.

In 1937 Gamma Cas brightened to magnitude 1.6. By the end of that year it returned to its usual 2.2, then in 1940 it faded to 3rd magnitude. Slowly recovering, the star reached magnitude 2.5 in 1954 and has been hovering near 2.2 for over a decade. There's no telling when Gamma Cas will brighten again. To check it with the naked eye – easy to do any time you look up in the fall and winter – compare it to Alpha, magnitude 2.2. If you see much difference between them, Gamma is acting up.

Two nebulae lie near Gamma and clearly appear to be illuminated by it. IC 59 and IC 63 are large but faint. The original *Index Catalogue* calls both "pretty faint," which is near middle ranking in the NGC and IC brightness descriptions. (The next description up the scale of 10 is "pretty bright.") I can't see a trace of them with the 6-inch reflector through moderately light-polluted skies. A nebula filter on a larger aperture might make the difference.

6. DELTA (δ) CASSIOPEIAE

Our next stop is the 3rd-magnitude star forming the shallow point of Cassiopeia's W. It appears just a trace less blue than Gamma Cas in the 6-inch, and in fact is a white *A*5 star. It lies about 60 light-years away. With 20 times the luminosity of the Sun it is rather like a distant copy of Sirius. However, Delta Cas has shown slight variations (less than 0.1 magnitude) and may be an eclipsing binary with a period of 2 years.

7. NGC 457

Two degrees south-southwest of Delta Cas is this little cluster, one of my favorites in the whole sky. Lying on my back and gazing up with 7×50 binoculars, I can just make it out as a hazy streak extending northwestward from a pair of stars, the brighter of which is Phi (φ) Cassiopeiae. Viewing the cluster for the first time this way on a wild and windy October night years ago, I imagined it to be a wisp of candle flame blown from the two stars by the wind.

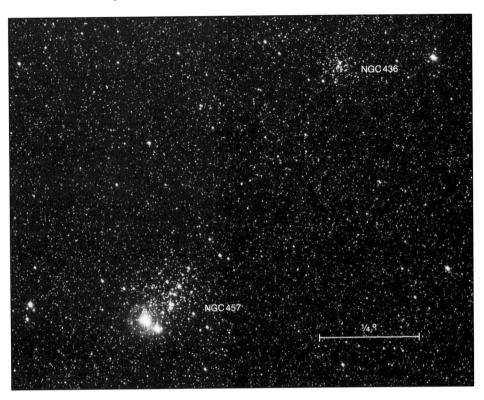

Any photograph of a bright star cluster is a poor thing compared to the original. No photo can capture the dynamic range of intensely bright star points on a velvet black background. Therefore, the star patterns that dominate a cluster are often different in the eyepiece than on a photo. In NGC 457 at lower left, the "E.T. cluster," the eyes of the humanoid figure described in the text are to the southeast (lower left); the feet are northwest. NGC 436 is at upper right. From a Palomar Sky Survey blue plate.

This is one of those clusters that especially provoke the human tendency to see animals, faces, and monsters in random patterns. Tom Lorenzin, author of *1000+: The Amateur Astronomer's Field Guide to Deep-Sky Observing*, calls NGC 457 the "E.T. cluster" after the extraterrestrial figure in the movie *E.T.* Writes Lorenzin: "E.T. waves his arms at you, and winks!" In the 6-inch the whole group does look like a gangly humanoid figure with arms splayed out and brilliant, unequal eyes far apart. He has a red star in his north armpit. The inner part of the cluster, E.T.'s body, looks to me like a long, hollow arrowhead pointing northwest. Others claim to see an owl here instead.

NGC 457 is thought to be 9,000 light-years distant. Bright Phi Cas may well be a member of the cluster, judging from its supergiant spectrum and the reddening and polarization that its light has undergone crossing thousands of light-years of interstellar dust. If so, it is one of the most luminous stars known, with an absolute magnitude of about –8.8, which is 250,000 times the light of the Sun.

Phi's color looks wrong to me – it is a dusky yellow-gold despite its *F*0 spectrum, which signifies a white star with perhaps just the palest trace of yellow. Indeed, Phi has a color index of 0.7, more typical of a *G* star. Here is a chance to view the reddening effect of interstellar dust directly.

Less than a degree northwest of NGC 457 is the much more subdued cluster NGC 436, a big, dim glow underlying a few fairly bright stars. It forms a gentle contrast to its flashy neighbor.

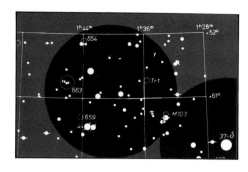

The field of star clusters east of Delta (δ) Cassiopeiae, beginning with bright M103. Adapted from Uranometria 2000.0.

Finder charts for the tiny planetary IC 1747. The gray circle on the left chart shows the field at right.

8. THE M103 FAMILY OF CLUSTERS

East of Delta Cas the star clusters fairly swarm. Five of them are in a 2° circle, as best shown on the *Uranometria 2000.0* chart at left.

First pick up M103, which is 1° northeast of Delta. This smart, bright triangle of a cluster rivals NGC 457 for splash and dazzle, with glimmering starry depths behind a few bright luminaries. It too contains a bright star on one edge – the double Struve (Σ) 131, magnitudes 7.3 and 10.5, separation 13.8″, position angle 142° (meaning the faint star is southeast of the bright one).

Moving north-northeast, Trumpler 1 is an odd little clump – very small and dominated by a bright linear streak. In the 6-inch the streak looks like nothing I've seen anywhere else in the sky, an anomaly begging for more aperture and resolution. Photographs or a larger aperture show it to be a chain of stars lined up close together.

NGC 654 is a hazy, uniform glow faintly resolved into tiny stars, just north of a pair of much brighter stars that seem to lend it an artistic touch.

NGC 663 is a surprise after these weaker clusters! In the 6-inch it's a big, fully resolved, elongated lozenge oriented northwest-southeast with a dark gulf in its middle. With 80 stars in an area ¼° across and a total magnitude of 7.1, this one deserved to be a Messier object.

NGC 659, on the other hand, is just a small glow behind a star or two.

All five of these clusters are only 15 to 26 million years old according to *Sky Catalogue 2000.0*, Volume 2.

9. EPSILON (ε) CASSIOPEIAE AND IC 1747

The eastern end of the Cassiopeia W is the star Epsilon, magnitude 3.4, a blue-white *B3* star some 450 light-years distant with 700 times the Sun's luminosity. It serves as a guide to our last object of the night, which is a real challenge.

IC 1747 is a tiny, faint planetary nebula listed as only 13th magnitude and 13″ across. The first challenge is merely to detect it as a "star." The next is to find evidence of its nebular nature.

On the little chart from *Uranometria 2000.0* at left, the gray circle indicates the field of the 12′ drawing at its right, which will help pinpoint the nebula's position. The drawing, from the *Webb Society Deep-Sky Observer's Handbook*, Volume 2, was made by E. S. Barker of Herne Bay, England, using an 8½-inch telescope at 204 power. He called the nebula "slightly extended" northwest to southeast with a "very slight hint of darker centre."

I can't see anything here at all with the 6-inch in suburban skies. But IC 1747 is easy in my 12.5-inch under the same conditions – a lovely little round glow. Use your highest possible power and try a nebula filter if you have one. Move the filter in and out of the view between your eye and the eyepiece; this should make faint stars blink in and out of view while a nebula stays more or less the same brightness.

Like all planetary nebulae, IC 1747 consists of the outer layers of a red giant that were puffed into space as the star shrank toward becoming a white dwarf. This planetary is calculated to be 7,000 light-years away, which would make it half a light-year in diameter. Were it not so near a landmark star, it would be utterly lost to the attention of most amateurs amid the swarming riches of the Milky Way.

Appendix A:
The Greek Alphabet

α	Alpha	ι	Iota	ρ	Rho
β	Beta	κ	Kappa	σ	Sigma
γ	Gamma	λ	Lambda	τ	Tau
δ	Delta	μ	Mu	υ	Upsilon
ε	Epsilon	ν	Nu	φ	Phi
ζ	Zeta	ξ	Xi	χ	Chi
η	Eta	o	Omicron	ψ	Psi
θ	Theta	π	Pi	ω	Omega

(These are the lowercase letters.)

Appendix B: Constellation Names

Abbr.	Name	Latin Genitive	Meaning
And	Andromeda	Andromedae	Andromeda
Ant	Antlia	Antliae	(Air) Pump
Aps	Apus	Apodis	Bird of Paradise
Aqr	Aquarius	Aquarii	Water Bearer
Aql	Aquila	Aquilae	Eagle
Ara	Ara	Arae	Altar
Ari	Aries	Arietis	Ram
Aur	Auriga	Aurigae	Charioteer
Boö	Boötes	Boötis	Herdsman
Cae	Caelum	Caeli	Engraving Tool
Cam	Camelopardalis	Camelopardalis	Giraffe
Cnc	Cancer	Cancri	Crab
CVn	Canes Venatici	Canum Venaticorum	Hunting Dogs
CMa	Canis Major	Canis Majoris	Big Dog
CMi	Canis Minor	Canis Minoris	Little Dog
Cap	Capricornus	Capricorni	Sea Goat
Car	Carina	Carinae	Ship's Keel
Cas	Cassiopeia	Cassiopeiae	Queen Cassiopeia
Cen	Centaurus	Centauri	Centaur
Cep	Cepheus	Cephei	King Cepheus
Cet	Cetus	Ceti	Whale
Cha	Chamaeleon	Chamaeleontis	Chameleon
Cir	Circinus	Circini	Drawing Compass
Col	Columba	Columbae	Dove
Com	Coma Berenices	Comae Berenices	Berenice's Hair

Abbr.	Name	Latin Genitive	Meaning
CrA	Corona Australis	Coronae Australis	Southern Crown
CrB	Corona Borealis	Coronae Borealis	Northern Crown
Crv	Corvus	Corvi	Crow
Crt	Crater	Crateris	Cup
Cru	Crux	Crucis	Southern Cross
Cyg	Cygnus	Cygni	Swan
Del	Delphinus	Delphini	Dolphin
Dor	Dorado	Doradus	Goldfish
Dra	Draco	Draconis	Dragon
Equ	Equuleus	Equulei	Little Horse
Eri	Eridanus	Eridani	River Eridanus
For	Fornax	Fornacis	Furnace
Gem	Gemini	Geminorum	Twins
Gru	Grus	Gruis	Crane
Her	Hercules	Herculis	Hercules
Hor	Horologium	Horologii	Clock
Hya	Hydra	Hydrae	Sea Serpent
Hyi	Hydrus	Hydri	Water Snake
Ind	Indus	Indi	Indian
Lac	Lacerta	Lacertae	Lizard
Leo	Leo	Leonis	Lion
LMi	Leo Minor	Leonis Minoris	Little Lion
Lep	Lepus	Leporis	Hare
Lib	Libra	Librae	Scales
Lup	Lupus	Lupi	Wolf
Lyn	Lynx	Lyncis	Lynx
Lyr	Lyra	Lyrae	Lyre

Abbr.	Name	Latin Genitive	Meaning
Men	Mensa	Mensae	Table Mountain
Mic	Microscopium	Microscopii	Microscope
Mon	Monoceros	Monocerotis	Unicorn
Mus	Musca	Muscae	Fly
Nor	Norma	Normae	Level
Oct	Octans	Octantis	Octant
Oph	Ophiuchus	Ophiuchi	Snake Holder
Ori	Orion	Orionis	Orion
Pav	Pavo	Pavonis	Peacock
Peg	Pegasus	Pegasi	Pegasus
Per	Perseus	Persei	Perseus
Phe	Phoenix	Phoenicis	Phoenix
Pic	Pictor	Pictoris	Easel
Psc	Pisces	Piscium	Fishes
PsA	Piscis Austrinus	Piscis Austrini	Southern Fish
Pup	Puppis	Puppis	Ship's Stern
Pyx	Pyxis	Pyxidis	Ship's Compass
Ret	Reticulum	Reticuli	Eyepiece Reticle
Sge	Sagitta	Sagittae	Arrow
Sgr	Sagittarius	Sagittarii	Archer
Sco	Scorpius	Scorpii	Scorpion
Scl	Sculptor	Sculptoris	Sculptor's Apparatus
Sct	Scutum	Scuti	Shield
Ser	Serpens	Serpentis	Serpent
Sex	Sextans	Sextantis	Sextant
Tau	Taurus	Tauri	Bull
Tel	Telescopium	Telescopii	Telescope
Tri	Triangulum	Trianguli	Triangle
TrA	Triangulum Australe	Trianguli Australis	Southern Triangle
Tuc	Tucana	Tucanae	Toucan
UMa	Ursa Major	Ursae Majoris	Big Bear
UMi	Ursa Minor	Ursae Minoris	Little Bear
Vel	Vela	Velorum	Ship's Sails
Vir	Virgo	Virginis	Virgin
Vol	Volans	Volantis	Flying Fish
Vul	Vulpecula	Vulpeculae	Little Fox

Appendix C:
Rate Your
Observing Site

Every astronomer longs for the unattainable – bigger aperture, more perfect optics, an end to light pollution, travel to the stars – and learns to make do with what's available. Astronomy teaches humility and patience. So it is with our observing sites. Virtually no amateur has the ideal place to view the skies, and most of us don't even come close.

We face light pollution overhead and floodlights blazing next door. We dodge trees, buildings, nosy strangers, and meddlesome police, only to confront the natural problems of dew, frost, cold, and mosquitoes. To get to a good observing site, some of us put up with a long nighttime commute.

But before you curse the place that life has thrust you and do something unreasonable, like move to a mountaintop or quit skywatching, ask whether your glass is half empty or half full. No matter how bad your situation, there's always some amateur who has it worse and yet still manages to do plenty of astronomy and enjoy it greatly. You may even discover that certain observing-site problems carry blessings in disguise.

To help judge the qualities of the places you skygaze – and what can be done about them – here is my own list of the six things that matter. They are: lights nearby, light pollution in the sky itself, how much sky is visible, convenience, privacy/safety, and the location's overall esthetics. If you like to put numbers on things, you can rate each on a scale of 0 to 10 from hopeless to ideal, respectively. Some of the factors may mean more to you than others. If so, rate the important ones toward the high or low extremes of the scale and the less important ones toward the middle. We'll compute a final score at the end.

1. Lights nearby are the most annoying and destructive problem. A telescope near a streetlight is almost useless for anything but the Moon and planets. But this problem is often the most avoidable. Dark corners offer refuge. With a little ingenuity you might be able to rig up a shade. Block that light! Try a tarpaulin on ropes or elastic bungee cords that loop onto hooks screwed into walls or trees. Some light-plagued amateurs view with black cloths draped over their heads and eyepieces like old-time photographers. The most convenient way to use the cloth is to wear it as a cape; it can be flipped up over your head when needed.

Perhaps you can talk a light-hoggish neighbor into letting you turn off the problem with an outdoor switch whenever you observe. Break the ice by offering looks through your telescope some evening. Or talk up the *energy-saving, inexpensive, high-security* motion detectors sold at hardware and electronics stores. They turn on floodlights only when someone walks into the yard, a far more effective security device than a light that burns all night. Some amateurs have offered to go halves on paying for a neighbor's motion detector, or have paid for the whole thing and installed it too.

In severe cases of "light trespass" by uncooperative neighbors, property owners have gone to court and won orders requiring the neighbors to shield the offending fixtures. You have a basic legal right to keep other people's nuisances off your property. Information on ameliorating all kinds of light problems, from local to global, is available from the International Dark-Sky Association, 3545 N. Stewart Ave., Tucson, AZ 85716. It's a vital organization that deserves the financial backing of all astronomers. Write for the current membership fee and other information.

Rubber eyecups on your eyepieces will help keep local lights from glinting into your view. To preserve dark adaptation, keep your observing eye closed when not looking into the telescope; use your other eye to get around. A tip for binocular users comes from Philip Harrington. Take an old pair of rubber swimmer's goggles, remove the glass windows, and spray-paint the insides flat black. The goggles serve as excellent light baffles around the binoculars' eyepieces.

Rate your site with 10 points if the brightest lights don't outshine Venus. If your worst unavoidable light outshines the quarter Moon, you get a 3 or 2; the full Moon, 1.

2. Light pollution refers to the glow of the sky itself. It is usually rated by the "sky transparency," how faint a star you can see with the naked eye. To judge this properly you need normal or well-corrected vision and good dark adaptation. Use the chart below, which shows the magnitudes of stars in and around the Little Dipper. What is the faintest star you can see here?

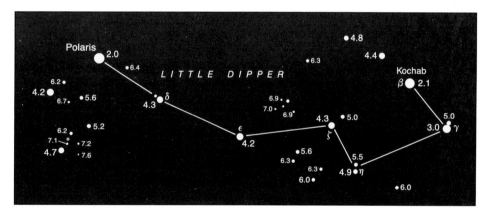

What's the faintest star you can see through your light pollution? To rate the sky transparency at your site, examine the Little Dipper. Stars are marked with their visual magnitudes.

Where there's no light pollution at all, the limiting magnitude is usually assumed to be 6.5, though many people can see fainter. Under such conditions the sky is packed with stars, the Milky Way is a mass of swirling, jumbled detail, and any clouds appear blacker than the sky itself. At a limiting magnitude of 5.5, clouds are brighter than the sky because they are lit from below. The Milky Way is still visible but far less detailed. All of the Little Dipper can be made out fairly readily. At limiting magnitude 4.5, the Milky Way is barely detectable as a faint, featureless band. The stars of the Little Dipper's handle are quite difficult, and the faintest star of its bowl is gone completely. Sadly, our rule of thumb at *Sky & Telescope* magazine is that the average reader lives under a 4.5-magnitude sky.

City dwellers typically face a limit of 3.5. The Milky Way is completely invisible, and all that remains of the Little Dipper are Polaris and the two stars at the end of the bowl. At magnitude 2.5 stars are very few and far between. Of the Little Dipper only Polaris and Kochab can be detected, assuming you can even figure out where they are.

The good news about light pollution is that you *can* see through it. A pair of binoculars in downtown Manhattan shows fainter stars than you can see with the naked eye in the most desolate mountains of New Mexico. The basic strategy for coping with light pollution is to penetrate it with high powers – even when looking for dim, extended objects such as galaxies. It is a myth that deep-sky objects (aside from the very largest ones) require low power.

To let you observe comfortably at high powers, your telescope needs a very stable, rigid mounting with smooth motions, preferably an equatorial mount with a clock drive. You'll also need a large finderscope in perfect alignment with the main scope, as well as excellent maps and map-using skills. Acquire these things and you may be surprised at how much your telescope will show from the city or suburbs.

If you haunt the hours after midnight, you'll find the sky darkens slightly as lights get turned off. Light-pollution filters offer some additional relief depending on the object under study. They work well on bright nebulae, including planetary nebulae, but do little or nothing for galaxies and clusters.

It also pays to minimize the light from a bright sky that bounces around inside your scope. Extend the front of the tube with a long dewcap, such as a tube of paper or cardboard blackened on the inside and held on with elastic. On a reflector, add a ring of black paper behind the main mirror so light from the ground doesn't come in around the mirror's edge. (Leave room for air to circulate). You can reduce reflections into the eyepiece by lining the inside of the eyepiece holder with black velvet below where your longest eyepiece or Barlow lens fits in. A couple drops of glue will hold it in place.

The worse your light pollution, the more night-to-night variation in it you can expect. So keep an eye out for those unusually clear, deep-blue afternoons that presage the best starry nights.

Give your site a 10 if the usual limiting magnitude is 6.5 or fainter, 7 if it's 5.5, 4 for 4.5, and 2 for 3rd magnitude or worse. Rate less harshly if you specialize in the Moon and planets, because light pollution has no effect on them at all.

3. Sky area visible. Your dream observing site has horizon-to-horizon views all around, right? If your dream ever comes true you'll discover the advantages of a sky that's partially blocked. Trees and buildings, curse them all you will, provide shelter from the wind. They shade you from nearby lights. They darken your immediate area even if the only light is from the sky, aiding night vision. And a limited view of the sky actually improves your observing skills. You have to use maps and reference books to ransack the small area visible for whatever is there, rather than just look all around at the easiest objects.

Years ago when I had to make do with narrow zones of sky between treetops, I was mystified by astronomers' complaints about dew. I never had dew problems at all. But when I moved to a more open area, the scope would become so drenched that I had to towel it off. Only then did I realize that sky obstructions act as a giant dewcap. They shield your scope, charts, and other gear from the radiational cooling into space that would allow them to chill below the dew point.

Not all parts of the sky are equally valuable. The south is the most important because that is where objects south of the celestial equator are at their highest. Half the ecliptic, with the Moon and planets, is south of the celestial equator. Next most important is the east. This is where planets shine in the evening when near opposition and where constellations make their first appearance each year. Next comes the west, where more of the ecliptic lies. Last is the north, a rather barren and changeless area of sky. True, Polaris is there, but you *can* polar-align an equatorial telescope without it.

Give yourself 4 points for a good view to the south, another 3 for the east, 2 for the west, and 1 for the north.

4. Convenience and comfort. How hard is it to get your gear to the site? Can you just carry the telescope a few feet from a shed or porch? Or is transporting everything a lengthy task you dread? The quicker and easier you can set up, the more often you'll observe.

Fortunately this is largely under your control. Charts, reference books, notebook, pencils, eyepieces, filters, lights, batteries, and other impedimenta should be kept neatly in an observing kit you can carry with one hand. The foldup table you put them on (you *do* have an observing table, right?) should be light enough to carry in the other hand. And the more inconvenient the site, the more manageable the telescope had better be. Do all that you possibly can to make setup and takedown neat and easy. An afternoon spent tinkering at the workbench to save two minutes in your setup routine is worth it.

As for the site itself, deduct points for wind, dust, bad footing, bugs, and other hassles. A well-designed observatory rates a 10. Give yourself a 2 if getting the telescope to the site requires two people shouting orders at each other to maneuver it down stairs.

Relaxing at dawn under Venus after an all-nighter on North Carolina's Grandfather Mountain, "the darkest site I can easily drive to." Self-portrait by Johnny Horne.

5. Privacy and safety. Privacy means different things to different people. If you are one of those expansive souls who like to set up the telescope on the front lawn and show the sights to any neighbor who passes by, you will go through life rich in the ways that matter. Other observers dread being questioned or stared at.

There are times when discretion is wise for anyone. Hide binoculars under your coat. If you are seen carrying binoculars to the neighborhood vacant lot at night, you are a Peeping Tom until you prove otherwise. When the police find you it won't help to be wearing the black cape and swimmer's goggles. Every longtime amateur seems to have at least one tale of an encounter with police in which a display of star charts saved a dicey situation. Do bring them.

Then there are *real* criminals with whom you may find yourself sharing the night. A woman I know observed quite successfully from her row-house roof-top in a big city, despite severe light pollution, until she realized her row of roofs was becoming a nighttime trade route for persons she did not wish to meet. It's nice to know you'll be alone if you want to be.

Rate your site with a 10 if you could leave a telescope and eyepieces unattended all night without worrying, a 9 if a neighbor has never encountered you but might, and a 5 if the occasional spectators are friendly.

6. Esthetics. Your surroundings color your experience of the universe. Even the dingiest neighborhood takes on a magical aura in the late-night starry stillness when you're alone with the crickets, peeptoads, and galactic immensities. But it's nicer if the scenery accords with the grandeur of the show.

One of my most memorable sites was a desolate beach where, year after year, the constellations of autumn twinkled to the endless booming of Atlantic surf invisible in the dark. Another was the verge of a black pond in a Victorian-era cemetery, where willows and cypress stood silhouetted against the stars over white marble tombs ghostly in the shade – a scene of melancholy beauty that would have inspired Lovecraft or Poe. But this site would get a bad rating on item 5, because at regular intervals I had to crouch behind bushes with my binoculars and *Norton's Star Atlas* to hide from the headlights of a security guard. Trespassing was forbidden after dark and I, a teenager, would have been instantly presumed guilty of all sorts of things. Who would believe that I just wanted a place to see the tail of Scorpius?

Your grand score. If you add up your points, 60 is a perfect score and 30 represents average quality. But this simple total is misleading because one bad factor at a site devalues all the rest. Everything is connected to everything else. So *multiply* your six numbers together and take the cube root of the result. In this more realistic rating, the perfect score is 100 and average quality gets a 25.

Any score above, say, 10 means that astronomy is *possible*. So no excuses – get out and use what you've got.

Appendix D: Recommended Reading

Naked-Eye Constellation Guides

The Stars: A New Way To See Them, H. A. Rey (Houghton Mifflin Co., 1952). Many skywatchers consider this popular classic (over 320,000 sold, and still selling) to be the easiest and most user-friendly guide to the constellations. I'm partial to it because it's the book I learned the sky with at age 14. Even then I thought its age level was a bit below me. Rey connects the stars of each constellation into a stick-figure pattern that actually resembles, in a cartoonish way, the person or creature the constellation is supposed to represent. Rey does have his critics. Some of his constellation patterns are just too complicated to see easily, and they often rely on faint stars that have become all but invisible in the spreading light pollution since the book was published in 1952. But Rey's explanation of the "whys and hows" of sky motions is still the best around.

Find the Constellations, H. A. Rey (Houghton Mifflin Co., 1954). A more juvenile reworking of Rey's *The Stars,* using the same constellation patterns.

Sky & Telescope (see **Magazines** below) has an excellent color map in the center of each issue showing the evening sky for the current month. It's similar to the 12 all-sky maps on pages 16 to 27, but larger and more elaborate. Stars are plotted to magnitude 4.5.

Planispheres

A planisphere is a flat "star wheel" with a movable disk. You turn the disk to set your time and date; the result is a map of your whole sky (usually with severe distortion in the southern area). A planisphere is always handy to have around. Hundreds have been published, ranging in clarity from excellent to nearly useless. Be sure to get one that's made for your approximate latitude on Earth.

Sky & Telescope Star Finder (Sky Publishing Corp.). This planisphere has a very clear star map and a couple of extra features: it shows the horizon for different latitudes from 30° to 50° north, and it allows you to build in time corrections for your longitude and daylight saving time.

The Night Sky, David Chandler. This well-designed, low-cost planisphere has a special feature: it's two-sided. The back side shows the southern sky with distortion minimized – a big advantage over ordinary planispheres when it comes to constellation-spotting.

Precision Planet and Star Locator, David Kennedal (Sky Publishing Corp.). Called "the Mercedes of planispheres" in its ads, it is indeed the best of the lot. For years I've had one in daily use at home and at work. It displays altitude and azimuth lines on the sky – a vital help for showing a star's actual height and compass direction. It comprises five plastic disks for setting not only time and date but corrections for your longitude and daylight saving time, and you can also dial a moving marker on the sky to any right ascension and declination you want, such as that of the Sun, a planet, or comet.

Binocular Observing

Exploring the Night Sky With Binoculars, David Chandler. This pamphlet-size companion to the Night Sky planisphere introduces the basics of binocular observing and points the way to a few of the brightest and most interesting objects.

Leslie Peltier's Guide to the Stars, Leslie C. Peltier (Cambridge University Press, 1986). A friendly and thoughtful introduction to naked-eye constellations and binocular observing, especially of variable stars, by the author of *Starlight Nights* (listed on page 152).

Touring the Universe Through Binoculars, Philip S. Harrington (John Wiley & Sons, 1990). This large, detailed guide marked a big step up for binocular astronomy when it appeared. Its heart is a constellation-by-constellation listing of over 1,000 deep-sky sights, many of them with paragraph-length descriptions. Many are faint enough to require very large (70- or 80-millimeter) binoculars. Contains no charts; you need a separate star atlas.

Binocular Astronomy, Craig Crossen and Wil Tirion (Willmann-Bell, Inc., 1992). Another big, new guide, tying Harrington's book above for the title of the best. This one includes star maps: the 6th-magnitude charts of the *Bright Star Atlas 2000.0* described below. The chapters are organized by season rather than by constellation, which to me seems to make things harder to find. Compared to Harrington's guide, this one dwells more on the couple hundred brighter binocular objects to the exclusion of the faintest ones; it was written with 10 × 50 binoculars in mind. It also spends more time on the constellations themselves.

Star Atlases

6th magnitude

Bright Star Atlas 2000.0, Wil Tirion (Willmann-Bell, Inc., 1990). This low-cost but high-quality atlas was drawn by the renowned Dutch sky cartographer Wil Tirion. It plots all stars to magnitude 6.5 along with deep-sky objects that are visible in binoculars and small telescopes. Facing each of the 10 charts are tables of data about the interesting objects plotted on it. These charts have been incorporated into several other books.

Norton's 2000.0 Star Atlas and Reference Handbook, Ian Ridpath (Longman Scientific & Technical, 18th edition, 1989). This reworking of the venerable 1910 *Norton's Star Atlas* includes newly drafted charts similar in quality to those of the *Bright Star Atlas 2000.0,* but at a slightly larger scale and using a better map projection. Again, data tables list the vital statistics of interesting objects on each chart. Old-timers can be heard grousing that more was lost than gained in the redrafting of the charts. I tend to agree. There are 135 pages of basic astronomical reference material.

8th magnitude

Sky Atlas 2000.0, Wil Tirion. (Sky Publishing Corp., 1981). This big, fine atlas plots 43,000 stars and 2,500 deep-sky objects on 26 large charts. It has become *the* basic star atlas for amateur telescope users and supplied all the 8th-magnitude charts in this book. It comes in three basic editions: the Desk and Field editions are loose sheets of stiff paper with black printing on a white background (Desk) or white printing on a black background (Field). Both of these editions are available in a spiral-bound, laminated format for maximum protection against weather and wear. The Deluxe edition presents the same maps about 8 percent larger, color-codes the different kinds of deep-sky objects, includes a clear plastic coordinate-grid overlay for finding exact positions, and comes spiral-bound in tough, flexible covers. There is no text; use it with a reference like *Burnham's Celestial Handbook.*

9th magnitude

Uranometria 2000.0, Wil Tirion, Barry Rappaport, and George Lovi (Will-mann-Bell, Inc., 1987). Wil Tirion's magnum opus plots 332,000 stars to about magnitude 9.5, and 10,300 deep-sky objects, on 473 charts. All the 9.5-magnitude charts in this book are adapted from *Uranometria.* It consists of two large hardbound volumes, one covering the northern celestial hemisphere, the other the southern. This atlas is highly desirable for users of 6-inch and larger telescopes who know their way around the sky well enough not to get lost among the 473 charts.

Deep-Sky References

Burnham's Celestial Handbook, Robert Burnham, Jr. (Dover, 1978). An extraordinary constellation-by-constellation travelogue through the deep sky. This 2,138-page, three-volume labor of love was assembled over a 25-year period by a staff astronomer at Lowell Observatory who had a poetic sensibility and sometimes quirky interests. It has become a standard on every telescope owner's bookshelf – not just for planning observing sessions like the ones in this book, but for endless bedtime reading on cloudy nights. It has no large-scale sky charts; its natural companion is *Sky Atlas 2000.0.* Some of the scientific material is growing dated, but the visual descriptions, history, folklore, and poetry will keep this a classic for decades.

The Messier Album, John H. Mallas and Evered Kreimer (Sky Publishing Corp., 1978). A handy little reference book with a photograph, drawing, finder chart, visual description, and basic data for each of the 110 Messier objects. Includes a facsimile reprint of Charles Messier's original catalog (in French) from the 1780s.

Messier's Nebulae and Star Clusters, Kenneth Glyn Jones (Cambridge University Press, 2nd edition, 1991). The most in-depth reference book about the 100-plus Messier objects (those cataloged by the late-18th-century astronomer Charles Messier) and their observational history.

Sky Catalogue 2000.0, Vols. 1 and 2. The massive data tables forming these two volumes may make the telephone book look like interesting reading, but they present the most complete and up-to-date information on the most celestial objects available to amateurs. *Volume 1: Stars to Magnitude 8.0* (edited by Alan Hirshfeld, Roger W. Sinnott, and François Ochsenbein; Sky Publishing Corp., 2nd edition, 1991) lists names, catalog designations, exact positions, magnitudes, spectra, colors and distances (when known) of the 50,000 stars magnitude 8.0 and brighter. The data quality is much improved over the first edition, which appeared in 1982. *Volume 2: Double Stars, Variable Stars, and Non-Stellar Objects* (edited by Alan Hirshfeld and Roger W. Sinnott; 1985) contains well-thought-out tables of data for 15 classes of objects. Both books are carefully edited, professional-quality works. They provided most of the facts in the star-hop chapters of this book.

Observing Handbook and Catalogue of Deep-Sky Objects, Christian Luginbuhl and Brian Skiff (Cambridge University Press, 1990.) Gives detailed visual descriptions of 2,000 objects noted at the eyepieces of amateur telescopes of various sizes under dark skies. This is the most thorough collection of descriptions of how deep-sky objects actually look.

The Deep-Sky Field Guide to Uranometria 2000.0, Murray Cragin, James Lucyk, and Barry Rappaport (Willmann-Bell, Inc., 1993). For each of the 473 charts in *Uranometria 2000.0,* this big book presents data tables and abbreviated descriptions of every deep-sky object plotted. The data are well researched from primary sources.

Amateur Astronomy Guides

Nightwatch, Terence Dickinson (Camden House Publishing, revised edition, 1989). This has been called "the introductory astronomy book to get if you're getting only one." It covers a little of everything, including beautiful naked-eye star maps for each season, telescopes and their use, a rundown of where we are in space, and some detailed charts of selected sky areas; all very well done. Any book by Dickinson can be counted on to be good.

The Backyard Astronomer's Guide, Terence Dickinson and Alan Dyer (Camden House Publishing, 1991). A more thorough introduction to the hobby, beautifully designed and illustrated, and written to avoid duplicating *Nightwatch.* Unlike other amateur guides, this one is oriented squarely toward understanding the modern commercial telescope market and pulls no punches in evaluating products. It is also a good how-to introduction to all aspects of practical observing, including sky photography.

The Guide to Amateur Astronomy, Jack Newton and Philip Teece (Cambridge University Press, 1988). A more traditional, less colorful, and less expensive introduction to amateur astronomy. This is a good, heavy book that crowded out a slew of more stolid guides from the 1950s, 60s, and 70s (most of them British) as soon as it appeared. It includes sections on telescope making and sky photography.

How To Use an Astronomical Telescope, James Muirden (Linden Press, 1985). Though it's a bit old-fashioned (and British) and not well illustrated, this beginner's guide to amateur astronomy provides a firm grounding in almost all aspects of observing at a low price.

General

Exploring the Night Sky, Terence Dickinson (Camden House Publishing, 1987). If you're looking for a high-quality astronomy book to give to a 6th- to 8th-grader, this is it.

The Astronomical Calendar, Guy Ottewell (The Astronomical Workshop, Furman University). Published annually in November or December. Guy Ottewell has a knack for creating big, lovingly detailed, and highly informative diagrams, often computer generated, that illuminate a variety of celestial phenomena and events. It features a daily calendar of sky happenings for the current year. Ottewell is a poet and classicist as well as an astronomer, giving his publications unusual depth.

Starlight Nights, Leslie Copus Peltier (Macmillan, 1965; reprinted by Sky Publishing Corp., 1981). The autobiography of an Ohio farm boy who by 1940 had become a world-class comet discoverer and variable-star observer. Peltier was a shy but keenly observant student of nature influenced by the likes of Henry Thoreau and Edwin Way Teele. His pastoral reminiscences of life with his beloved telescopes have been very influential. *Sky & Telescope* columnist Walter Scott Houston wrote that *Starlight Nights* had "the widest impact of any astronomy book since Garrett P. Serviss wrote at the turn of the century." It had an impact on me as a teenager; it helped deepen what might have been a passing fancy into a lifelong pursuit. *Starlight Nights* is out of print as this is written (1993) but may be republished.

Any freshman college astronomy textbook. Astronomy divides into two branches, often too disconnected from each other: practical sky observing outdoors, and "what science knows about the universe today." The books listed here deal mostly with the former; many others offer good summaries of the latter. One source is your local college bookstore, where you'll find at least one first-year astronomy textbook. (Many textbooks also have a half-size "lite" one-semester edition under a different title.) At least two dozen freshman textbooks are in print; they're generally more alike than different. They also tend to be expensive, but for practically nothing you can pick up a previous edition only a few years old that is essentially just as good. New editions of college textbooks are issued frequently with only minor changes and updates, but with renumbered pages to thwart the student used-book trade.

Magazines

Sky & Telescope (Sky Publishing Corp., P. O. Box 9111, Belmont, MA 02178; phone 617-864-7360). Anyone holding this book will be eager to discover the hobby's premier magazine, from which almost every chapter originated. *Sky & Telescope* presents popular feature articles and news of current astronomical research, often written by the researchers themselves; a monthly all-sky chart with evening sky description; observing projects and upcoming celestial events; telescope making, computing, sky photography, and news from the world of organized amateurdom. Published monthly since 1941. Check your newsstand or library, or contact the publisher directly.

Astronomy (Kalmbach Publishing Co., 21027 Crossroads Cir., Waukesha, WI 53187; phone 414-796-8776.) *Astronomy* has a format similar to *Sky & Telescope,* with a strong hobby orientation, but less news coverage. Published monthly since 1973.

Mercury (Astronomical Society of the Pacific, 390 Ashton Ave., San Francisco, CA 94112). Bimonthly. This nearly advertising-free glossy magazine is put out by the nonprofit Astronomical Society of the Pacific, a dynamic outfit that serves as a great educational resource for members of the public interested in the universe. *Mercury* is always a good read and is especially strong on astronomical history.

Griffith Observer (Griffith Observatory, 2800 E. Observatory Rd., Los Angeles, CA 90027). Monthly. A small but always interesting glossy magazine that has been published since 1937 by the Griffith Observatory in Los Angeles, one of the country's leading planetariums.

Star Date (McDonald Observatory, RLM 15.308, University of Texas at Austin, Austin, TX 78712). Bimonthly. This is another slim, glossy magazine from a nonprofit institution. It started as a newsletter for listeners of the Star Date program on public radio, but it has grown into a respectable outlet for quality feature articles on modern astronomical topics – though sometimes with a heavy emphasis toward its parent institution, the University of Texas at Austin.

The Planetary Report (The Planetary Society, 65 N. Catalina Ave., Pasadena, CA 91106). The Planetary Society, perhaps best known for its president Carl Sagan, is a large membership organization that advocates for solar system exploration, the search for intelligent life in the universe, and science education. The glossy magazine that comes with membership has first-rate articles on planetary science and related topics for interested laypeople.

Many of the books described in this appendix are available by mail order from Sky Publishing Corp., P. O. Box 9111, Belmont, MA 02178 (phone 617-864-7360). Write or call for prices or a free catalog.

Object Index

Bold numbers indicate illustrations

Phecda, 102
Phi Aurigae, **67**, 69
Phi Cassiopeiae, 139
Plaskett's star, 83
Polaris, 145
Pollux, 85

R

Rho Aurigae, 67
Rho Ophiuchi, 110
Ring nebula, the, 117, **117**
Rosette nebula, 83, **84**
RS Cygni, 126

S

S Monocerotis, 80
SAO 67287, 115
SAO 114146, 83
SAO 132270, 62
"Scorpius" asterism, the, 130
Scorpius-Centaurus Association, the, 108
Sharpless 2-82, 121, **121**
Sigma Aurigae, 67
Sigma Geminorum, 50
Sigma Orionis, 63
Sigma Scorpii, 110
South 529, 80
South 726, 128
Stephenson 11, 117
Stock 8, **67**, 69
Struve 687, 69
Struve 698, **67**, 69
Struve 747, **62**
Struve 939, 83
Struve 953, 81
Struve 954, 80
Struve 1124, 87
Struve 1603, 102
Struve 1645, 94
Struve 2338, 115
Struve 2392, 115
Struve 2525, 119
Struve 747, 61

T

T Lyrae, 116
Theta Serpentis, 107
Theta^1 Orionis, 61, 76
Theta^2 Orionis, 61
Trapezium, 76
Trumpler 1, 140

U

Upsilon^1 Cassiopeiae, 137
Upsilon^2 Cassiopeiae, 137
Upsilon Geminorum, 50

V

Van den Bergh 126, 121, **121**
Vega, 113
Vega B, 114
Vega E, 114
Virgo (Local) supercluster, 89

W

Whirlpool galaxy, the, 89

X

Xi Cygni, 132
Xi Geminorum, 78
XY Lyrae, 115

Y

Y Canum Venaticorum, 94

Z

Z Ursae Majoris, 101
Z Vulpeculae, 120
Zeta Aurigae, 66
Zeta Lyrae, 116

General Index

Lucyk, James *see* Cragin, Murray
Luginbuhl, Christian, 80, 86, 93, 151
Lynds, Beverly T., 121
Lyra, 113–118; **103**, **114**

M

magnitudes, 31
    see also color index
Mallas, John H., 151
maps, all-sky *see* all-sky maps
Mare Tranquillitatis, 33
maria, 33
Mars, 34, 47
Mercury, 33
Mercury, 153
Messier Album, The, 151
Messier's Nebulae and Star Clusters, 151
mirror image, 41, 51
    celestial poles in, 97
Monju, Joe, **48**
Monoceros, 78–84; **79**
Moon, the, **33**
    binoculars, as seen in, 32–33
    drawing, 47–48
    sizing, 28
Muirden, James, 48, 152

N

nebulae, planetary, 140
    high magnification, viewing with, 88
Neptune, 34
New General Catalogue (NGC), 61, 81, 121, 126
Newton, Jack, 152
Newtonian telescope, **40**
Night Sky, The, 149
night vision, *see* dark adaptation
Nightwatch, 152
North Star, the, *see* Polaris
Norton's 2000.0 Star Atlas and Reference Handbook, 150

O

observing
    amateur astronomy guides for, 152
    binoculars, with, 35, 59–60, 150
    combatting nearby lights and, 144–145
    deep-sky objects, 57–58, 146
    faint objects, 98
    flashlights for, 54
    planning for, 78
    safety tips for, 147–148
    setting up for, 147
    telescopes, with, 46–48
Observing Handbook and Catalogue of Deep-Sky Objects, **80**, **86**, **93**, 151
Oceanus Procellarum, 33

Ochsenbein, François, *see* Hirshfeld, Alan
Ophiuchus, 103–107; **103**, **104**
Orion, 56, 59–63; **59**, **60**, **79**

P

Palomar Observatory Sky Survey, **76**, **77**, **80**, **82**, **107**, **121**, **126**, **128**, **138**, **139**
Peltier, Leslie C., 150, 152
peripheral vision, 55
photons, 56
Planetary Report, The, 153
planets
    Earthlike, 119, 137
    finding, 28
    sketching, 47
    Vega, of, 113
    see also individual listings
planispheres, 149
Poczobut, Abbé, 106
Polaris, finding, 29–30, 51, 75, 96
power
    binocular, 36
    deep-sky observing, for, 55–57
    faint objects, for viewing, 98
    telescope, 39–40, 45, 146
Precision Planet and Star Locator, 149
Proctor, Mary, 103, 113

R

Rappaport, Barry, *see* Tirion, Wil, 151
red dwarfs, 105–106
red giants, 116
redshift, 94
reflectors, 41, **41**
refractors, 40–41; **40**, **41**
retina, 54
Rey, H. A., 49, 149
Ridpath, Ian, 150
right ascension, 30, 75
Roberts, Isaac, 122
Rosse, Lord, 99
Rounsaville, Phil, **44**

S

Sagitta, **120**, **122**
Salvage Scope, The, **48**
Saturn, 34
Schmidt-Cassegrain telescopes, **40**, 41–42, 43
Scorpius, 108–112; **108**, **109**
seeing, 85
    atmospheric, 44, 47, 74
    celestial objects, 32, 58
    faint objects, 55
Serenitatis, 33
show objects, 34, 72, 89, 114, 119

Sinnott, Roger W., *see* Hirshfeld, Alan
Skiff, Brian, *see* Luginbuhl, Christian
Sky & Telescope,   9, 10, 12, 33, 34, 106, 110, 127, 145,
        149, 153
Sky & Telescope Star Finder,   149
Sky Atlas 2000.0,   150
        see also star charts
Sky Catalogue 2000.0,   77, 108, 112, 127, 133, 140, 151
sky dome,   14–15
sky, the
        brightness of and deep-sky observing,   53
        Earth, as seen from,   14
        distances and directions in,   28–30, 49–52
        visible area of, rating,   146
Smithsonian Astrophysical Observatory Star Catalog (SAO),   30
Smyth, William Henry,   103, 104, 122
solar filters,   **45**
spectral types,   31, 64–65
star chains,   81
star charts
        Sky Atlas 2000.0, from,   49, **50, 66, 73, 86, 104, 109,
                116, 120, 124, 136**
        Uranometria 2000.0, from,   **68, 79, 94, 97, 108, 114,
                122, 130, 140**
        using,   129
        see also sky, the: distances and directions in
Star Date,   153
star diagonals,   51–52, 75
star names,   30–31, 78, 103
star triangles,   52, 69
star-hopping,   9–10
        light-polluted areas, tour for,   124–128
        planning for,   77
        practice tour,   50–51
        starting out right,   11, 15–28
Starlight Nights,   152
stars
        atlases of,   150–151
        catalogs of,   30
        estimating brightness of with naked eye,   103
        evolution of,   78–79
        loose groupings of,   77
        telescopes, as seen in,   53
        see also individual listings in Object Index
Stars, The: A New Way To See Them,   49, 149
Stellafane convention,   **13**
Struve, Wilhelm,   31
Summer Triangle,   119
Sun, the
        observing,   **45**, 46
        sizing,   28
        spectral types and,   31, 64

T

Taurus,   **55**

Teece, Philip, *see* Newton, Jack
telescope mounts,   42–43, 46
telescopes
        all-purpose,   43
        buying,   43–44
        equipment for,   45–46
        Gregorian,   **44**
        homemade,   **42**, 46
        observing tips for,   46–48
        optical quality of,   44
        star colors in,   80
        star magnitudes in,   31
        starter,   12, 39, 78
        storing,   43
        types of,   40–42
termintator,   33
Tirion, Wil,   12, 49, 150, 151
        see also Crossen, Craig
Titan,   34
Touring the Universe Through Binoculars,   12, 150
trapezium,   76

U

Uranometria 2000.0,   12, 151
        see also star charts
Uranus,   34

V

variable stars,   31
Vehrenberg, Hans,   **67, 91, 94**, 122
Venus,   33–34
Viscome, George R.,   87
Visual Astronomy of the Deep Sky,   55
Vulpecula,   **120**, 122

W

Warkoczewski, S. J.,   111
waste light,   12
wavelengths,   31
Webb Society Deep-Sky Observer's Handbook,   110, 112,
        137, 140
Webb, Rev. Thomas W.,   69
Winter Triangle,   79
wire rings,   50–51; **50**
Wright, Darnley,   80

Z

zenith,   15
Zussman, Kim,   **100, 117, 122**